Milnsbridge Drill Hall War Memorial 1914-1921

7th Battalion The Duke of Wellington's (West Riding Regiment)

Milnsbridge Drill Hall War Memorial 1914-1921

7th Battalion The Duke of Wellington's (West Riding Regiment)

Compiled by
Scott Flaving, Michael and Susan Green

A
VALENCE HOUSE
Publication

First published in Great Britain in 2022
By Valence House Publications
Valence House, Becontree Avenue,
Dagenham, Essex RM8 3HT

www.valencehousecollections.co.uk

The text has been compiled by the authors as an educational, non-profit making publication to inform relatives and researchers of the 'Dukes' soldiers commemorated on the 7th DWR War Memorial in Huddersfield Drill Hall.

Images courtesy of the Trustees of the DWR Museum and Archive, unless otherwise annotated.

Maps and Images of the Tablets © Richard Harvey, DWR Volunteer Archivist.

The publisher is not responsible for the accuracy or continued existence of any websites referenced.

ISBN - 978-1-911391-97-5

All proceeds will be shared between Valence House Volunteers and the Huddersfield Drill Hall and Trust, Charity Number 224671.

Cover Image: Central panel of the 7th DWR War Memorial Tablets, 2020.

Back cover image: Wellington Cemetery, 2021.

All rights reserved. No part of this publication may be reproduced, stored in a retrieval system, or transmitted, in any form or by any means, electronic, mechanical, photocopying, recording or otherwise, without the prior permission of the copyright owner.

VALENCE HOUSE
a place of discovery

CONTENTS

List of Plates, Illustrations and Maps.	3
Foreword	6
Dedication	7
Introduction	8
Glossary	15
Order of Battle – 49th Division and 62nd Division	17
Roll of Honour	24
Addenda	155
The Battles	159
Weapons	166
Poem - Shell Hole Boy	168
Heritage and Legacy	170
Acknowledgements	171
Bibliography	172
Statistics	174

LIST OF PLATES, ILLUSTRATIONS AND MAPS

PLATES:

Front Cover:

Image and design – Scott Flaving, 2021.

Back Cover:

Wellington Cemetery – Regimental collection, c1918.

Wellington Cemetery – Michel L'Espagnol, 2021.

Other Plates:

J H Lobley painting – by kind permission of Kirklees Art Gallery and Library Service. Displayed in the Drill Hall (image supplied by Andrew Best and enhanced by Richard Harvey).

Memorial Tablets unveiling ceremony, 1921.

War Memorial Tablets, centre gallery – Richard Harvey, 2021.

Drill Hall Interior and 5th and 7th Battalions' War Memorials – Scott Flaving.

A7V tank – courtesy of M L'Espagnol.

All other images – courtesy of the Trustees of the Huddersfield Drill Hall, the Trustees of the Museum and Archives of The Duke of Wellington's Regiment or the authors.

MAPS:

Bullecourt, Somme and Ypres sketch maps – © Richard Harvey (2018-2019).

Nieuport – extract from Capt P G Bales History.

Bligny – extract from the *Official History of the War*, Historical section of the Committee for Imperial Defence, Macmillan and Co (1938).

Iwuy – DWR Archives map collection.

DWR Soldiers on the front line, Ypres Sector, December 1915
Painting by J H Lobley

The Drill Hall War Memorial tablets
commemorating the men of the 7th Battalion,
below the 5 DWR War Memorial boards
in Huddersfield Drill Hall
Mr Derek Alexander providing the scale.

FOREWORD

Again I am honoured to have been asked to write a forward to another book compiled by Mr Flaving and his fellow archivist volunteers. Having created a book (2019) giving information about those listed on the 5th Battalion DWR War Memorial boards, the team decided to complete a similar exercise for the 7th Bn DWR War Memorial tablets which are displayed below those of the 5th Bn DWR memorial boards, which form the front of the balcony in St Paul's Street Drill Hall.

This sequel to their previous book brings to life those whose names are carved into the stone tablets mounted on the wall below the balcony at the southern end of the main hall.

It is difficult to imagine the amount of research that must be undertaken to establish the identity and background information relating to each individual remembered on these boards. I would not even know where to start. However, once again Mr Flaving and his team have done just that, through endless hours of painstaking work. In so doing they have not only given us a superb reference book relating to those who served and died as members of 7th Bn, but have honoured the memory of those brave soldiers of the Great War.

Again, there appear to be some anomalies and some names missed off which perhaps should have been inscribed when the tablets were commissioned. The Trustees of Huddersfield Drill Hall hope to be able to rectify this by adding the missing names at an appropriate date in the future.

I can recommend this book to anyone with an interest in the 7th Bn DWR, the Huddersfield Drill Hall or a more general interest in the Great War and the part played by men of the local area.

Major (Retired) S M Armitage TD
Chairman of the Drill Hall Trustees
May, 2021.

DEDICATION

This book is dedicated to the men recorded on this memorial who suffered so much,
and their families, who grieved so much,
during and after the Great War

May they be ever remembered by future generations

LEST WE FORGET

INTRODUCTION

7th Battalion The Duke of Wellington's (West Riding Regiment)
World War One War Memorial
housed in Huddersfield Drill Hall

The origins of this book.

This book naturally follows on from the previous book dedicated to the commemoration of the men of the 5th Battalion The Duke of Wellington's Regiment (West Riding), who are listed on their war memorial in the Huddersfield Drill Hall. The fallen of the 7th Battalion are commemorated on the engraved War Memorial tablets, unveiled in 1921 at Scar Road Drill Hall, Milnsbridge, but are now located directly underneath the 5th Battalion War Memorial in St Paul's Street Drill Hall, it was decided a companion book be compiled to provide some basic background information on these men as well to help their surviving relatives to understand more about their experiences and sacrifice.

You will note that the (West Riding) in brackets differs from the title of the book. This is because in January, 1921, the end portion of the Regimental title was changed from ...(West Riding Regiment) to ...Regiment (West Riding).

The origins of the 7th Battalion.

Between 1883 and 1908 three local Volunteer Battalions were formed from a number of the previous Rifle Volunteer Corps and Administrative Battalions in the West Riding, some of which were directly linked to the Napoleonic War Volunteers, technically disbanded between 1803 and 1859, when a new fear of a possibility of a French invasion arose. These Battalions were numbered 1st, 2nd and 3rd Volunteer Battalions, based in Halifax, Huddersfield and Skipton, respectively, and linked to the Duke of Wellington's (West Riding Regiment), a title given by Queen Victoria on 18th June, 1853, in honour of the Great Duke's long and distinguished connection with the 33rd Regiment of Foot. The 33rd and 76th Regiments had been amalgamated in 1881 as they shared links, including the Great Duke, and had shared a Regimental Depot and recruiting area based in Halifax since 1877.

In April, 1908, another momentous reorganization of the Army was carried out and, as part of this, the Volunteer Battalions were transformed into the Territorial Force, modeled on the organization of the Regular Army. The new West Riding Brigades were each composed of four Battalions, so the 2nd West Riding Brigade required a fourth 'Dukes' Battalion to bring it up to strength. Lt Col F W Beadon VD, was appointed the commanding officer with effect 1st April, 1908, and the new battalion took over four Drill Halls from the 5th Battalion (Lees, Mossley, Saddleworth and Slaithwaite) and had to raise four more Companies (Golcar, Marsden, Micklehurst and Milnsbridge) as well creating new Drill Halls (Mossley, Uppermill, Marsden, Greenfield and Golcar/Milnsbridge).

Having taken over a total of 117 men and officers, the 7th Battalion was given official recognition on reaching the target of 330 men, towards the establishment of 1,000, on 7th July, 1908. Great efforts were made in the next few years to increase the strength of the unit and building the new Drill Halls. Major W Cooper, 5 DWR, an architect in civilian life, was responsible for many of these new buildings, and had designed the St Paul's Street Drill Hall for the Volunteers, opened in 1902.

By 1913, the Battalion took 19 officers and 652 men to camp at Aberystwith, second only to the 6th Battalion, 733 men, in the 2nd West Riding Brigade. It is not recorded if this total includes 'Bugler' Ian Clarke, nine years and six months old, 3ft 10inches, who, presumably, accompanied his father.

The origins of the War Memorial.

During the First World War, many ideas for locally commemorating those who had fallen were discussed and memorials were even erected in many churches; local firms, working men's clubs and local communities also created their own memorials and rolls of honour. The various local communities in and around Huddersfield also designed and built their own War Memorials and Cenotaphs, in a wave of national commemoration in the months and years following the Armistice. Much of this was described in the pages of the Huddersfield Examiner between 1919 and 1921, and no less than ninety five articles were published between these dates, from the Milnsbridge Library memorial proposal (9th Jan 1919) to the Oddfellows Memorial in Holmfirth (13th December, 1921).

The War Memorial was executed by George Iredale, sculptor, and was unveiled and dedicated in Milnsbridge Drill Hall on 3rd December, 1921, by Major General H R Davies CB, the commander of the 49th (West Riding Division).

The Memorial consists of seven Yorkshire stone tablets, each of three panels, the first tablet contains 90 names, tablet two 129 names, tablet three 118 names, tablet four 116 names and tablets five to seven each contain 129 names, a total of 840 names. To this may be added a further 21 names on tablet one, bringing this tablet's total up to 44 and the memorial total to 861 (see Addenda, page 155).

Laying of Foundation Stone for Drill-Hall for A. & B. Companies by John Sykes Esq. JP. 4 – 3 – 11.

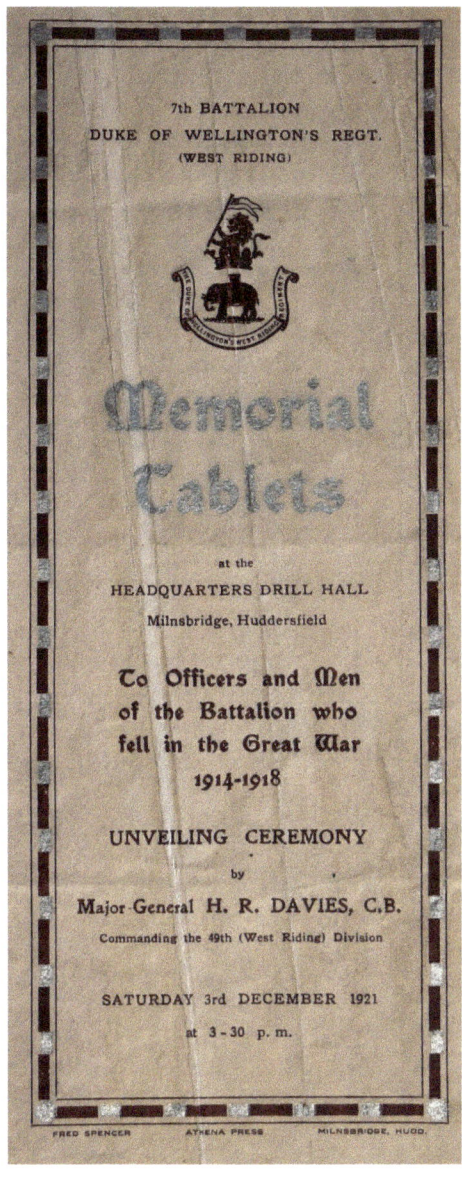

Image of the cover of the four page brochure issued for the unveiling ceremony in 1921.

Major General H R Davies commanded the 49th (West Riding) Division on the reforming of the Territorial Army (successor to the Territorial Force of 1909), himself succeeding Major General N J G Cameron, who had commanded the Division since 20th October, 1917.

Courtesy of Richard Harvey
Volunteer Archivist, DWR Musuem

Extracts from Mossley & Saddleworth Newspaper
November & December, 1921.

The following extracts describe the unveiling and dedication of the War Memorial in 1921 the first is the 'administrative instruction' issued to the men of the Battalion by the Adjutant, a common way of promulgating orders to the Territorials at that time.

The second extract is a press report of the day describing the background and the unveiling ceremony.

Courtesy of the British newspaper Archive:

7th Duke of Wellington's Regiment

Unveiling of Battalion War Memorial - the memorial tablets at Headquarters will be unveiled by Major General H R Davies CB, commanding 49th (West Riding) Division on Saturday, Dec 3rd, 1921, at 15.30 hours. The battalion will parade as strong as possible on that date outside Golcar Station at 14.00 hour, and march by way of James Street, Golcar, to Headquarters. Capt C Mallalieu, of C Coy, will be in command of the battalion until its arrival at Headquarters.

The guard of honour, consisting of two Sergeants and 24 file, under command of Capt C Mallalieu, will fall in facing the main entrance at Headquarters at 14.50 hours. 2nd Lieut G S Armitage will also parade with the guard of honour.

The Colour party with the guard of honour will be: 2nd Lieut G Taylor, CSM W R Smith, C Coy, and CQMS C H Lewis, C Coy. Lieut J H Charlesworth will receive the King's Colour of the 2/7th Duke of Wellington's Regiment from Major General H R Davies CB and the escort to the colour will be CSM G Collins, A Coy, and CSM H Ball, B Coy. Dress: Service Dress, stiff caps, belt and sidearms (rifles will be drawn from the armoury, H Q Drill Hall, by the guard of honour).

Train services will be as under: Oldham (Glodwick Road), 13.12 hours; Lees, 13.16; Mossley, 13.20; Slaithwaite, 13.25, Golcar, 13.57.

The Commanding Officer desires all Company officers to ensure as strong a parade as possible of men of the battalion on that date to do honour to their fallen comrades.

Drum Inspection - The Adjutant will inspect the drums art Saddleworth Drill Hall on Tuesday, Nov 29th at 20.00 hours. The Sergt Drummer will arrange for all men of the Drums to be on parade in uniform and to have with them all instruments with which they have been issued.

R Taylor, Major and Adjutant
7th Duke of Wellington's Regt TA
(West Riding)

Mossley and Saddleworth Reporter, 26 Nov 1921.

2nd extract:

There was an imposing ceremony when the Yorkshire Stone tablets containing the names of the 840 men of the 7th Battalion Duke of Wellington's (West Riding Regiment) who fell in the war, were unveiled in the Milnsbridge Drill Hall on Saturday by Major General H R Davies CB, commanding the 49th (West Riding) Division. The men of the battalion assembled in full force, accompanied by the band, and a guard of honour was formed for Major General Davies. The hall was crowded, special seats being reserved for the relatives of fallen soldiers.

The proceedings opened with the singing of Kipling's appropriate hymn, Lest We Forget.

Colonel G Tanner DSO TD, who presided, said it was a red letter day in the history of the battalion. It was also unique in that they were going to unveil tablets erected in memory of their comrades who fell in the Great War. It was well to point out that the 7th was an active service battalion which had distinguished itself well on many fields. The battalion was mobilised when war broke out in 1914 and went to France and Flanders in April, 1915, after a period of intensified training. Before the first line went out a second had been raised. They also underwent a period of intensified training and left for France in February, 1917. The names on the tablets to be unveiled belonged to one or other of the two battalions. Before 1914, the 7th Duke of Wellington's had no history and very little tradition. It was quite true that the 2nd Volunteer Battalion Duke of Wellington's which they (the 7th) had succeeded, had active service in South Africa but that was a Huddersfield battalion and the operations were on a small scale. Now the 7th had made history and created traditions which would have a lasting effect. Eight hundred and forty men of the battalion gave their lives for their country. Many could live for their country but very few had the honour of dying for their country and, while they felt sad at having lost so many of their old comrades, yet they had feelings of pride in their achievements and it was to all of them of them to follow the example which had been set and do their duty, no matter what the cost.

Considering what those men who had lost their lives had done, there was little for those at home to bicker about. But what did they find? Once the war was over everybody was trying to get the better of someone else or to get something for nothing. Their comrades gave their lives for their country; it was now for us left to pull together and make the country fit for heroes to live in. Major General Davies, whom he had pleasure in introducing, was in command of the 49th Division, and had undertaken the task of organisation.

Major General Davies said it was a pleasure for him to be amongst them on such an occasion. Had eight years ago someone had told them that they would at this day be unveiling tablets to the memory of 840 fallen soldiers, it would have been looked on as incredible. It was fitting that the tablets should be erected in the Headquarters of the battalion, because they would serve as an object lesson to those who came after them. There were many in that room who had lost loved ones. There were few, indeed, in this country who had not lost relatives or friends and the while occasion of that sort were in a measure and they could not but bring feelings of pride, and in generations to come people who viewed those tablets would point, with proud feelings, to a name which belonged to an ancestor or family connection. War was a terrible thing but it produced a spirit of self sacrifice, and sacrifice could never be wasted in this world or the next. As to the future, the 7th had ceased to be regarded merely as Territorials; they could now stand with pride alongside the regular battalions of the Regiment and it was for them to uphold the traditions of the battalion. Should another war break out nothing could be more inspiring to the men of the battalion than the sight of those behind.

He pulled a string, and the whole of the tablets were brought to view, making a touching sight as they covered the whole of the end of the Drill Hall.
The Last Post and Reveille were sounded by the bugles.
Mrs Shaw, of Botham Hall, Golcar, formally presented the tablets.
The Rev T W Hunt, Chaplain to the 7th Battalion, dedicated the tablets and the company joined in the singing of 'For all the Saints'.

The King's Colour for the 2/7th was presented by General Davies. He pointed out that the 2/7th had now ceased to exist, but he had not doubt if another war ever broke out the battalion would be re-formed and the colours used. Explaining the uses of Colours, he said they represented the King for the Regiment. A statesman, however great, only represented a section, but the King represented the whole country, and not only this country, but the whole of the British Empire.
Many decorations were distributed. Colonel Tanner received the Territorial Decoration.

Mossley and Saddleworth Reporter, 10 Dec 1921.

A note on sources:

For the Colne Valley Battalion, in addition to the incredibly detailed and well researched book left to us by the late Margaret Stansfield, covering Huddersfield, we are also indebted to Rita Vaughan and Kathryn Young, who have extensively researched the men of the Mossley district, including Carrbrook and Luzley. This was originally published in a pamphlet entitled Remember all the Boys and a copy of this was kindly donated to the DWR Regimental Archives in 2011. Since then a major update has been completed and extracts of the relevant DWR entries have been donated. These have been published online as .pdf documents and can be accessed through the DWR website - dwr.org.uk, family history page. We have also drawn on the research done by Mr Ron Hartley, who has looked into the men of the 7th Battalion for many years and has been an invaluable source of detail and problem solving. In addition, much useful detail has been sent to us by Mr Paul Sims, from his extensive research on embarkation rolls of the first line Territorial Force Battalions of the Regiment.

For a more comprehensive list of other sources, please see the bibliography.

Layout:

The layout of each entry follows as closely as possible to the following sequence:

1. Names are listed alphabetically, for ease of reference, although they are not in alphabetical order on the War Memorial boards. Some of the common problems are Hinchcliffe/Hinchliffe; Brook/Brooke, Cook/Cooke, etc. Often the sources are at variance, and, where this cannot be rectified from further research, through census returns, etc, the CWGC version has been taken as the most likely correct version. Some of those named cannot be verified as having been killed during the war, or immediately afterwards, and we have found no trace as to why they are included.

2. Numbers. Regimental numbers were originally issued by each battalion of a Regiment, but this proved to be unwieldy during the early part of the war when men were posted between battalions and Regiments. In the short term the Battalion number was used as a prefix, i.e. 3/1234 but this was not effective in the cases of cross Regimental postings. As a result, in April 1917, the Territorial Forces were issued with new six figure numbers, blocks of numbers being allocated to each Battalion of a Regiment. Where known, we have listed both the old four and five figure numbers, as well as the later six figure numbers. Officers were not issued with numbers until after the war.

3. Ranks are shown in full.

4. Place of birth (family, if known), residence and enlistment; date of embarkation.

5. Battalion, Company (if known); fate of soldier; date(s) of wounding (where known); death; age (where known) and the Battle or Sector in which he fell, where appropriate.
(Please note that the format of the dates is the result of a number of earlier automatic computer updates, which changed the usual date formats from 1901 to 2001, etc, on more than one occasion. This led to the addition of 100 years to all the Boer War dates, for example, on the Regimental Master Index at least twice over a period of two or three years. Many months were spent amending thousands of dates to a format not recognised by the computer during subsequent updates. This has worked so far and so has been adopted).

6. **Burial**, where applicable. A large proportion of the men have no known grave. Some of them are undoubtedly buried in unmarked graves – 'known unto God' – and it will be of comfort to relatives to know that work on identifying these men is still ongoing. Two 'Dukes' soldiers buried in unmarked graves in Talana Farm Cemetery, Belgium, have been tentatively identified by a local historian, who is

currently working on submitting his findings to the CWGC so that these men can be positively identified and new, named, headstones procured. However, this is a far from simple procedure. There are a number of images of headstones in the Archives collection, we have not included them in this book as the quality varies and it is now possible to order high resolution images through the Commonwealth War Graves Commission website - cwgc.org.uk.

7. **Commemorations**: we have included as many commemorations as can be traced. A large number of national and local War Memorials are yet to be fully transcribed and the names of 'Dukes' are being added to a growing database, which the Regimental Archives Team has been working on for many years. Mrs Stanfield's book was instrumental in providing a great number of the local Huddersfield Memorials and Rolls of Honour, on which the men are also commemorated, and Rita Vaughan's booklet has added many more from the Mossley area. The final commemoration for each entry, also in bold, shows the relevant panel and column on the Drill Hall Memorial as an aid to finding the names, especially as the majority are not listed in alphabetical order.

8. Details of mentions in other publications are listed, especially the Goodall collection and local newspapers, as well as the Unit War Diaries and a wealth of locally produced publications that we have had access to (please see the bibliography for details of these).

9. The original DWR battalions (i.e. 1/7th and 2/7th Battalions, pre 1918) and former Regiments, where men had been posted into the 'Dukes' from elsewhere, either by commissioning or, more commonly, whilst in transit through the Infantry Base Depots on the French coast, are included to aid research. A number of men were transferred to the 10th Battalion, in which they were serving when they fell. Exhaustive research has been carried out on the men of the 10th Battalion and this work has been published online by Dr Bill Smith, a member of the Regimental Archives Team, as part of ***tunstillsmen.blogspot.com.***

10. Finally, we have included epitaphs which were submitted by families in the 1920s to be carved at the base of the CWGC headstones. Families were invited to send in their messages to be carved into the Portland stone, at a cost of 3½d per letter.

Example of a full entry:

> **MOORE John Colin Dawson** – 2nd Lieutenant.
> Son of Emanuel and Emma E Moore, of Keighley.
> 7th Battalion DWR; died of wounds (air raid) 20 7 1918, aged 22.
> **Buried** – St Imoges Churchyard, France, C, 10.
> **Commemorated** - 5 DWR Drill Hall WM panel 8, column 2; 62nd Division History, page 201, and the **7 DWR Drill Hall WM panel 3, column 3.**
> Formerly 2579 LCpl, 5 DWR.
> Mentioned in 5th DWR Unit War Diary (died of wounds) 31 7 1918. HDH Album 7 DWR Volume 2 (wounded, air raid, 12 1917), page 27.
> *"BECAUSE I LIVE, YE SHALL LIVE ALSO"*

Legacy

It is hoped that this book will help the relatives of those men who are commemorated on the Drill Hall War Memorial to find out more about their forebears who sacrificed their lives for King and Country. It is also intended to reassure readers that these men, and others, from the Regiment are not forgotten by their comrades who have followed them into the ranks of the Duke of Wellington's Regiment, as well as the friends and supporters working to sustain the history and heritage of the Regiment into the future.

GLOSSARY

Common Military terms used:

Cenotaph	Stone monument erected in a local community to commemorate the men from that community who fell in war and whose remains are elsewhere.
DWR	The Duke of Wellington's Regiment. The Regiment was raised as Huntingdon's Regiment in 1702 and numbered 33rd from 1751. Named The Duke of Wellington's Regiment (DWR) on 18th June, 1853. Amalgamated with 76th Regiment in 1881, forming the 1st and 2nd Battalions of the Regiment. Was known as the West Riding Regiment (W Rid R) in the Boer War and Great War. Its soldiers have been proud to bear the nickname 'Dukes' for many years.
First Line	The original Territorial Force battalions, renamed 1/5th, etc, on the raising of the second line units in August, 1914.
Formation	A grouping of a number of units, a number of Brigades or a number of Divisions.
Great War	The common name for the conflict until WW2. Later WW1, possibly from September 1939, although it had been referred to as a World War towards the end of the conflict.
Ranks	Private (Pte), Lance Corporal (LCpl), Corporal (Cpl), Lance Sergeant (LSgt), Sergeant/Serjeant (Sgt), Company/Regimental Quarter Master Sergeant (CQMS/RQMS), Company/Regimental Sergeant Major (CSM/RSM), 2nd Lieutenant (2Lt), Lieutenant (Lt), Captain (Capt), Major (Maj), Lieutenant Colonel (Lt Col), Brigadier General (Brig Gen), Major General (Maj Gen).
Regiment	Originally raised as a single battalion size unit named after the Colonels who had been commissioned to raise them. From 1751 the regiments were numbered in order of precedence in the Army List; DWR was numbered 33rd. From 1881, as part of the amalgamations of the Cardwell Reforms, Regiments were grouped in two regular battalions, one for home service, and one for overseas service, usually with a Militia Battalion. In 1883, the Volunteer Battalions were formally linked to their local Recruiting District regular units. In 1908 the Volunteers were reorganised into the Territorial Force. In August, 1914, Regiments were ordered to double the number of their Territorial Force battalions as well as raise further Service (Kitchener) battalions. DWR raised 23 battalions during the war, 2 Regular, 1 Militia, 12 TF, 7 Service, 1 Young Soldiers.
Roll of Honour	A list of men who fell, who served, or a combination of these, usually on scrolls, in books or on plaques.
Second Line	The newly raised Territorial Force battalions, named 2/7th, etc, on the splitting of the first line units in August, 1914, in order to double their strength.
Third Line	The second line battalions were originally used to train and send drafts to the first line units. In 1915 they were ordered to raise third line training battalions to continue this function, in order to carry out collective training for operations. The 3/7th Battalion was initially posted to Clipstone Camp, moving to Rugeley in October, 1916.

Unit	A battalion size grouping, approx 1,000 men in the Infantry.
War Memorial	Normally a stone structure, usually carved or bearing a plaque, with the names of the fallen. However, in many places wooden or metal plaques, lychgates, stained glass windows and even village halls have been erected as war memorials.

Holme Valley Memorial Hospital War Memorial, central panel

ABBREVIATIONS

Abbreviations have been kept to the minimum and appear mostly in the Mentions section of each entry:

ADS	Advanced Dressing Station
Bn	Battalion.
CPGW	Craven's Part in the Great War, publication and website.
CWGC	Commonwealth War Graves Commission, publications and website.
Dates	Dates are given in the format dd m yyyy, see introduction.
GOC	General Officer Commanding.
MGC	Machine Gun Corps.
Ranks	*See Glossary.*
Regt	Regiment
RFC	Royal Flying Corps – until April, 1918, then Royal Air Force (RAF).
RoH	Roll of Honour.
SDGW	Soldiers Died in the Great War publication.
WM	War Memorial.

ORDER OF BATTLE

49th (WEST RIDING) DIVISION
62nd (PELICAN) DIVISION

In September, 1914, each of the original Duke of Wellington's (West Riding Regiment) Territorial Force battalions were ordered to raise a second, mirror image, unit in order to double their strength, using a cadre from each battalion to take in and begin training the crowds of volunteers clamouring to join the army and have a crack at the foe before it was "all over by Christmas".

Thus the 1st West Riding Division (TF) produced the 2nd West Riding Division (TF) in this fashion, and the 2nd West Riding Infantry Brigade, comprising of four first line 'Dukes' battalions, generated the 2/2nd West Riding Infantry Brigade, comprising of the newly created, second line 'Dukes' Battalions.

On 12th May, 1915, the two Divisions were re-designated as **49th (West Riding) Division**, with 147th Infantry Brigade (1/4th, 1/5th, 1/6th & 1/7th Battalions DWR) and **62nd (West Riding) Division**, including the 186th Infantry Brigade (2/4th, 2/5th, 2/6th & 2/7th Battalions DWR).

The various components of the British Army in 1914 were made up of:

Unit/Formation	Number (approx)	Commander
Section	15	Corporal.
Platoon	60	2nd Lieutenant/Lieutenant.
Company	200	Captain.
Battalion	1,000	Lieutenant Colonel.

(Infantry Regiments consisted of various numbers of battalions, each allocated to Brigades in various Divisions).

Brigade	5,000	Brigadier General.
Division	18,000	Major General.
Corps	two or more Divisions	Lieutenant General.
Army	two or more Corps	General.
Expeditionary Force	two Corps (1914) five Armies (1916)	Field Marshal.

An Infantry Battalion was made up of four Rifle Companies; Battalion Headquarters (including the Battalion Orderly Room); Headquarters Company, consisting of the Signals Platoon, Bombers, Machine Gun Platoon, Quartermasters Department, Catering Platoon and Transport Section. Most of these specialist platoons were split between the four Companies when in the Field, according to the tactical situation and operations being undertaken.

The Battalions, Brigades and Divisions were moved frequently between different formations, so a Corps, in particular, could command many Divisions for a particular operation.

The two Divisions in which the men of the 5th Battalion served were the 49th and 62nd Divisions:

49th (WEST RIDING) DIVISION
Symbol: White Rose of Yorkshire.

In 1914, this division was an existing Territorial Force Division, one of many created by the foresight of Lord Haldane in the reforms of 1908, and the establishment of the Territorial Force, which was well trained (by the standards of the day) for the previous war – the Boer War – at annual camps, including Redcar, Marske, the Isle of Man, Ripon, Flamborough and Aberystwyth. This Division, approximately 15,000 strong, was drawn from the West Riding of Yorkshire, with Divisional Headquarters in York. The three Brigade Headquarters were in York, Skipton and Sheffield and the twelve infantry battalions were located in York, Bradford, Leeds (two), Halifax, Huddersfield, Skipton, Milnsbridge, Wakefield, Doncaster, Sheffield and Rotherham.

Towards the end of July, 1914, the various units of the Division left their Drill Halls for a gloriously hot summer camp at Marske. On the 4th August the Division received orders to return to their Headquarters, with the exception of the 2nd West Riding Brigade, which was ordered to proceed direct from camp for immediate duty. The same day, mobilisation was ordered and what became known as the Great War had begun. Units then proceeded to their allotted war stations as part of the Central Force, Home Defence, and progressive training for war was carried out whilst initially also guarding the east coast in case of the much feared German invasion. The Division was eventually concentrated on Doncaster Race Course for collective training.

On 31st March, 1915, the 1st West Riding Division was informed that it had been selected to proceed to France as a complete Division and embarkation would take place in April.

On 7th April, 1915, a small advance party left Doncaster for Le Havre and, on 12th April, the Division began to entrain to proceed to France and, on 13th April, Divisional Headquarters and the Divisional Artillery left Doncaster and crossed from Folkestone to Boulogne. The infantry also crossed from Folkestone to Boulogne, but the mounted troops, Royal Engineers, Signal Company, Field Ambulances, Sanitary Section, Veterinary Section and the Train, all went from Southampton to Le Havre. By the 19th April the Division completed its concentration behind the River Lys, in the area Estaires – Merville – Neuf Berquin. The infantry began their trench warfare indoctrination in the Fleurbaix Sector.

The Division started out with twelve infantry Battalions, each with two machine guns, by 1916 Machine Gun Companies (MG Coy) and Trench Mortar Batteries (TMB) had been added to each Brigade (Bde) and, in 1918, the number of battalions was reduced to nine per Division. In addition, each Division had under command a Pioneer Battalion (infantry), three Brigades of Field Artillery, one Howitzer Brigade and one Heavy Battery; three Trench Mortar Batteries (from June, 1916); two Field Companies of Royal Engineers, one Cavalry Squadron, one Signals Company; three Field Ambulance units; a Sanitary Section, a Veterinary Section and the Divisional Train (Transport and Supply), as well as the Artillery Ammunition Columns. The Machine Gun Company was added in 1916 (199th MG Coy from June, 1917), later replaced by a Battalion (49th Battalion, MG Corps from March, 1918). The Infantry battalions were from the West Yorkshire Regiment (Depot in York), the West Riding Regiment (Depot in Halifax), the King's Own Yorkshire Light Infantry (Depot in Pontefract) and the York and Lancaster Regiment (Depot in Sheffield):

INFANTRY UNITS	**146 Bde**	**147 Bde**	**148 Bde**
	1/5 W Yorks	1/4 W Rid	1/4 KOYLI
	1/6 W Yorks	1/5 W Rid	1/5 KOYLI
	1/7 W Yorks	1/6 W Rid	1/4 Y & L
	1/8 W Yorks	1/7 W Rid	1/5 Y & L
In Jan 1918 Brigades were reorganised on a three battalion basis:-	**146 Bde**	**147 Bde**	**148 Bde**
	1/5 W Yorks	1/4 W Rid	1/4 KOYLI
	1/6 W Yorks	1/6 W Rid	1/4 Y & L
	1/7 W Yorks	1/7 W Rid	1/5 Y & L

Each Bde had a MG Coy and TM Bty attached	146 MG Coy (27 Jan 16)	147 MG Coy (28 Jan 16)	148 MG Coy (6 Feb 16)
	146 TMB	147 TMB	148 TMB

The Divisional and Brigade General Officers Commanding (GOC) during the war were:

GOC			From	To	
49 Div (1st W Rid)	Maj Gen	Baldock	19 9 1911	16 7 1915	(wounded)
	Maj Gen	Perceval	17 7 1915	19 10 1917	
	Maj Gen	Cameron	20 10 1917		
146 Bde (1st W Rid)	Brig Gen	MacFarlane	11 5 1912		
	Lt Col	Legge	20 12 1915		(acting)
	Brig Gen	Goring-Jones	17 1 1916		
	Brig Gen	Rennie	18 10 1917		
147 Bde (2nd W Rid)	Brig Gen	Brereton	11 5 1912		
	Brig Gen	Lewes	13 9 1916		
	Brig Gen	Morant	02 9 1818		
148 Bde (3rd W Rid)	Brig Gen	Dawson	01 4 1912		
	Brig Gen	Adlercron	07 6 1916		(DWR)
	Brig Gen	Green-Wilkinson	24 10 1917		

The 49th Division served on the Western Front in France and Belgium throughout the Great War and was engaged in the following operations:

1915						
09 5 1915		Battle of Aubers Ridge		4th Corps		1st Army
19 12 1915		First Phosgene Gas Attack		4th Corps		2nd Army
1916						
01 7 1916	03 7 1916	Battle of Albert		10th Corps		4th Army
14 7 1916	17 7 1916	Battle of Bazentine Ridge		10th Corps		Res Army
23 7 1916	18 8 1916	Battle of Pozieres Ridge		10th Corps	to 24 7	Res Army
27 8 1916	03 9 1916	Battle of Pozieres Ridge		2nd Corps		Res Army
15 9 1916	22 9 1916	Battle of Flers Courcelette		2nd Corps		Res Army
1917						
12 7 1917	23 9 1917	Operations on Flanders Coast		15th Corps		4th Army
09 10 1917		Battle of Poelcappelle		2nd Anzac Corps		2nd Army
1918		**Battles of the Lys**				
10 4 1918	11 4 1918	Battle of Estaires	147 Bde	15th Corps		1st Army
10 4 1918	11 4 1918	Battle of Messines	148 Bde	9th Corps		2nd Army
13 4 1918	15 4 1918	Battle of Bailleul		9th Corps		2nd Army
13 4 1918	14 4 1918	Defence of Neuve Eglise	148 Bde			

17 4 1918	19 4 1918	First Battle of Kemmel Ridge	9th Corps	2nd Army
		(146 Bde under 22nd Corps)		
25 4 1918	26 4 1918	Second Battle of Kemmel Ridge	22nd Corps	2nd Army
29 4 1918		Battle of Sherpenberg	22nd Corps	2nd Army

Advance to Victory

10 10 1918	12 10 1918	Pursuit to the Celle	Cdn Corps	1st Army

The Final Advance in Picardy

17 10 1918	18 10 1918	Battle of the Celle	22nd Corps	1st Army
01 11 1918	02 11 1918	Battle of Valenciennes	22nd Corps	1st Army

At the end of the Battle of Valenciennes, the 49th Division was relieved in the front line. On 5th November the Division moved back to the north of Douai and was transferred to 8th Corps. It was still resting on the 11th November. The Division remained in the Douai area, where, on 16th December, the Division was inspected on a ceremonial parade by Lieutenant General Sir A J Godley, commanding 22nd Corps.

Demobilisation began in January, 1919, and went steadily on until 30th March, by which date the Division had been reduced to a cadre. The Division was reformed in England in 1920.

62nd (WEST RIDING) DIVISION
Symbol: Pelican, with raised foot
(also 62nd (Pelican) Division)

The 2nd (West Riding) Division was formed at the outbreak of war as a second line Territorial Force Division by the creation of the 2/1st, 2/2nd and 2/3rd (West Riding) Infantry Brigades. The units of these Brigades were formed in their home Drill Halls as the result of an Army Order of 31st August, 1914 and created from a nucleus of the parent Division. Originally, the second line units were designated as Home Service but, later, renamed Reserve and, eventually, 2nd Line, in February, 1915. At this stage they were used to provide drafts of reinforcements to the 1st Line battalions for possible service overseas, the men having volunteered to change their terms of service. In return, the 2nd Line units had soldiers transferred into them who had not volunteered or were considered unfit for active service. Later, these men were transferred to Provisional Battalions used for coastal defence duties, and the newly raised 3rd Line Battalions which then became responsible for training and drafting volunteers, and conscripts from March, 1916.

The Divisional Headquarters assembled at Doncaster on 17th February, 1915. In March the Divisional HQ moved to Matlock and the various Brigades and supporting arms concentrated in the area Matlock, Derby, Belper, Nottingham and Bakewell. From May, 1915, the Division moved to various training areas, including Thoresby Park, Retford, and Newcastle. In early 1916, the Division moved to Salisbury Plain. In June, 1916, the Division moved to Norfolk, based in the Lowestoft area, moving to Bedford in October. In December, 1915, the Division received orders to embark for France and Flanders in January, 1917.

As for the 49th Division, the 62nd Division consisted of four battalions per infantry Brigade until February, 1918, when the number was reduced to three battalions per Brigade. They had the same complement of supporting arms as 49th Division, except that the Pioneer Battalion (1/9th DLI) did not join them until March, 1918:

INFANTRY UNITS	185 Bde	186 Bde	187 Bde
	2/5 W Yorks	2/4 W Rid	2/4 KOYLI
	2/6 W Yorks	2/5 W Rid	2/5 KOYLI
	2/7 W Yorks	2/6 W Rid	2/4 Y & L
	2/8 W Yorks	2/7 W Rid	2/5 Y & L
on 03 2 1918 Brigades were reorganised on a three battalion basis:-	**185 Bde**	**186 Bde**	**187 Bde**
	2/5 W Yorks	2/4 W Rid	2/4 KOYLI
	2/7 W Yorks	5 W Rid	5 KOYLI
	8 W Yorks	2/7 W Rid to 18 6 1918	2/4 Y & L
		2/4 Hants from 14 6 1918	
Each Bde had a MG Coy and TM Bty attached	212 MG Coy (09 3 1917)	213 MG Coy (09 3 1917)	208 MG Coy (04 3 1917)
	185 TMB (1 1917)	186 TMB (1 1917)	187 TMB (1 1917)

Note that the 2/7th Battalion was disbanded on 18 6 1918.

2/7th Battalion Officers 1915

The General Officers Commanding (GOC) the Division and Brigades were:

GOC			From	To	
62 Div (2nd W Rid)	Maj Gen	Sir K J Trotter	17 2 1915	22 12 1915	
	Maj Gen	W P Braithwaite	23 12 1915	27 8 1918	
	Maj Gen	Sir R D Whigham	28 8 1918		
185 Bde (2nd/1st W Rid)	Col	H W N Guiness	11 2 1915		
	Brig Gen	V W de Falbe	04 1 1916	21 8 1917	(invalided)
	Brig Gen	Viscount Hampden	21 8 1917		
186 Bde (2nd/2nd W Rid)	Col	H G Mainwaring	02 3 1915		
	Brig Gen	F F Hill	09 12 1915		
	Brig Gen	R B Bradford VC	10 11 1917	30 11 1917	(killed)
	Lt Col	H E P Nash	30 11 1917		(acting)
	Brig Gen	J L G Burnett	03 12 1917		
187 Bde (2nd/3rd W Rid)	Col	H B Lasseter	04 3 1915		
	Brig Gen	R O'B Taylor	22 5 1916	08 2 1918	(sick)
	Lt Col	B J Barton	02 2 1918		(DWR, acting)
	Lt Col	W K James	28 3 1918		(acting)
	Brig Gen	A J Reddie	03 4 1918		

The 62nd Division served on the Western Front in France and Belgium throughout the Great War and was engaged in the following operations:

1917

15 2 1917	13 3 1917	Operations on the Ancre	5th Corps	Fifth Army
14 3 1917	19 3 1917	German Retreat to the Hindenburg Line	5th Corps	Fifth Army
11 4 1917		First Attack on Bullecourt	5th Corps	Fifth Army
15 4 1917		German Attack on Lagnicourt (186 Bde)	5th Corps	Fifth Army
03 5 1917	17 5 1917	Battle of Bullecourt	5th Corps	Fifth Army
20 5 1917	28 5 1917	Actions at the Hindenburg Line	5th Corps	Fifth Army

Battle of Cambrai

20 11 1917	21 11 1917	The Tank Attack	4th Corps	Third Army
27 11 1917	28 11 1917	Capture of Bourlon Wood	4th Corps	Third Army

1918 — **First Battles of the Somme**

25 3 1918		Battle of Bapaume	4th Corps	Third Army
28 3 1918		Battle of Arras	4th Corps	Third Army

Advance to Victory
Battles of the Marne

20 7 1918	30 7 1918	Battle of Tardenois	22nd Corps	Fifth (Fr) Army

		Second Battle of Arras		
26 8 1918	30 8 1918	Battle of the Scarpe	6th Corps	Third Arm
02 9 1918		Battle of Drocourt-Queant Line	6th Corps	Third Arm
		Battles of the Hindenberg Line		
12 9 1918		Battle of Havringcourt Wood	6th Corps	Third Arm
27 9 1918	30 9 1918	Battle of the Canal du Nord	6th Corps	Third Arm
		The Final Advance in Picardy		
17 10 1918	23 10 1918	Battle of the Selle	4th Corps	Third Arm
20 10 1918		Capture of Solesmes	4th Corps	Third Arm
04 11 1918		Battle of the Sambre	4th Corps	Third Arm

After the battle of the Sambre, the Division remained in the front line and fought its way forward toward Maubeuge, advancing past Mecouignies and Neuf Mesnil (8th Nov). On the 9th the southern outskirts of Maubeuge was entered, the River Sambre crossed, Louvroil and St Lazare were captured and the line of the Maubeuge – Avesnes road was reached. On the 11th November, an outpost line was established along the River Soire, with piquets to the east of the river, but no signs of the enemy were encountered by cyclist patrols who pushed on as far as Cerforntaine and Recquignies (3 miles east of Maubeuge). At 11 am the Armistice came into force and hostilities ceased.

With acknowledgements to Ray Westlake, Kitcheners Armies, *(Spellmount, 1998) , Captain Wilfred Miles, compiler of the* Official History of the Great War, Military Operations, *(Macmillan and Co, 1938) and Major Tom Goodall,* The Goodall Collection.

Slaithwaite Drill Hall

THE WAR MEMORIAL TABLETS

INTRODUCTION:

The entries below are in alphabetical order for ease of looking up the names, which is not actually the case on the War Memorial Tablets, which are in no discernible order. Although some regard to the chronology of the Army numbering system (early four figure and later six figure) can be made out, it would appear that the tablets may have been originally fixed in Milnsbridge Drill Hall in a different order to how they appear now. Note that some duplicated names appear on different columns. There are also a number of spelling errors (see Sgt Duehurst/Dewhurst) which we have tried to correct, using contemporary sources, wherever possible. We have placed these in the order of what we believe is the correct name, a separate entry using the name on the War Memorial to point to the correct entry.

ABBOTTS, Frank – 16063 (later 308122) Private.
Born and resided in West Bromwich. Enlisted at Smethwick.
2/7th Battalion DWR; killed in action 14 5 1917 (Battle of Lagnicourt).
Commemorated – Arras Memorial, France, and the **7 DWR Drill Hall WM panel 1, column 2.**

ADAMS, Henry – 23865 Private.
Born in Eccleshill, Bradford, the son of Jonathan and Fanny Adams. Resided with his wife, Mary, at 1 Station Road, Chapeltown, Sheffield. Enlisted at Sheffield.
1/7th Battalion DWR; killed in action 01 11 1918 (Advance to Victory).
Buried – Auberchicourt British Cemetery, France, 4, A, 1.
Commemorated – the **7 DWR Drill Hall WM panel 2, column 2.**
"TO MEMORY EVER DEAR"

AGNEW, James – 7066 (later 307924) Private.
Born at Cambois, Northumberland the son of James and Margaret Agnew, of 12 Boat House Terrace, Northumberland. Resided in Cambois. Enlisted at Blyth.
1/7th Battalion DWR; killed in action 03 5 1917, aged 23 (Battle of Bullecourt).
Buried – St Vaast Post Military Cemetery, France, 4, G, 6.
Commemorated – the **7 DWR Drill Hall WM panel 6, column 1.**
Formerly 4000 Pte N Fus.
"HE GAVE HIS LIFE FOR OTHERS"

AINLEY, Jack – 235329 Private.
Born Huddersfield, the son of Sam Ainley and Annie (later Bower), of 20 Bankfield Terrace, Outcote Bank, Huddersfield. Enlisted at Huddersfield.
1/7th Battalion DWR; killed in action 01 11 1918, aged 21 (Advance to Victory).
Buried – Famars Communal Cemetery Extension, France, 25.
Commemorated – M Stansfield, page 3, and the **7 DWR Drill Hall WM panel 1, column 1.**
Mentioned in the Huddersfield Examiner (killed in action) 30 12 1918; listed in Huddersfield voters.
M Stansfield shows name as Jock.

AINLEY, William (Willie) – 307740 (307749?) Private.
Born on 18 7 1892, the son of John and Ellen Ainley, of 20 Rose Street, Turnbridge. Enlisted at Huddersfield on 09 2 1916. Wounded on 03 7 1916.
1/7th Battalion DWR; killed in action 09 4 1917, aged 24 (Battle of Arras).
Buried – St Vaast Post Military Cemetery, France, 4, F, 8.
Commemorated – Northumberland Street Primitive Methodist Church RoH; M Stansfield, page 4, and the **7 DWR Drill Hall WM panel 6, column 3.**
Mentioned in the Huddersfield Examiner (killed in action) 02 5 1917.
WM & NA Roll show number as 307749.

AINSCOUGH, Ernest – 25458 Private.
Born and enlisted at Liverpool.
1/7th Battalion DWR; killed in action 11 4 1918 (German Spring Offensive).
Commemorated – Tyne Cot Memorial, Belgium, and the **7 DWR Drill Hall WM panel 2, column 2.**
Formerly 46528 Pte Cheshire Regt; 46528 Pte Liverpool Regt & 217455 Labour Corps.
WM shows initials as J R.

AINSCOUGH, J R - 25458 - see **AINSCOUGH Ernest.**
Commemorated – the **7 DWR Drill Hall WM panel 2, column 2.**

AKEROYD, A - 306640 - see **AKEROYD Willie.**
Commemorated – the **7 DWR Drill Hall WM panel 7, column 2.**

AKEROYD, Willie – 306640 Private.
Enlisted at Birstall.
2/7th Battalion DWR; killed in action 26 3 1918 (German Spring Offensive).
Buried – Pommer Communal Cemetery, France, 17.
Commemorated – the **7 DWR Drill Hall WM panel 7, column 2.**
WM shows initial A.

ALLAN (ALLEN?), Albert – 47336 Private.
Born and enlisted at Nottingham.
1/7th Battalion DWR; died of wounds 12 10 1918 (Advance to Victory).
Buried – Bucquoy Road Cemetery, Ficheux, France, 3, G, 6.
Commemorated – the **7 DWR Drill Hall WM panel 2, column 1.**
Formerly R/4/235645 Private, Army Service Corps.
CWGC shows name as ALLEN.

ALLAN (ALLEN?), Hildred – 305544 Sergeant; Military Medal.
Son of Thomas and Maud Allan, of 1 Meg Lane, Longwood, Huddersfield. Enlisted at Slaithwaite on 31 8 1914. Embarked for France & Flanders on 10 1 1917. Twice wounded.
2/7th Battalion DWR; died, suffocation from brazier in dug-out, on 18 5 1918, aged 20.
Buried – Bienvillers Military Cemetery, France, 14, D, 10.
Commemorated – Slaithwaite WM; St. Mark's Parish Church, Longwood, RoH; St James's Church, Slaithwaite, RoH; CVA; M Stansfield, page 4, and the **7 DWR Drill Hall WM panel 3, column 2.**
Mentioned in the Unit War Diary (wia on patrol by bayonet) 24 7 1917; (patrol action) 26 9 1917; (patrol action) 28 9 1917; (GOC's recognition of patrol work) 9 1917; the Huddersfield Examiner (wia, official casualty list), 12 6 1917; (wia, official casualty list) 04 9 1917; (died, accident, 6 1918) 05 6 1918; J Fisher (honoured by Brighouse Town Council), page 86; London Gazette (MM award), 28 9 1917, page 10021; L Magnus (medal roll), page 297;
CWGC and other sources show name as ALLEN.
"NEVER ABSENT FROM THE HEARTS AND MINDS OF THOSE WHO LOVED HIM"

ALLAN (ALLEN?), Thomas – 306361 Private.
Resided in Athlone, Ireland. Enlisted at Slaithwaite.
2/7th Battalion DWR; killed in action 27 11 1917 (Battle of Cambrai).
Commemorated – Cambrai Memorial, Louverval, France, and the **7 DWR Drill Hall WM panel 7, column 3.**
CWGC and SDGW shows name as ALLEN.

ALLEN (ALLAN?), Joshua – 5098 Private.
Son of John Alfred and Hannah Allen, of 4 Fox Street, Bingley. Enlisted at Bingley.
1/7th Battalion DWR; died of wounds 08 9 1916 (Battle of the Somme).
Buried – Bingley Cemetery, Yorkshire, N3, 109.
Commemorated – **7 DWR Drill Hall WM panel 6, column 1.**
SDGW shows name as Allan.

ALLISON, Andrew – 203232 Private.
Brother of John H Allison, of 15 Glebe Road, Harrowgate Hill, Darlington. Enlisted at Darlington.
1/7th Battalion DWR; killed in action 11 10 1918 (Advance to Victory, Battle of Iwuy).
Buried – Wellington Cemetery, Rieux-en-Cambresis, France, 3, B, 4.
Commemorated – the **7 DWR Drill Hall WM panel 1, column 1.**

ANDERSON, Alexander – 26370 Private.
Born in Aberdeen. Resided in Sibton, Suffolk. Enlisted at Chelmsford.
2/7th Battalion DWR; killed in action 27 11 1917 (Battle of Cambrai).
Commemorated – Cambrai Memorial, Louverval, France, and the **7 DWR Drill Hall WM panel 2, column 2.**
Formerly 111 Private, Army Service Corps.

ANDERSON, Harry – 367053 Lance Sergeant.
Born at Bingley, the son of John and Mary E Anderson. Enlisted at Keighley.
1/7th Battalion A Company, DWR; killed in action 11 10 1918 (Advance to Victory, Battle of Iwuy).
Buried – Wellington Cemetery, Rieux-en-Cambresis, France, 2, B, 7.
Commemorated - the **7 DWR Drill Hall WM panel 1, column 3.**
CWGC & SDGW show number as 267053.

APPLEBY, Arthur Lumley – 205104 Private; Military Medal.
Born in Hampsthwaite, the son of William and Priscilla Appleby. Husband of Eva, of Quarry Cottage, Menston-in-Wharfedale. Enlisted at Keighley.
1/7th Battalion DWR; killed in action 11 10 1918, aged 29, (Advance to Victory, Battle of Iwuy).
Buried – Wellington Cemetery, Rieux-En-Cambresis, France, 2, C, 2.
Commemorated - the **7 DWR Drill Hall WM panel 6, column 2.**
Mentioned in the Unit War Diary (MM award) 29 5 1918; LG (MM award) 13 9 1918; L Magnus (medal roll) page 257.
"UNTIL WE MEET AGAIN"

ASHURST, Sharrock – 205120 Private.
Born at Barrow-in-Furness. Resided with his wife, at 'Bellmount House' Luck Lane, Marsh, Huddersfield. Enlisted at Huddersfield.
1/7th Battalion DWR; killed in action, shellfire, 09 10 1917, aged 36 (3rd Battle of Ypres, Passchendaele).
Commemorated – Tyne Cot Memorial, Belgium; All Saint's Church, Paddock, RoH (now in Huddersfield Drill Hall); M Stansfield, page 9, and the **7 DWR Drill Hall WM panel 6, column 3.**

BACON, Frederick (Fred) – 1166 Private.
Born in Norwich. Resided in Mossley. Enlisted at Micklehurst, Lancs.
1/7th Battalion DWR; killed in action 04 7 1916 (Battle of the Somme).
Buried – Authuile Military Cemetery, France, F, 1.
Commemorated – R Vaughan, pages 25 & 168, and the **7 DWR Drill Hall WM panel 5, column 3.**
NA Roll shows a duplicate entry with number 1164. R Vaughan also shows number as 1164.

BAGGLEY, John (Jonathan?) – 202304 Private.
Son of Simpson and Annie Baggley, of 4 George Street, Tunstall, Stoke-on-Trent. Enlisted at Tunstall.
1/7th Battalion DWR; died of wounds 21 10 1918 (Advance to Victory).
Buried – St Sever Cemetery Extension S, Rouen, France, 2, R, 5.
Commemorated – the **7 DWR Drill Hall WM panel 6, column 3.**
WM shows name as BAGLEY.
"ETERNAL REST GIVE UNTO HIM O LORD R.I.P."

BAGSHAW, Henry Kenyon – Lieutenant.
Son of the Reverend Henry Fosbery and Margaret Bagshaw, of 'The Vicarage', Chatteris, Cambs.
1/7th Battalion DWR; killed in action 13 4 1918 (German Spring Offensive).
Commemorated – Tyne Cot Memorial, Belgium, and **7 DWR Drill Hall WM panel 3, column 3.**
Mentioned in Unit War Diary (joined Bn) 20 8 1917; HDH Album 7 DWR Vol 2 (from ASC, kia 13 4 1918) pages 27 & 33.
Formerly 2Lt, 97th Coy, Army Service Corps.

BAILEY, John – 13184 Private.
Born and resided in Baildon. Enlisted at Keighley.
2/7th Battalion DWR; died of wounds, 22 11 1917, aged 23 (Battle of Cambrai).
Buried – Rocquigny-Equancourt Road British Cemetery, Manancourt, France, 2, F, 21.
Commemorated – 7 DWR Drill Hall WM panel 2, column 1.
Also served in the 10th Battalion, see - tunstillsmen.blogspot.com (last accessed August, 2020).
"TOO DEARLY LOVED TO BE FORGOTTEN"

BAILEY, Thomas Hartley – 265737 Private.
Son of Mr and Mrs W H Bailey, of Longroyd Road, Earby. Resided in Colne, Lancs. Enlisted at Skipton.
1/7th Battalion DWR; killed in action 14 4 1918, aged 31 (German Spring Offensive).
Commemorated – Tyne Cot Memorial, Belgium; Earby WM & Earby Parish RoH, page 104; CPGW, page 343, with photograph, and the **7 DWR Drill Hall WM panel 7, column 2.**

BAKER, Tom – 305801 Private.
Resided at 17 Gladstone Buildings, Marsden. Enlisted at Milnsbridge in November, 1914.
1/7th Battalion DWR; died, accidentally drowned, 21 10 1917, aged 27.
Buried – Trouville Communal Cemetery, France, Military Plot.
Commemorated – Marsden WM; M Stansfield, page 16, and the **7 DWR Drill Hall WM panel 6, column 3.**
CWGC & SDGW show name as BAKER, WM shows BARKER.
"NOT MY WILL, BUT THINE OH LORD BE DONE"

BALL, Francis Matthew – 268629 Private.
Son of Arthur and Mary Booth Ball, of Warsop, Mansfield, Notts. Enlisted at Mansfield.
2/7th Battalion DWR; died of wounds 22 5 1918, aged 20, (German Spring Offensive).
Buried – Doullens Communal Cemetery, France, 2, C, 3.
Commemorated - the **7 DWR Drill Hall WM panel 3, column 2.**

WM shows initials F W.
"JUST WHEN HIS HOPES WERE BRIGHTEST GOD CALLED HIM HOME TO REST"

BALMFORTH, Tom – 306576 Private.
Son of Squire and Levena Balmforth, of Lower Shay Clough, Denholme. Enlisted at Shipley.
2/7th Battalion DWR; died at home 08 8 1917, aged 21.
Buried – Denholme Gate (St Paul's) Churchyard, Yorkshire, K, K, 25.
Commemorated - the **7 DWR Drill Hall WM panel 3, column 1.**

BARBER, William – 267108 Private.
Born in Armley, Leeds, the son of Mrs Barber, of 42 Westgate Street, Skipton. Enlisted at Skipton.
1/7th Battalion DWR; died of wounds 31 10 1918 (Advance to Victory).
Buried – St Sever Cemetery Extension, Rouen, France, S, 3, 1, 23.
Commemorated – CPGW, page 365, with photograph, and the **7 DWR Drill Hall WM panel 2, column 1.**

BARKER, Henry – 306750 Private.
Enlisted at Bradford.
2/7th Battalion DWR; killed in action 26 11 1917 (Battle of Cambrai).
Commemorated – Cambrai Memorial, Louverval, France, and the **7 DWR Drill Hall WM panel 3, column 1.**

BARKER Thomas – 305892 Private.
Born in Sunderland to Thomas and Sarah Ann Barker, native of Seaham, County Durham. Resided in Mossley. Enlisted at Milnsbridge.
1/7th Battalion DWR; died, accident, 05 8 1917, aged 32, (Nieuport Sector).
Buried – Coxyde Military Cemetery, Belgium, 2, H, 20.
Commemorated – Micklehurst Conservative Club WM; All Saints Church WM; R Vaughan, pages 24 & 90, **and** the **7 DWR Drill Hall WM panel 6, column 1.**
Mentioned in HDH Album 7 DWR Vol 2, page 25 (drowned 06 8 1917).
"THE LORD BE WITH YOU"

BARKER, Tom – 305801 Private - see **BAKER T.**

BARLOW, George – 2595 Private.
Son of George Barlow, of 3 House, 2 Court, Bardsey Street, Waterhead, Oldham. Enlisted at Milnsbridge.
1/7th Battalion, C Company, DWR; died of wounds 23 8 1916, aged 21, (Battle of the Somme).
Buried – Oldham (Hollinwood) Cemetery, J2, 59.
Commemorated – the **7 DWR Drill Hall WM panel 4, column 2.**
"AT REST"

BARRAN, A – 307693 – see **BARON Albert.**
Commemorated – the **7 DWR Drill Hall WM panel 6, column 2.**
CWGC shows name as BARON, SDGW shows name as BARRON.

BARRACLOUGH, George Will – 2nd Lieutenant; Military Cross.
Born at Almondbury, the son of Mr H Barraclough, of Grove Street, Dewsbury.
1/6th Battalion DWR; killed in action 29 9 1918, aged 22, (Advance to Victory).
Buried – Grand Ravine British Cemetery, France, C, 13.
Commemorated – 5 DWR Drill Hall War Memorial, panel 1, column 3; CPGW, page 77, with photograph: M Stansfield, page 23, and the **7 DWR Drill Hall WM panel 3, column 3.**

Mentioned in Unit War Diary (MC award) 31 10 1918; the London Gazette (MC award) 01 2 1919, page 1641.
Formerly 7536 (203567) Sgt G W Barraclough, 1/5th DWR, commissioned into 1/6th DWR 28 8 1917, also att 2/4th DWR.
SDGW shows name as BARMCLOUGH.

BARON, Albert –307693 Private.
Born at Keighley, the son of Elizabeth Ann Baron, of Swartha Farm, Swartha, Silsden, Keighley. Enlisted at Keighley.
1/7th Battalion DWR; died of wounds (shellfire) 18 4 1917, aged 24.
Buried – La Gorgue Communal Cemetery, France, 3, B, 5.
Commemorated – the **7 DWR Drill Hall WM panel 6, column 2.**
WM shows name as BARRAN. 1659 Albert BARRON was wounded in action, on 02 7 1916, with 1/6th DWR, may have transferred to 1/7th DWR after recovery.
"HE LIES WITH ENGLAND'S HEROES IN THE WATCHFUL CARE OF GOD"

BARRATT, Frederick William Richard – 16070 (later 308129) Private.
Born and enlisted at Walsall, Staffs.
2/7th Battalion DWR; killed in action 03 5 1917 (Battle of Bullecourt).
Commemorated – Arras Memorial, France, and the **7 DWR Drill Hall WM panel 2, column 2.**
CWGC and SDGW show name as BARRETT.

BARRETT, John Hartley – 306416 Private.
Born at Connonley, Yorks. Enlisted at Keighley.
1/7th Battalion DWR; killed in action 13 4 1918 (German Spring Offensive).
Commemorated – Tyne Cot Memorial, Belgium, and the **7 DWR Drill Hall WM panel 6, column 2.**
CWGC & SDGW show name as BARRITT.

BARRETT, Leonard – 241939 Private.
Born at Meltham, the son of William and Emily Barrett, of Greenside, Meltham, Yorks. Enlisted at Huddersfield.
1/7th Battalion DWR; killed in action 29 4 1918, aged 25 (German Spring Offensive).
Commemorated – Tyne Cot Memorial, Belgium; St Bartholomew's Church, Meltham; M Stansfield, page 24, and the **7 DWR Drill Hall WM panel 6, column 3.**
Mentioned in the Huddersfield Examiner (killed in action) 30 5 1918.

BARTLE, Frederick De Forge – 306527 Private.
Enlisted at Heckmondwike.
2/7th Battalion DWR, killed in action 03 5 1917 (Battle of Bullecourt).
Commemorated – Arras Memorial, France, and the **7 DWR Drill Hall WM panel 2, column 2.**
WM shows initials F B F.

BARTON, Bertram – 306979 Sergeant.
Resided in Silloth, Cumberland. Enlisted at Sheffield.
2/7th Battalion DWR; killed in action 21 11 1917 (Battle of Cambrai).
Commemorated – Cambrai Memorial, Louverval, France, and **7 DWR Drill Hall WM panel 7, column 2.**

BATES, George William – 306552 Private.
Enlisted at Bradford.
1/7th Battalion DWR; killed in action 01 11 1918 (Advance to Victory).
Buried – Famars Communal Cemetery Extension, France, 34.

Commemorated – the **7 DWR Drill Hall WM panel 1, column 2.**

BATTAMS, Charles Ernest – 33850 Private (later 42920 Private).
Enlisted into DWR, transferred to the Bedfordshire and Hertfordshire Regt.
Killed in action 12 10 1918 (Advance to Victory).
Commemorated: Arras Memorial, France, and the **7 DWR Drill Hall WM panel 2, column 2.**
Not shown in CWGC or SDGW.

BAXTER, Frederick – 306015 Lance Sergeant; Military Medal.
Son of William H Baxter, of Linthwaite. Husband of Ann, of 4 Spring Buildings, Hoyle House, Linthwaite. Enlisted at Derby. Embarked for France & Flanders in January, 1916.
1/7th Battalion DWR; killed in action 11 10 1918, aged 37, (Advance to Victory, Battle of Iwuy).
Buried – Wellington Cemetery, Rieux-En-Cambresis, France, 2, C, 4.
Commemorated – Linthwaite WM; M Stansfield, page 28, and the **7 DWR Drill Hall WM panel 6, column 3.**
Mentioned in the Unit War Diary (MM award) 08 6 1918; the London Gazette (MM award) 13 9 1918, page 10760; L Magnus (medal roll), page 298.
"NOT MY WILL BUT THINE O LORD BE DONE"

BAXTER, Harry - 267644 Private.
Born in Halifax. Resided at 6 Hadassah Street, Siddal, Halifax. Enlisted at Halifax.
2/7th Battalion DWR; killed in action 03 5 1917, aged 37 (Battle of Bullecourt).
Commemorated – Arras Memorial, France; Halifax Civic Book of Remembrance; CWD, page 53, and the **7 DWR Drill Hall WM panel 3, column 1.**
Mentioned in Halifax Courier 21 3 1918.

BEAN, Herbert Major – 7083 (later 307938) Private.
Born in Eagle, Lincs, the son of John and Emma Bean. Enlisted at Lincoln.
1/7th Battalion DWR; died of wounds 15 8 1917, aged 24 (Nieuport Sector).
Buried – Adinkerke Military Cemetery, Belgium, C, 20.
Commemorated – the **7 DWR Drill Hall WM panel 6, column 3.**
Formerly 4052 Northumberland Fusiliers.

BEARDSALL, Harry – 101 Drummer.
Born at Marsden, the son of Mr and Mrs James Beardsall, of Oliver Lane. Enlisted at Marsden, aged 14, in 1908. Pre war local Territorial, mobilised on 05 4 1914.
1/7th Battalion DWR; killed in action, shrapnel, 04 7 1916, aged 22, (Battle of the Somme).
Commemorated – Thiepval Memorial, France; Marsden WM; M Stansfield, page 31, and the **7 DWR Drill Hall WM panel 4, column 3.**
Mentioned in the Colne Valley Almanac, date of death shown as 05 7 1916, the Huddersfield Examiner (killed in action) 25 7 1916; J Fisher, page 110.

BEAUMONT, Albert – 306870 Private.
Born in Halifax, the son of Benjamin and Elizabeth Beaumont, of Holroyd Square, Stainland. Enlisted at Stainland.
2/7th Battalion DWR; killed in action 03 5 1917, aged 26, (Battle of Bullecourt).
Commemorated – Arras Memorial, France; St. Andrew's Church, Stainland, Halifax; CWD, page 348, and the **7 DWR Drill Hall WM panel 2, column 3.**

BEAUMONT, G – 5245 Private.
No trace, CWGC or SDGW, possibly a duplicate of G A BEAUMONT, below:

BEAUMONT, George Arthur – 307241.
Born and enlisted at Ossett.
1/7th Battalion DWR; killed in action 05 4 1917 (Battle of Arras).
Buried – St Vaast Post Military Cemetery, France, 4, F, 6.
Commemorated – the **7 DWR Drill Hall WM panel 7, column 2.**
Formerly 27766 Private, Kings Own Yorkshire Light Infantry.

BEAUMONT, Harry – 307751 Private.
Born in Bradford to Eliza Beaumont, of 67 Tumbling Hill Street. Enlisted at Halifax.
1/7th Battalion DWR; died of wound, 15 8 1917 (Nieuport Sector).
Buried – Coxyde Military Cemetery, Belgium, 2, H, 15.
Commemorated – the **7 DWR Drill Hall WM panel 6, column 2.**
CWGC & SDGW show number as 307757.

BEAUMONT, James Hutchings – Lieutenant.
Son of John and Bertha Beaumont, of Dogley Villa, Fenay Bridge, Huddersfield. Commissioned in February 1915.
2/7th Battalion DWR; died of wounds 24 6 1917, at Boulogne Base Hospital, aged 22.
Buried – Boulogne Eastern Cemetery, France, 7, B, 24.
Commemorated – Kirkburton WM; All Hallow's Church, Kirkburton; headstone in Kirkburton Cemetery; Almondbury Grammar School RoH; M Stansfield, page 35, and the **7 DWR Drill Hall WM panel 3, column 3.**
Mentioned in the Huddersfield Examiner (died of wounds) 05 7 1917. J Fisher, page 133.
"HE DIED FOR KING & COUNTRY"

BEDFORD, Clement – 267305 Private.
Born in Halifax. Resided at Lee House Farm, Ovenden Wood, Halifax. Enlisted at Halifax.
2/7th Battalion DWR; died of wounds at 30 CCS on 18 1 1918.
Buried – Anzin St Aubin British Cemetery, France, 3, A, 9.
Commemorated – Mount Tabor, Halifax, Wesleyan Methodist Church RoH; Halifax Civic Book of Remembrance; CWD, page 55, and the **7 DWR Drill Hall WM panel 1, column 3.**
Mentioned in the Halifax Weekly Guardian (died) 03 2 1918.

BELL, Henry – 34069 Private.
Born in Preston, the son of Peter and Alice Bell, of 17, Oakley Street. Enlisted at Preston.
1/7th Battalion DWR; killed in action 11 10 1918 (Advance to Victory, Battle of Iwuy).
Buried – Wellington Cemetery, Rieux-en-Cambresis, France, 1, E, 7.
Commemorated – the **7 DWR Drill Hall WM panel 2, column 3.**
"GOD OF MERCY, JESUS BLEST GRANT THY SERVANT PEACE AND REST"

BENNETT, Wylie – 1201 Private.
Born at Marsden, the son of Mr and Mrs Harry Bennett, of Shepherds Bush, London. Resided in Rock Ferry, Cheshire. Enlisted at Slaithwaite in 1912. Pre war local Territorial, mobilised on 05 4 1914.
1/7th Battalion DWR; died of wounds at Rouen Base Hospital 25 9 1915, aged 20.
Buried – St Sever Cemetery, Rouen, France, A, 11, 15.
Commemorated – Marsden WM; 5 DWR Drill Hall WM, panel 1, column 4; M Stansfield, page 40, and the **7 DWR Drill Hall WM panel 4, column 2.**

BENSON, Alexander (Alec) – 305517 Private.
Born in 1897 in Mossley, the son of Alexander and Mary Benson, of 'Springfield', Micklehurst Road. Enlisted at Mossley. Embarked for France & Flanders in Jan 1917.
2/7th Battalion DWR; killed in action 03 7 1917.

Buried – Noreuil Australian Cemetery, France, G, 6.
Commemorated – All Saints Church WM; St George's Church WM; Abney (Derbyshire) Congregational Church RoH and window; R Vaughan, pages 86 & 154, and the **7 DWR Drill Hall WM panel 7, column 1.**
"LOVING THOUGHTS OF ONE SO DEAR OFTEN BRING A SILENT TEAR"

BERRY, Fred – 2238 (later 268555) Private.
Born on 15 12 1896, at 51 Oak Road, Bradley. Resided in Rawmarsh. Enlisted at Milnsbridge.
1/7th Battalion DWR; killed in action 09 4 1917, aged 20.
Buried – St Vaast Post Military Cemetery, France, 4, G, 1.
Commemorated – St Thomas's Church, Bradley, RoH; Learoyd Brothers' Mill RoH; M Stansfield, page 41, and the **7 DWR Drill Hall WM panel 5, column 1.**

BERRY, Fred – 306556 Private.
Son of Jim and Hannah Mary of Craven Terrace, Gomersal. Resided in Gomersal, Bradford. Enlisted at Heckmondwike.
2/7th Battalion DWR; killed in action 03 5 1917, aged 20 (Battle of Bullecourt).
Commemorated – Arras Memorial, France; Bailiffe Bridge WM; Spenborough WM; Firth's Carpets, Cleckheaton, RoH; and the **7 DWR Drill Hall WM panel 3, column 2.**
WM shows number as 306566.

BERRY, Frederick Arthur – 4957 Private.
Born and resided in Bradford, the son of William and Mary Ann Berry, of 12 Rodney Street. Enlisted at Bradford.
1/7th Battalion DWR; killed in action 17 9 1916, aged 37 (Battle of the Somme, Leipzig Salient).
Commemorated – Thiepval Memorial, France, and the **7 DWR Drill Hall WM panel 5, column 3.**

BERRY, George Arthur – 308115 Private.
Born in Liversedge. Resided at 4 Shakespeare Street, Halifax. Enlisted at Halifax in October, 1916.
2/7th Battalion DWR; killed in action 16 4 1917, aged 33 (Battle of the Scarpe),
Commemorated – Arras Memorial, France, Halifax Civic Book of Remembrance; CWD, page 58, and the **7 DWR Drill Hall WM panel 1, column 1.**
Mentioned in the Halifax Weekly Guardian, 5 & 12 5 1917, with photograph.

BERRY, John Leslie – 2nd Lieutenant (formerly 2737 & 266723 Pte, 1/6th DWR).
Born 24 10 1897, the son of John and Margaret Berry, of 48 Broughton Road, Skipton.
Resided in Gargrave. Enlisted 28 6 1915. Commissioned into 9 DWR, 27 5 1918.
1/7th Battalion DWR; killed in action 12 10 1918, aged 20 (Advance to Victory, Battle of Iwuy).
Buried – Selridge British Cemetery, Montay, France, 1, C, 17.
Commemorated – Gargrave WM; CPGW, page 74, and the **7 DWR Drill Hall WM panel 3, column 3.**
Mentioned in the Craven Herald (killed in action) 25 10 1918; S Barber, page 39; From Mills to Marching and Back Again, page 270.
"UNTIL THE DAY DAWNS AND THE SHADOWS FLEE AWAY"

BERRY, Joseph – 240283 Private; Military Medal.
Born on 11 6 1898, the son of Arthur and Annie Berry, of Lockwood, 35 Lockwood Road, Huddersfield. Enlisted at Huddersfield in May, 1914. Pre war local Territorial, mobilised on 05 4 1914.
1/7th Battalion DWR; died of wounds at CCS (gunshots to lungs and chest) 13 10 1918, aged 20. (Advance to Victory, Battle of Iwuy).
Buried – Bucquoy Road British Cemetery, Ficheux, France, 4, F, 41.

Commemorated – St Stephen's Church, Rashcliffe, M Stansfield, page 41, and the **7 DWR Drill Hall WM panel 6, column 2.**
Mentioned in the Unit War Diary (MM award for raid of 04 7 1918) 14 7 1918, the London Gazette (MM award) 21 10 1918, page 12401; Huddersfield Voters; Huddersfield Examiner (in memoriam) 13 10 1919; L Magnus (medal roll), page 256.
"STILL OURS IN MEMORY THOUGHT AND LOVE"

BESWICK, Henry – 1110 Private.
Born in 1894 in Mossley. Resided in Mossley. Enlisted at Micklehurst.
1/7th Battalion DWR; died of wounds, shellfire, 24 8 1915 (Ypres Salient).
Buried – Lijssenthoek Military Cemetery, Belgium, 3, C, 27A.
Commemorated – All Saints Church WM; St George's Church WM; R Vaughan, page 38, and the 7 **DWR Drill Hall WM panel 4, column 2.**
SDGW shows number as 1166.

BETTS, Thomas – 307931 Private.
Born and resided in Bulwell, Notts. Enlisted at Nottingham.
1/7th Battalion DWR; killed in action 13 4 1918 (German Spring Offensive).
Buried – Mont Noir Military Cemetery, France, 1, E, 9.
Commemorated – the **7 DWR Drill Hall WM panel 7, column 1.**
Formerly 38903 Private, Northumberland Fusiliers.

BIDDLES, Joseph Henry - 306600 Private.
Son of Florence M Biddles, of 186 Ripon Street, Otley Road, Bradford. Enlisted at Bradford.
2/7th Battalion DWR; killed in action 03 5 1917, aged 22 (Battle of Bullecourt).
Commemorated – Arras Memorial, France, and the **7 DWR Drill Hall WM panel 7, column 3.**

BILL, John Samuel – 305383 Private; Territorial Force War Medal.
Born in 1896 in Maple, Staffs. Resided in Mossley. Enlisted at Uppermill. Embarked for France & Flanders in Jan 1917.
2/7th Battalion DWR; reported missing (killed in action) 03 5 1917 (Battle of Bullecourt).
Commemorated – Arras Memorial, France; St John the Baptist Church WM; R Vaughan, pages 18, 74 & 175, and **7 DWR Drill Hall WM panel 3, column 1.**
Mentioned in the Huddersfield Examiner (wounded in action) 01 6 1917.

BILTCLIFFE, Percy – 305846 Lance Corporal.
Born at Marsden, the son of Thomas and Rachel Biltcliffe, of 3 Argyle Street, Marsden. Resided in Marsden. Enlisted at Milnsbridge in August, 1914. Embarked for France & Flanders in January, 1917.
2/7th Battalion DWR; killed in action 03 5 1917, aged 21 (Battle of Bullecourt).
Commemorated – Arras Memorial, France: Marsden WM; M Stansfield, page 43, and the **7 DWR Drill Hall WM panel 5, column 2.**
Mentioned in the Huddersfield Examiner (wounded in action) 01 6 1917.
CWGC & SDGW show number as 305486.

BINGHAM, Walter – 205110 Private.
Born in Sheffield. Enlisted at Sheffield.
1/7th Battalion DWR; killed in action 25 11 1917 (Battle of Cambrai).
Buried – Perth Cemetery (China Wall), France, 5, J, 7.
Commemorated – the **7 DWR Drill Hall WM panel 7, column 1.**

BINKS, George – 307091 Private.
Born and enlisted in Leeds.

1/7th Battalion DWR; killed in action 14 4 1918 (German Spring Offensive).
Commemorated – Tyne Cot Memorial, Belgium, and the **7 DWR Drill Hall WM panel 7, column 3.**
WM shows 307191.

BINTCLIFFE, John Henry – 306909 Private.
Son of Reuben and Zillah Bintcliffe, of Green Gate Head, Sowood, Stainland, Halifax. Resided in Stainland. Enlisted at Halifax on 27 3 1916.
2/7th Battalion DWR, C Company, died of septic poisoning, 18 2 1918, aged 25.
Buried – Aubigny Communal Cemetery Extension, 3, C, 23.
Commemorated – St Andrew's Church, Stainland, Halifax; CWD, page 351; M Stansfield, page 43, and the **7 DWR Drill Hall WM panel 5, column 2.**
Mentioned in the Brighouse Echo (died) 08 3 1918.
"UNTIL THE DAY BREAKS AND THE SHADOWS FLEE AWAY"

BIRCH, Arthur Leonard – 307112 Private.
Born in Nottingham, to James and Lucy Birch, of 9 Coleridge Street, Radford, Nottingham. Enlisted at Nottingham.
1/7th Battalion DWR, A Company, died of wounds 29 4 1918, aged 21 (German Spring Offensive).
Buried – Lijssenthoek Military Cemetery, Belgium, 28, E, 11.
Commemorated – the **7 DWR Drill Hall WM panel 6, column 3.**
"BEAUTIFUL MEMORIES LEFT BEHIND – MOTHER"

BIRCH, Henry Edward – 1789 (later 242126) Sergeant.
Born and resided in Grimsby. Enlisted at Bradford.
1/7th Battalion DWR; killed in action 11 10 1918 (Advance to Victory, Battle of Iwuy).
Buried – Wellington Cemetery, Rieux-En-Cambresis, 3, B, 4.
Commemorated – the **7 DWR Drill Hall WM panel 1, column 1.**

BLADES, Albert – 306999 Private.
Son of Walker and Isabella Blades, of Glen Cottage, Bradley, Keighley. Resided in Bradford. Enlisted at Skipton.
2/7th Battalion DWR; died of wounds 14 4 1917.
Buried – Mory Abbey Military Cemetery, Mory, 1, B, 2.
Commemorated – CPGW website and the **7 DWR Drill Hall WM panel 1, column 1.**
"LOVED AND REMEMBERED"

BLAKEY, James – 1789 Private.
Born in Bradford. Resided in Bradford and at Warrington Terrace, Marsden. Enlisted at Milnsbridge, a local Territorial before outbreak of war.
1/7th Battalion DWR; killed in action 29 10 1915, aged 25 (Ypres Salient).
Buried – Talana Farm Cemetery, Belgium, 3, D, 3.
Commemorated – Marsden WM; M Stansfield, page 46, and the **7 DWR Drill Hall WM panel 4, column 2.**

BLAKEY, Walter – 4785 Private.
Born in Driffield, to George and Eliza Blakey. Enlisted at Leeds.
2/7th Battalion DWR; died at home 31 5 1916, aged 28.
Buried – Forest Town (St Alban's) Churchyard, Nottinghamshire.
Commemorated – the **7 DWR Drill Hall WM panel 5, column 3.**

BLAND, Ackroyd – 306561 Private.
Son of Mrs Alice Farrar Bland, of 32 Lidget Place, Lidget Green, Bradford. Enlisted at Bradford.

2/7th Battalion DWR; killed in action 16 4 1917, aged 28 (Battle of the Scarpe).
Commemorated – Arras Memorial and the **7 DWR Drill Hall WM panel 1, column 1.**
NA Roll shows 306551.

BLAND, Fred – 269058 Private.
Born and enlisted at Sheffield.
1/7th Battalion DWR; 13 4 1918 (German Spring Offensive).
Commemorated – Tyne Cot Memorial, Belgium, and the **7 DWR Drill Hall WM panel 7, column 1.**
WM shows 269858.

BLAND, Nelson – 6636 (later 307755) Private; Territorial Force War Medal.
Born Halifax on 21 3 1898, to Walter and Jane Bland, of 3 Alfred Street, Halifax. Resided at 368 Queens Road, Halifax. Enlisted at Halifax. Reservist, called up in August 1914.
1/7th Battalion DWR; killed in action 29 7 1917, aged 19 (Nieuport Sector).
Buried – Oostende New Communal Cemetery, Belgium, B, 7.
Commemorated – Halifax Civic Book of Remembrance; CWD, page 61, and the **Drill Hall WM panel 7, column 3.**
Mentioned in the Halifax Weekly Guardian (died) 11 8 1917.

BODDY, Mark – 307874 Private.
Born in Rotherham, to John and Alice Boddy, of Lorne Street, Waterloo Street, Hull. Enlisted at Hull.
1/7th Battalion DWR; killed in action 11 10 1918, aged 23 (Advance to Victory, Battle of Iwuy).
Buried – Wellington Cemetery, Rieux-En-Cambresis, France, 2, C, 2.
Commemorated the **7 DWR Drill Hall WM panel 1, column 1.**
"BELIEVE IN ME" SAID THE LORD "FOR I AM THE WAY, THE TRUTH AND THE LIFE"
WM shows 307834

BOFFEY, W – 4176 Private.
Son of Ada Boffey, of 7 Plais Street, Rowbarton, Taunton. Enlisted into 1/7th Battalion Northumberland Fusiliers.
Attached to 7th Battalion, DWR; died 15 8 1916 (Battle of the Somme).
Buried – Lonsdale Cemetery, Authuile, France, 7, H, 9.
Commemorated – the **7 DWR Drill Hall WM panel 5, column 2.**

BOLLAND, Arthur – 7074 Private.
Born in Benington, Boston, Lincs, to Emma Bolland, of Sea End, Benington. Enlisted at Boston.
1/7th Battalion DWR; died of wounds at home 27 11 1916, aged 23 (Battle of the Somme).
Buried – Benington (All Saints) Churchyard, Lincolnshire.
Commemorated – Arras Memorial, France, and the **7 DWR Drill Hall WM panel 5, column 1.**
Formerly 4033 Private, Northumberland Fusiliers.
WM shows surname spelt ROLLOND.

BOOTH, Frederick Arthur – 2nd Lieutenant, Distinguished Conduct Medal.
Born at Higher Crumpsall, to Mr & Mrs F W Booth of 'Moorside', Crumpsall Lane, Crumpsall, Manchester.
Attached to 1/7th Battalion DWR: killed in action 11 10 1918 aged 23, (Advance to Victory, Battle of Iwuy).
Buried – Wellington Cemetery, Rieux-En-Cambresis, 2, A, 12.
Commemorated - the **7 DWR Drill Hall WM panel 3, column 3.**
Mentioned in HDH Album 7 DWR Vol 2, page (killed in action, Battle of Iwuy, 10 1918).
Formerly 19229 Lance Sergeant, Manchester Regiment (DCM), from 2Lt, 8 West Yorkshire Regiment.
"TILL THE DAY BREAKS AND THE SHADOWS FLEE AWAY"

BOOTH, Harry – 2846 Private.
Resided in Oldham. Enlisted at Milnsbridge.
1/7th Battalion DWR; killed in action 17 9 1916 (Battle of the Somme, Leipzig Salient).
Commemorated – Thiepval Memorial, France, and the **7 DWR Drill Hall WM panel 5, column 2.**

BOOTH, Lawrence Ewart – 2314 Private.
Born at 19, Lowergate, Longwood on 13 5 1898, the son of Harry and Charlotte Ann Booth, of, 46 Rufford Road, Sear Lane, Milnsbridge. Resided at 51, Crow Lane Terrace, Milnsbridge. Enlisted at Milnsbridge on 07 10 1914, embarked for France & Flanders in April, 1915.
1/7th Battalion DWR; killed in action (shot by sniper) 27 5 1915, aged 17.
Buried – Rue-David Military Cemetery, Fleurbaix, France, 1, B, 15.
Commemorated – Shared Church, Paddock RoH, St John's Church, Golcar, RoH; Crow Lane Board School, Milnsbridge, RoH; M Stansfield, page 49, and the **7 DWR Drill Hall WM panel 4, column 3.**
Mentioned in the Huddersfield Examiner (shot when leaving trenches) 02 6 1915.
"FOR KING AND COUNTRY TILL WE MEET AGAIN"

BOOTH, Samuel – 307617 Private.
Born in Bradford. Husband of Edith Spalding (formerly Booth), of 55 Airedale Cottages, Kildwick, Keighley. Enlisted at Keighley.
2/7th Battalion DWR; killed in action 03 5 1917 (Battle of Bullecourt).
Commemorated – Arras Memorial, France, and the **7 DWR Drill Hall WM panel 3, column 1.**

BOOTHROYD, Harry – 269184 Private.
Born on 16 3 1882, Swan Lane, Lockwood, the son of George Boothroyd. Resided with spouse, Edith Annie, at 63 Blackhouse Road, Fartown, Huddersfield. Enlisted at Huddersfield on 17 3 1917.
1/7th Battalion DWR; killed in action 14 4 1918, aged 36 (German Spring Offensive).
Commemorated – Tyne Cot Memorial, France; Christ Church, Woodhouse Hill, RoH; Fartown & Birkby WM; Lockwood Cemetery WM; M Stansfield, page 52, and the **7 DWR Drill Hall WM panel 7, column 2.**

BOSTOCK, Frederick – 307152 Private.
Born in Nottingham, the son of Arthur James Bostock, of 4 Conway Street, St Ann's Road, Nottingham. Enlisted at Nottingham.
1/7th Battalion DWR; killed in action 23 2 1918.
Buried – Duhallow ADS Cemetery, Belgium, 8, F, 15.
Commemorated – the **7 DWR Drill Hall WM panel 7, column 3.**

BOTTOMLEY, Edgar – 5968 Private West Yorkshire Regiment, formerly 5111 Pte, DWR.
Resided in Northowram, Halifax. Enlisted at Halifax.
2/7th Battalion West Yorkshire Regiment; killed in action 17 2 1917.
Buried – Waggon Road Cemetery, Beaumont-Hamel, France, E, 42.
Commemorated – the **7 DWR Drill Hall WM panel 5, column 3.**

BOTTOMLEY, Lewis – 268580 Private.
Born in Marsden, the son of John and Ellen Bottomley, of 61 Higher Ardwick, Manchester. Resided in Fern Lea, Marsden. Enlisted at Milnsbridge in October, 1914, aged 16.
1/7th Battalion DWR; killed in action 29 4 1918, aged 20.
Commemorated – Tyne Cot Memorial, France; Marsden WM; St Mark's Parish Church, Longwood; Marsden Churchyard (parents' headstone); Marsden Conservative Club RoH; M Stansfield, page 54, and the **7 DWR Drill Hall WM panel 6, column 2.**
WM shows 268588.

BOTTOMLEY, Oswald – 307753 Private.
Only son of Sam and Alice Bottomley, of 4 Stod Fold, Mixenden, Halifax. Enlisted at Halifax in 1914.
1/7th Battalion DWR; killed in action 13 4 1918, aged 20 (German Spring Offensive).
Commemorated – Tyne Cot Memorial, Belgium; St Mary's Church, Illingworth, Halifax, RoH; Halifax Civic Book of Remembrance; CWD, page 61, and the **7 DWR Drill Hall WM panel 7, column 2.**
Mentioned in Brighouse Echo 17 5 1918.

BOTTOMLEY, T N – 23868 Private.
Commemorated - the **7 DWR Drill Hall WM panel 1, column 1.**
No trace of this man by name or number in CWGC, SDGW or Regimental records.

BOTTOMLEY, William – 305936 Private.
Resided in Oldham. Enlisted at Milnsbridge.
2/7th Battalion DWR; killed in action 27 11 1917 (Battle of Cambrai).
Commemorated – Cambrai Memorial, Louverval, France, and the **7 DWR Drill Hall WM panel 7, column 2.**

BOWER, John (Jonathan?) Thomas – 3024 Private. Silver War Badge awarded.
Born at Damside Road, Huddersfield, on 07 7 1892, the son of Mr & Mrs John Bower, of 2 Graham's Yard, Milford Street, Huddersfield. Husband of Ida Bower of 3 Bent Street, King's Mill Lane, Huddersfield. Enlisted on 02 6 1915. Wounded (spine) in September 1916, taken to Royds Hall Hospital, Huddersfield, in January 1917.
1/7th Battalion DWR; died at Royds Hall War Hospital on 27 4 1918, aged 26 (Battle of the Somme).
Buried – Huddersfield (Edgerton) Cemetery, Screen Wall 2B, 116.
Commemorated – South Crosland and Netherton WM; Huddersfield Corporation RoH; M Stansfield, page 55, and the **7 DWR Drill Hall WM panel 4, column 2.**
Mentioned in the Huddersfield Examiner (shell shock) 02 10 1916, (shrapnel wound) 03 10 1916).

BOWYER, Albert – 20708 Corporal.
Born at Charlton, London. Resided in North Shields. Enlisted at London.
1/7th Battalion DWR; killed in action 29 4 1918 (German Spring Offensive).
Commemorated – Tyne Cot Memorial, Belgium, and the **7 DWR Drill Hall WM panel 2, column 1.**

BOYES, Norman – 267803 Private.
Born in Bradford, the son of Mr F Boyes of 13 Lemon Street, Little Horton, Bradford. Enlisted at Bradford.
1/7th Battalion DWR; died of wounds 14 10 1918 (Advance to Victory, Battle of Iwuy).
Buried – Naves Communal Cemetery Extension, France, 5, A, 17.
Commemorated - the **7 DWR Drill Hall WM panel 6, column 2.**

BRADBURY, Robert – 1343 Private.
Born at Springhead, Lancashire, to John and Mary Ann Bradbury. Native of Lees, Lancs. Enlisted at Lees.
1/7th Battalion DWR; died of wounds at Base Hospital on 25 9 1915.
Buried – Etaples Military Cemetery, France, 4, G, 15A.
Commemorated – the **7 DWR Drill Hall WM panel 4, column 2.**
WM shows initial P.

BRADBURY, Thomas Piers – Lieutenant.
Son of Joseph and Mrs Bradbury, of 'Ardeme', Uppermill, Yorkshire.
7th Battalion DWR; killed in action 26 4 1918, aged 23 (German Spring Offensive).

Commemorated – Tyne Cot Memorial, Belgium, and the **7 DWR Drill Hall WM panel 3, column 3.**
Mentioned in the Unit War Diary (joined 1/7th in 5 1915) 25 6 1915; J Fisher, with photograph, pages 55 & 133; Mentioned in HDH Album 7 DWR Vol 2, pages 5, 34 & 35, with photo (joined 1/7th 25 6 1915, to 1/4thYork and Lancaster Regt, killed in action 26 4 1918). G Howcroft, (joined 1/7th 1915), page 12, (details of action in 1918, with photograph), pages 123 & 124.

BRAMBINI, Augustine – 306637 Private.
Born in Bradford, the son of Agostino and Frances Brambini, of 49 Woodland Street, City Road, Bradford. Enlisted at Bradford.
2/7th Battalion DWR; killed in action 01 6 1918, aged 25.
Buried – Bienvillers Military Cemetery, France, 21, A, 11.
Commemorated – the **7 DWR Drill Hall WM Panel 3, column 1.**
CWGC & SDGW show name as BRAMBANI.
"INTO THY HANDS O LORD"

BRAMHALL, Albert Bishop – 34074 Private.
Born at Salford, the son of Albert Griffiths and Ellen Bramhall, of 17 Higher West Street, Eccles New Road, Weaste, Salford. Enlisted at Manchester.
1/7th Battalion DWR; killed in action 11 10 1918, aged 18 (Advance to Victory, Battle of Iwuy).
Buried – Wellington Cemetery, Rieux-En-Cambresis, France, 2, C, 6.
Commemorated – the **7 DWR Drill Hall WM panel 3, column 2.**
WM shows name as Bramhall A J; CWGC shows initials as A B; SDGW shows surname as BRAMBALL.
"A SILENT SIGH, A HIDDEN TEAR, A SACRED MEMORY OF ONE SO DEAR"

BRANNAN, Joseph – 34647 Private.
Born and enlisted at Newcastle-on-Tyne.
1/7th Battalion DWR; killed in action 11 10 1918 (Advance to Victory, Battle of Iwuy).
Buried – Wellington Cemetery, Rieux-En-Cambresis, 2, B, 5.
Commemorated – the **7 DWR Drill Hall WM panel 2, column 3.**
Formerly 69090 Pte Northumberland Fusiliers.
CWGC show name as BRANNEN.

BRANT, W 17075 – see **GRANT, William**.
Commemorated – the **7 DWR Drill Hall WM panel 2, column 1.**
CWGC and SDGW shows name as Grant.

BRAY, Walter Booth – 28585 Private.
Born and resided in Thongsbridge, Huddersfield. Enlisted at Huddersfield in January, 1917.
2/7th Battalion DWR; killed in action 27 3 1918 (German Spring Offensive).
Buried – Pommier Communal Cemetery, France, 1.
Commemorated –All Saints Churchyard, Netherthong, Memorial; Hospital (Netherthong & Thongsbridge Plaque) WM; Netherthong Working Men's Club RoH; M Stansfield, page 61, and the **7 DWR Drill Hall WM panel 3, column 1.**
CWGC & M Stansfield, page 61, shows number as 23585.

BREEZE, William Edward – 306958 Private.
Resided in Attercliffe, Sheffield, the son of James and Clara E A Breeze, of 46 Edward Road, Attercliffe. Enlisted at Sheffield.
2/7th Battalion DWR; killed in action 03 5 1917, aged 20 (Battle of Bullecourt).
Commemorated – Arras Memorial, France, and the **7 DWR Drill Hall WM panel 2, column 1.**

BRENNAN, Harold James – 307697 Drummer.
Born in Pietermatitzburg. Resided in Bradford, the son of William Edward and Annie Leng Brennan. 7, Whetley Grove, Whetley Lane, Manningham, Bradford. Enlisted in Guiseley.
1/7th Battalion DWR; killed in action 11 10 1918, aged 20 (Advance to Victory, Battle of Iwuy).
Buried – Wellington Cemetery, Rieux-En-Cambresis, 2, C, 5.
Commemorated - the **7 DWR Drill Hall WM panel 1, column 3.**

BRIERLEY, Oliver – 2162 Private.
Resided in Delph. Enlisted at Milnsbridge.
1/7th Battalion DWR; died of wounds 17 11 1916 (Battle of the Somme).
Buried –Warlincourt Halte British Cemetery, France, 4, A, 15.
Commemorated – the **7 DWR Drill Hall WM panel 5, column 1.**

BRIERLEY, William – 394 Private.
Born in Longwood, Huddersfield, the son of Mr and Mrs Roland Brierley, of 202 Cliffe End, Longwood. Enlisted at Milnsbridge, a local pre-war Territorial. Embarked for France & Flanders in April, 1915.
1/7th Battalion DWR; reported missing, presumed killed in action, 03 9 1916, aged 24 (Battle of the Somme, Thiepval).
Commemorated – Thiepval Memorial, France, St Mark's Parish Church, Longwood, RoH; M Stansfield, page 62, and the **7 DWR Drill Hall WM panel 5, column 1.**
Mentioned in the Huddersfield Examiner (killed in action) 02 11 1916.

BRIGGS, Henry – 306574 Lance Corporal.
Brother of James Briggs, of Northfield, Eccleshill, Bradford. Enlisted at Bradford.
2/7th Battalion DWR; killed in action 03 5 1917 (Battle of Bullecourt).
Commemorated – Arras Memorial, France, and the **7 DWR Drill Hall WM panel 1, column 2.**

BRIXTON, W - see BUXTON, William.
CWGC & SDGW show name as BUXTON.

BROADBENT, Herbert Lionel (Bertie) – 2240 Private.
Born on 05 1 1899, the son of Superintendant and Mrs A Broadbent, of 6 Woodthorpe Terrace, Bankfield Road, Huddersfield. Enlisted at Milnsbridge in September, 1914. Embarked for France & Flanders in April 1915.
1/5th Battalion DWR; killed in action 30 7 1915 aged 16 (Ypres Salient).
Buried – Colne Valley Cemetery, Belgium, D, 7.
Commemorated – St Thomas's Church, Longroyd Bridge; M Stansfield, page 63, and the **7 DWR Drill Hall WM panel 4, column 1.**

BROADBENT, John Franklin – 306241 Private.
Born in Marsden. Resided in Huddersfield, the son of Augustus Henry Broadbent, of 22, Ottiwell's Terrace, Marsden, Huddersfield. Enlisted at Milnsbridge on 15 9 1915.
1/7th Battalion DWR; killed in action 03 9 1916, aged 21 (Battle of the Somme, Thiepval).
Commemorated – Thiepval Memorial, France; Marsden War Memorial; M Stansfield, page 63, and the **7 DWR Drill Hall WM panel 6, column 2.**

BROADLEY, Arnold Howard – 34648 Private.
Born in Morley. Resided in Batley. Enlisted at Dewsbury.
1/7th Battalion DWR; killed in action 11 10 1918 (Advance to Victory, Battle of Iwuy).
Buried – Wellington Cemetery, Rieux-En-Cambresis, France, 2, C, 10.
Commemorated - the **7 DWR Drill Hall WM panel 1, column 1.**

Formerly 69093 Pte, Northumberland Fusiliers.

BROOK, Amon – 306795 Private.
Born at Shelf, Halifax. Resided in 54 Burnett Avenue, Bradford. Enlisted at Halifax.
2/7th Battalion DWR; killed in action 14 5 1917.
Commemorated – Arras Memorial, France; Shelf Primitive Methodist Church; Shelf Wesleyan Methodist Church; CWD, page 357, and the **7 DWR Drill Hall WM panel 1, column 1.**
Mentioned in Bradford Weekly Telegraph (died) 08 6 1917.

BROOK, Harold – 307759 Private.
Born on 24 9 1897, the son of Mr and Mrs G Brook of 200 Manchester Road, Huddersfield. Enlisted at Huddersfield.
1/7th Battalion DWR; died of wounds (gas poisoning) 30 7 1917, aged 19.
Buried – Coxyde Military Cemetery, Belgium, 3, A, 6.
Commemorated – St Thomas's Church, Longroyd Bridge; M Stansfield, page 67, the **7 DWR Drill Hall WM panel 6, column 2.**
Mentioned in the Huddersfield Examiner (casualty list) 04 9 1917.

BROOK, Harry – 305197 Sergeant.
Born in Marsden. Resided in 35 Royds Terrace, Marsden, Huddersfield, the son of Benjamin and Elizabeth Brook, of 35 Royds Terrace, Marsden. Enlisted at Marsden.
1/7th Battalion DWR; killed in action 08 10 1917, aged 23 (3rd Battle of Ypres, Passchendaele).
Commemorated – Tyne Cot Memorial, France; Marsden WM; M Stansfield, page 68, and the **7 DWR Drill Hall WM panel 6, column 1.**

BROOKS, Alfred – 2569 Private.
Resided in Stalybridge, the son of John and Sarah Brooks of 96 Brierley Street, Stalybridge. Enlisted at Milnsbridge.
1/7th Battalion DWR; killed in action 25 1 1917.
Buried – Berles-Au-Bois Churchyard Extension, France, Q, 6.
Commemorated – Stalybridge WM and the **7 DWR Drill Hall WM panel 5, column 2.**
"REST IN PEACE"

BROOKS, Joseph William – 307934 Private.
Born in Nottingham. Enlisted at Nottingham.
1/7th Battalion DWR; died of wounds 28 7 1917 (Nieuport Sector).
Buried – Coxyde Military Cemetery, Belgium 3, L, 7.
Commemorated – the **7 DWR Drill Hall WM panel 6, column 1.**
Formerly 38879 Private Northumberland Fusiliers.
CWGC & SDGW show name as BROOKES.

BROWN, Frank – 306572 Private.
Resided in Bradford. Enlisted at Harrogate.
2/7th Battalion DWR; killed in action 03 5 1917.
Commemorated – Arras Memorial, France, and the **7 DWR Drill Hall WM panel 3, column 2.**

BROWN, George – 268193 Private.
Born and enlisted at Bradford.
1/7th Battalion DWR; killed in action 31 7 1918.
Buried – Hagel Dump Cemetery, Belgium, 2, D, 7.
Commemorated – the **7 DWR Drill Hall WM panel 6, column 3.**

BROWN, John William – 306496 Private, Brighouse Tribute Medal.
Born in Brighouse, the son of Albert and Amelia Brown of 6 Crown Street, Highcliffe Road, Brighouse. Enlisted at Brighouse, March 1916.
2/7th Battalion DWR; killed in action 03 5 1917, aged 30 (Battle of Bullecourt).
Commemorated – Arras Memorial, France; Brighouse WM; Rastrick WM; CWD, page 359, and the **7 DWR Drill Hall WM panel 1, column 2.**
Mentioned in Brighouse Echo 18 & 25 5 1917, with photograph; the Huddersfield Examiner (casualty list) 01 6 1917.

BROWN, John William – 306821 Private.
Resided at 93, Highbury Place, Rastick, Brighouse, the son of Mr and Mrs Sam Brown, of Rastrick. Enlisted at Halifax.
2/7th Battalion DWR; died of wounds 27 3 1918, aged 42 (German Spring Offensive).
Buried – Bienvillers Military Cemetery, France, 12, A, 11.
Commemorated – Brighouse WM; Rastrick WM; CWD, page 359, and the **7 DWR Drill Hall WM Panel 3, column 1.**
Mentioned in the Brighouse Echo 19 4 1918.

BROWN, Joseph – 325033 Private.
Born in Bethnal Green, London. Resided in Walthamstow. Enlisted at London.
1/7th Battalion DWR; died of wounds 12 4 1918 (German Spring Offensive).
Buried – Meteren Military Cemetery, France, 4, A, 795.
Commemorated – the **7 DWR Drill Hall WM panel 7, column 1.**
Formerly SS/4663 Private RASC & 304066 Labour Corps.

BROWN, Joseph Francis – 16909 Sergeant, Distinguished Conduct Medal.
Born in Leeds. Resided in Bradford, the son of Emma Brown of 13 Dean Street, Brownroyd, Bradford. Enlisted at Bradford.
1/7th Battalion DWR; died of wounds, Base Hospital, 14 4 1918, aged 20 (German Spring Offensive).
Buried – Boulogne Eastern Cemetery, France, 8, I, 190.
Commemorated – the **7 DWR Drill Hall WM panel 2, column 1.**
Mentioned in the London Gazette (DCM award) 04 3 1918, page 2734.
"MY HOPE IS IN THEE"

BROWN, Trenholme – 267379 Private.
Resided in Bradford, the husband of Mary H Walker (formerly Brown), of 29, Farfield Terrace, Manningham, Bradford.
1/7th Battalion DWR; died of wounds, at home, on 27 11 1917, aged 28.
Buried – Bradford (Scholemoor) Cemetery, 5, C, 1714.
Commemorated – the **7 DWR Drill Hall WM panel 3, column 2.**

BRUMBILL, John – 203213 Private.
Born at Brownhills, Staffs. Resided in Aldridge. Enlisted at Lichfield.
1/7th Battalion DWR; killed in action 11 10 1918 (Advance to Victory, Battle of Iwuy).
Buried - Wellington Cemetery, Rieux-En-Cambresis, France, 3, C, 4.
Commemorated - the **7 DWR Drill Hall WM panel 1, column 3.**
Formerly 5043 Private, Durham Light Infantry.
WM shows BRUMBELL; SDGW shows number as 208213.

BRYDON, Joseph Henry – 34661 Private.
Born in Newcastle on Tyne, the son of Joseph Henry Septimus and Elizabeth Brydon, of 48 Isabella Street, Elswick, Newcastle-on-Tyne. Enlisted at Newcastle-on-Tyne.

1/7th Battalion DWR; killed in action 11 10 1918, aged 18 (Advance to Victory, Battle of Iwuy).
Buried – Wellington Cemetery, Rieux-En-Cambresis, France, 2, C, 8.
Commemorated - the **7 DWR Drill Hall WM panel 2, column 3.**
WM shows name as DRYDEN.
"THY WILL, BE DONE"

BUCKLEY, Abraham – 947 Private.
Born and resided at Oldham. Enlisted at Uppermill.
1/7th Battalion DWR; killed in action, shellfire, 20 12 1915 (Ypres Salient).
Commemorated – Ypres (Menin Gate) Memorial, Belgium, and the **7 DWR Drill Hall WM panel 4, column 3.**
Mentioned in Unit War Diary (killed in action) 20 12 1915.

BUCKLEY, Robert – 305878 Lance Sergeant.
Born in 1891 in Mossley. Resided in Mossley. Enlisted at Uppermill. Embarked for France & Flanders on 15 4 1915.
1/7th Battalion DWR; died of wounds 25 5 1917 (aged 25).
Buried – Vieille-Chapelle New Military Cemetery, Lacouture, France, 1, E, 1.
Commemorated – St John the Baptist Church WM; United Methodist Church WM; Abney (Derbyshire) Congregational Church WM; and the **7 DWR Drill Hall WM panel 2, column 2.**
Mentioned in Unit War Diary (wounded 24 5 1917, died of wounds 25 5 1917).

BUCKLEY, Thomas – 2360 Private.
Resided in Uppermill, the husband of Sarah Buckley, of 158 Derker Street, Oldham. Enlisted at Uppermill.
1/7th Battalion DWR; died of wounds 09 8 1915 (Ypres Salient).
Buried – Lijssenthoek Military Cemetery, Belgium, 1, C, 13.
Commemorated – the **7 DWR Drill Hall WM panel 4, column 2.**
Mentioned in Unit War Diary (killed in action) 08 8 1915.
"GONE FROM OUR HOME BUT NEVER FROM OUR HEARTS"

BUCKLEY, Thomas – 2604 Private.
Born in Holbeck, Leeds, the son of James and Louisa Buckley, of 47 Beech Street, Shaw, Lancashire. Resided in Oldham. Enlisted at Milnsbridge.
1/7th Battalion DWR; killed in action, shellfire, 24 8 1915, aged 22 (Ypres Salient).
Buried – Bard Cottage Cemetery, Belgium, 1, F, 31.
Commemorated – the **7 DWR Drill Hall WM panel 4, column 2.**
Mentioned in Unit War Diary (killed in action) 24 8 1915.

BUCKLEY, Wilfred Ward – 1839 Sergeant.
Born and resided at Diggle, the son of Thomas Ward Buckley, of 20 Hill View Council Houses, Diggle. Enlisted at Milnsbridge.
1/7th Battalion DWR; killed in action 03 9 1916, aged 24 (Battle of the Somme, Thiepval).
Commemorated – Thiepval Memorial, Somme, France, and the **7 DWR Drill Hall WM panel 5, column 2.**
Mentioned in J Fisher, page 113.
SDGW shows number as 1835.

BUMELL, Edward Arthur – see **BURNELL, Edward Arthur**.
CWGC shows name spelt BURNELL.

BURKE, George – 936 Private.
Resided in Huddersfield. Enlisted at Uppermill.
1/7th Battalion DWR; killed in action, shellfire, 20 12 1915 (Ypres Salient).
Commemorated – Ypres (Menin Gate) Memorial, Belgium; M Stansfield, page 76, and the **7 DWR Drill Hall WM panel 4, column 2.**
Mentioned in the Unit War Diary (killed in action) 20 12 1915; J Fisher (killed in action) page 110.

BURNELL, Edward Arthur – 26416 Private.
Born in Sampford Brett, Somerset. Resided in Williton. Enlisted at Taunton.
2/7th Battalion DWR; died of wounds 13 4 1918 (German Spring Offensive).
Buried – Doullens Communal Cemetery, France, 6, B, 18.
Commemorated – the **7 DWR Drill Hall WM panel 2, column 3.**
Formerly 33330 Pte, Somerset Light Infantry, 34312 Pte, 10 R Berkshire Regiment & 94890 Pte, Labour Corps.
WM shows name as BUMELL.

BURNS, James – 3476 Private.
Born in Mossley, the son of Thomas and Martha Burns. Resided in Mossley. Enlisted on 28 10 1915 at Milnsbridge.
1/7th Battalion DWR; died at home, No 1 General Hospital, Newcastle on Tyne, of pneumonia, on 04 12 1915.
Buried – Mossley Cemetery, R.C. 3074.
Commemorated – R Vaughan, pages 20 43 & 153; the **7 DWR Drill Hall WM panel 4, column 3.**
"St JOSEPH PRAY FOR HIM"

BURNS, Matthew – 306633 Private.
Son of Mr M Burns, of 52, Pollard Street, Bradford. Enlisted at Bradford.
2/7th Battalion DWR; killed in action 16 4 1917 (Battle of the Scarpe).
Buried – Ecoust Military Cemetery, Ecoust St Mien, France, 2, A, 32.
Commemorated – the **7 DWR Drill Hall WM panel 1, column 1.**

BUTTERWORTH, Ernest – 2165 Private.
Born and resided in Holmfirth, the son of Alfred H and Alice A Butterworth, of Park Riding, Holmfirth. Enlisted at Milnsbridge on the outbreak of war, with local Territorials.
1/7th Battalion DWR; killed in action (gunshot to head) 12 7 1915, aged 26 (Ypres Salient).
Buried – Colne Valley Cemetery, Belgium, D, 14.
Commemorated – Holmfirth WM; Upperthong WM; M Stansfield, page 79, and the **7 DWR Drill Hall WM panel 4, column 3.**
Mentioned in the Huddersfield Examiner (killed in action) 15 7 1915.

BUTTERWORTH, Wilfred – 34080 Private.
Born and resided at New Hey, Rochdale, the son of John S and Mary M Butterworth, of 20 Huddersfield Road, New Hey. Enlisted at Rochdale.
1/7th Battalion DWR, B Company; killed in action 11 10 1918, aged 18 (Advance to Victory, Battle of Iwuy).
Buried – Wellington Cemetery, Rieux-En-Cambresis, 3, B, 8.
Commemorated – the **7 DWR Drill Hall WM panel 2, column 2** and **panel 7, column 2.**
"HE LAID HIS RICHEST GIFT ON THE ALTAR OF DUTY, HIS LIFE"

BUXTON, W – 1748 Private.
Born at Blackley, Lancs, the son of Frederick and Mary Buxton, of 3 Seed Street, Radcliffe, Manchester. Resided in Denshaw, Lancs. Enlisted at Middleton, Lancs.

1/7th Battalion DWR; killed in action 10 8 1915, aged 23 (Ypres Salient).
Buried – Colne Valley Cemetery, Belgium, D, 4 (collective).
Commemorated – the **7 DWR Drill Hall WM panel 4, column 2.**
WM shows BRIXTON W. Duplicate Medal Index Card for Burton W, annotated see Buxton, the Buxton MIC shows 1718.
"HERE IS NOW THY HERO SLEEPING"

BYRON, Jesse Rose – 306754 Private.
Enlisted at Bradford.
2/7th Battalion DWR; killed in action 03 5 1917 (Battle of Bullecourt).
Commemorated – Arras Memorial, France, and **7 DWR Drill Hall WM panel 1, column 2.**

CADEN, Robert – 202312 Private.
Born in Halifax, the son of Patrick and Mary Caden, of 38 Back Foundry Street, Halifax. Enlisted at Halifax in March, 1916.
1/7th Battalion DWR; died of wounds 12 4 1918, aged 23 (German Spring Offensive).
Buried – Steenwerck, France, German Cemetery Memorial. 3.
Commemorated – Sacred Heart & St. Bernard's Roman Catholic Church, Halifax; Halifax Civic Book of Remembrance; CWD, page 77, and the **7 DWR Drill Hall WM panel 6, column 3.**
Mentioned in the Halifax Courier 28 5 1918; Hebden Bridge Times 31 5 1918.
"EVER REMEMBERED R.I.P."

CAMPBELL, Duncan Frederick – Lieutenant Colonel. Distinguished Service Order, Twice Mentioned in Despatches.
Son of Archibald Frederick and Helen Frances Campbell, of 304 Queen Street South, Hamilton, Ontario, Canada. Member of Parliament for North Ayrshire from 1911. Served in the South African Campaign.
2/7th Battalion DWR, Commanding Officer, died in Southwold Hospital on 04 9 1916, aged 39.
Buried – Kilmarnock Cemetery, Scotland, New portion. 28.
Commemorated – the **7 DWR Drill Hall WM panel 3, column 3.**
Formerly 3rd Battalion Black Watch (Royal Highlanders).
Mentioned in Goodall Collection, with obituary.

CAREY, John Allen – 2823 (later 305954) Private.
Born and resided in Oldham, the son of John and Anne Carey, of 13, Bankhill Street, Oldham. Enlisted at Milnsbridge.
1/7th Battalion DWR; died at home 03 1 1917, aged 19.
Buried – Whitby (Larpool) Cemetery, Yorkshire, Blue 4024.
Commemorated – the **7 DWR Drill Hall WM panel 3, column 2.**

CAREY, Stacey M – 33815 Private.
Born in Hammersmith, the son of Frank and Kate Carey, of 429, Latimer Road, North Kensington, London. Enlisted at Whitehall.
1/7th Battalion DWR, A Company; killed in action 11 10 1918, aged 18 (Advance to Victory, Battle of Iwuy).
Buried – Wellington Cemetery, Rieux-En-Cambresis, 2, B, 6.
Commemorated – the **7 DWR Drill Hall WM panel 2, column 3.**

CARTER, Alfred – 2832 Private.
Son of Samuel Carter of 2 Industrial Terrace, Greenside, Dalton. Enlisted at Milnsbridge in January 1915.
1/7th Battalion DWR; killed in action, shellfire, 20 12 1915, aged 22 (Ypres Salient).

Commemorated – Ypres (Menin Gate) Memorial, Belgium; St. Paul's Wesleyan Church, Dalton; M Stansfield, page 82, and the **7 DWR Drill Hall WM panel 4, column 2.**
Mentioned in the Unit War Diary (killed in action) 20 12 1915.

CARTER, Lionel – 2221 Private.
Resided in Delph. Enlisted at Milnsbridge.
1/7th Battalion DWR; killed in action 20 7 1915 (Ypres Salient).
Buried – Colne Valley Cemetery, Belgium, D, 11.
Commemorated – the **7 DWR Drill Hall WM panel 4, column 2.**

CARTER, Sydney Emsley – 4879 (later 306912) Private.
Son of William and Ellen Carter, of 10 Raikes Road, Skipton.
1/7th Battalion DWR; died of wounds 17 11 1916, aged 23 (Battle of the Somme).
Buried – Foncquevillers Military Cemetery 1, J, 30.
Commemorated – the **7 DWR Drill Hall WM panel 5, column 1 AND panel 7 column 3.**
WM shows 4873, panel 1 & 306912, panel 7.
"MAY HE REST IN PEACE"

CARTWRIGHT, Gordon – 2082 Private.
Born at Moldgreen, the son of Charles and Marion Cartwright of 109 Wakefield Road, Moldgreen.
Resided in Moldgreen, Huddersfield. Enlisted at Milnsbridge on 08 9 1914.
1/7th Battalion DWR; died of wounds (to head), at No.10 CCS, on 12 7 1915, aged 17 (Ypres Salient).
Buried – Lijssenthoek Military Cemetery, Belgium, 3, C, 3.
Commemorated – Christ Church, Mold Green, Kirkheaton Cemetery, headstone; M Stansfield, page 84, and the **7 DWR Drill Hall WM panel 4, column 3.**
"GONE BUT NOT FORGOTTEN"
Mentioned in the Huddersfield Examiner (died of wounds) 23 7 1915 & 04 8 1915.

CARTWRIGHT, Thomas – 1737 Private.
Son of Mrs E A Cartwright of 'The Shaws', Uppermill, Oldham. Enlisted at Uppermill.
1/7th Battalion DWR; killed in action 03 5 1917. aged 21.
Buried – Rue-David Military Cemetery, Fleurbaix, France, 1, A, 19.
Commemorated – the **7 DWR Drill Hall WM panel 4, column 1.**
Mentioned in HDH Album 7 DWR Vol 2, page 5 (1st 7 DWR casualty, 02 5 1915).
"REMEMBRANCE OF HIS LIFE IS OUR SWEETEST THOUGHT"

CASEMAN, Ernest – 34089 Private.
Born and enlisted at Rochdale.
1/7th Battalion DWR; killed in action 11 10 1918 (Advance to Victory, Battle of Iwuy).
Buried – Wellington Cemetery, Rieux-en-Cambresis, France, 1, E, 6.
Commemorated – **7 DWR Drill Hall WM panel 2, column 3.**

CASTLE, John Arthur – 12336 Private.
Born at Golcar, the son of Mr and Mrs Firth, of 316 Manchester Road, Milnsbridge. Enlisted at Huddersfield in September 1914. Twice wounded.
2/7th Battalion DWR; died of wounds 28 11 1917, aged 28 (Battle of Cambrai).
Commemorated – Cambrai Memorial, Louverval, France; Milnsbridge WM; CVA; M Stansfield, page 86, and the **7 DWR Drill Hall WM panel 2, column 1.**
Mentioned in the Huddersfield Examiner (official casualty list) 11 6 1917 (in memoriam) 28 11 1918, 28 11 1919 & 29 11 1920.

CATER, George Edward – 305484 Lance Corporal.
Born in Marsden, the son of Mr and Mrs W E Cater of Side Ing. Resided in Marsden. Enlisted at Milnsbridge in August, 1914. Embarked for France & Flanders in April, 1915.
1/7th Battalion DWR; killed in action 13 4 1918, aged 23 (German Spring Offensive).
Buried – Le Grand Beaumart British Cemetery, Steenwerck, France, Special Memorial A7.
Commemorated – Marsden WM; CVA; M Stansfield, page 86, and the **7 DWR Drill Hall WM panel 6, column 1.**
"THEIR GLORY SHALL NOT BE BLOTTED OUT"

CHAMPKIN, Laurence William – 305925 Sergeant.
Son of John and Elizabeth Champkin of Dunstable, Bedfordshire. Husband of Edith Lilian Boardman (formerly Champkin), of 62 Greengate Street, Oldham. Enlisted in December 1914.
2/7th Battalion DWR, C Company; died 14 2 1919, aged 49.
Buried – Oldham (Chadderton) Cemetery, Lancashire, E, 2, 176.
Served in the Royal Engineers, Sgt 48096, for a short time.
Commemorated – the **7 DWR Drill Hall WM panel 3, column 1.**

CHAPMAN, Arthur Allsop – 2nd Lieutenant.
Son of Henry and Sabina Chapman, of 20 Athlone Grove, Armley, Leeds.
7th Battalion, attached to 9th Battalion DWR; died 25 4 1917, aged 21.
Buried – Feuchy Chapel British Cemetery, Wancourt 5, G, 2.
Commemorated – Leeds University Roll of Honour and the **7 DWR Drill Hall WM panel 3, column 3.**
"DEARLY LOVED ONLY SON OF MR & MRS CHAPMAN, ARMLEY, LEEDS. REST IN PEACE"

CHAPMAN, Eli – 865 Private.
Born at Waterhead, the son of William and Mary Chapman, of 54 Shaws Road, Birkdale, Southport, Lancs. Resided in Oldham. Enlisted at Lees.
1/7th Battalion DWR; killed in action 17 9 1916, aged 24 (Battle of the Somme, Leipzig Salient).
Commemorated – Thiepval Memorial, Somme, France, and the **7 DWR Drill Hall WM panel 5, column 3.**

CHAPMAN, Stanley – 34092 Private.
Born at Manchester, the son of Charles and Sarah Ann Chapman, of 69 Fitzwarren Street, Seedley, Manchester. Resided in Manchester. Enlisted at Salford.
1/7th Battalion DWR; died of wounds 15 7 1918, aged 18.
Buried – Esquelbecq Military Cemetery, France, 3, E, 2.
Commemorated – the **7 DWR Drill Hall WM panel 2, column 1.**
"THY PURPOSE LORD WE CANNOT SEE, BUT ALL IS WELL THAT'S DONE BY THEE"

CHAPPELL, Harry – 3815 Private.
Son of Mr and Mrs Ben Chappell, of Bank Top, Hill Top, Slaithwaite. Resided in Slaithwaite, Huddersfield. Enlisted at Milnsbridge in March, 1916.
1/7th Battalion DWR; killed in action 08 8 1916, aged 26 (Battle of the Somme).
Buried – Lonsdale Cemetery, Authuile, France, 8, E, 1.
Commemorated – St James's Church, Slaithwaite, RoH; Slaithwaite WM; M Stansfield, page 89, and the **7 DWR Drill Hall WM panel 5, column 2.**
Mentioned in the Colne Valley Almanac (attached KOYLI, killed in action 09 8 1916).

CHERRY, William Henry – 5047 Private.
Son of William Bingham and Sarah Elizabeth Bingham (formerly Cherry), of 15 Lammas Street, Nottingham. Resided in Eakring, Nottingham. Enlisted at Mansfield.

1/7th Battalion DWR; died of wounds 31 10 1916, aged 27 (Battle of the Somme).
Buried – Warrington Cemetery C, CE, 828.
Commemorated – the **7 DWR Drill Hall WM panel 5, column 2.**
"GOD IS LOVE"

CHEW, J – 33008 Private.
Commemorated – the **7 DWR Drill Hall WM panel 3, column 1.**
No trace found.

CLARK, Edward – 268048 Corporal.
Born at Bradford, the son of Alfred and Ellen Clark, of 163 Southfield Lane, Great Horton, Bradford. Enlisted at Bradford.
1/7th Battalion DWR; died of wounds 30 4 1918, aged 25 (German Spring Offensive).
Buried – Boulogne Eastern Cemetery, France, 9, B, 17.
Commemorated – the **7 DWR Drill Hall WM panel 6, column 1.**
"ONLY THOSE WHO HAVE LOVED AND LOST CAN UNDERSTAND"

CLARKE, P – 306415 Private.
Unable to find this man by name or number. Not the same as CLARKE Peter 306994.
The only soldier of this name in DWR is: 6735 Sergeant Clarke P DCM, 2nd Battalion, aged 37, died 18 4 1915. The son of Patrick & Mary Ann Clarke, served as CARRINGTON.
Commemorated - Menin Gate Memorial, Belgium, and **7 DWR Drill Hall WM panel 6, column 1?.**
[*A search on the number only brought up two names: 1. T LEE, Kings Liverpool Regt. 2. A MITCHELL, Notts & Derby Regt*].

CLARKE, Peter – 306993 Private.
Resided in East Morton, Bingley, the son of Squire and Sarah Clark, of 'Hartley's Fold, Morton. Husband of Mary Hannah Clark, of 3 East Street, East Morton, Bingley. Enlisted at Bingley.
2/7th Battalion DWR; killed in action 20 11 1917, aged 38 (Battle of Cambrai).
Commemorated – Cambrai Memorial, Louverval, France, and the **7 DWR Drill Hall WM panel 3, column 1.**
CWGC & SDGW show his surname as CLARK.

CLARKE, William – 307052 Private.
Resided and enlisted at Bradford.
2/7th Battalion DWR; killed in action 21 11 1917 (Battle of Cambrai).
Commemorated – Cambrai Memorial, Louverval, France, and the **7 DWR Drill Hall WM panel 7, column 3.**

CLAYDEN, Albert – 325028 Private.
Born in Paddington, London. Resided in Earlsfield. Enlisted at London.
1/7th Battalion DWR; killed in action 11 10 1918 (Advance to Victory, Battle of Iwuy).
Buried – Wellington Cemetery, Rieux-En-Cambresis, France, 3, B, 9.
Commemorated - the **7 DWR Drill Hall WM panel 1, column 2.**
Formerly 10133 Pte, Army Service Corps and 299364 Pte, Labour Corps.
WM shows CLAYDON.

CLAYTON, Arthur – 307712 Private.
Enlisted at Skipton.
1/7th Battalion DWR; killed in action 12 4 1918 (German Spring Offensive).
Commemorated – Tyne Cot Memorial, Belgium, CPGW, page 344 & website, and the **7 DWR Drill Hall WM panel 6, column 1.**

CLAYTON, Firth – 306538 Private.
Son of Mrs A Clayton, of 32 Back Dudley Street, Tyersal, Bradford. Enlisted at Bradford.
2/7th Battalion DWR; died of wounds 17 5 1917, aged 23.
Buried – Achiet-Le-Grand Communal Cemetery, France 1, G, 26.
Commemorated – the **7 DWR Drill Hall WM panel 1, column 2.**
"MEMORIES CLING IN SILENT THOUGHTS"

CLAYTON, John William – 306813 Private.
Resided in Mount Tabor and at 7 Shelf Hall Lane, Shelf, Halifax. Enlisted at Halifax.
2/7th Battalion DWR; killed in action 03 5 1917 (Battle of Bullecourt).
Commemorated – Arras Memorial, France; St. John the Baptist Church, Coley, RoH and the **7 DWR Drill Hall WM panel 2, column 3.**

CLEW, S - see GLEW, Sam.
Commemorated – the **7 DWR Drill Hall WM panel 5, column 2.**

CLOUGH, Fred – 1913 Private.
Born at Lindley, Huddersfield, in September, 1890, the son of Mr and Mrs Harry Clough, of 3 East Street, Lindley. Resided in Huddersfield. Enlisted at Milnsbridge in September, 1914.
1/7th Battalion DWR; killed in action 12 7 1915, aged 24.
Buried – Colne Valley Cemetery, Belgium D, 13.
Commemorated – St Philip's Church, Birchencliffe, WM; Lindley Zion Methodist Church RoH; St Stephen's Church, Lindley, RoH; M Stansfield, page 97, and the **7 DWR Drill Hall WM panel 4, column 2.**
Mentioned in the Huddersfield Examiner (killed in action) 21 7 1915.

CLOUGH, Joseph – 24517 Private.
Born in Gomersal, the son of Arthur and Martha Clough, of Oxford Road, Gomersal, Leeds. Husband of Mary Clough, of Greystone Farm, Drighlington, Bradford. Enlisted at Heckmondwike.
2/7th Battalion DWR; died of wounds 02 12 1917.
Buried – Grevillers British Cemetery, France, 8, D, 8.
Commemorated – Spenborough WM and the **7 DWR Drill Hall WM panel 2, column 3.**
Also served in the 10th Battalion, see - **tunstillsmen.blogspot.com** *(last accessed August, 2020).*
"REST IN PEACE"

COCKROFT, Willie – 306790 Private.
Resided in Luddendenfoot, Halifax, the son of Job and Leah Cockroft, of 4 Stoney Booth, Luddendenfoot. Enlisted at Halifax.
2/7th Battalion DWR; died in Germany, as POW, on 27 6 1917, aged 31.
Buried – Mons (Bergen) Communal Cemetery, Belgium, 4, D. 10.
Commemorated – CWD, page 513, and the **7 DWR Drill Hall WM panel 1, column 3.**

COLL, John – 307249 Private.
Born in Dewsbury, the son of John and Annie Coll, of 102 Middle Road, West Town, Dewsbury. Enlisted at Dewsbury.
1/7th Battalion DWR; died of wounds 24 2 1918, aged 30.
Buried – Lijssenthoek Military Cemetery, Belgium, 27, E, 9.
Commemorated – the **7 DWR Drill Hall WM panel 7, column 3.**

COLLIER, George – 2705 Private.
Born at 13 Mitchell Street, Nursery Lane, Ovenden, Halifax. Resided with wife, Agnes Collier at 43 Baker Street, Oakes, Lindley, Huddersfield. Enlisted at Milnsbridge in October, 1914.

1/7th Battalion DWR; killed in action 03 7 1916, aged 29 (Battle of the Somme).
Commemorated – Thiepval Memorial, Somme, France; St Stephen's Church, Lindley RoH; M Stansfield, page 100, and the **7 DWR Drill Hall WM panel 5, column 1.**

COLLINS, Harold (M) Frank – 306707 Private.
Son of Arthur and Sarah Jane Collins, of Wolverhampton. Enlisted at Wolverhampton.
2/7th Battalion DWR; died of wounds 25 9 1917, aged 24.
Buried – Favreuil British Cemetery, France, 2, A, 3.
Commemorated – the **7 DWR Drill Hall WM panel 7, column 2.**
Initials variously recorded as F H, H F and H M.
"FOR US HE ALWAYS DID HIS BEST, GOD GRANT HIM ETERNAL REST"

COLLINS, William – 306410 Corporal.
Born in Bradford. Enlisted at Bradford.
1/7th Battalion DWR; killed in action 13 4 1918 (German Spring Offensive).
Commemorated – Tyne Cot Memorial, Belgium, and the **7 DWR Drill Hall WM panel 7, column 1.**

CONNOR, Harold – 3101 Lance Corporal.
Son of John Connor, of 23, Clegg Street, Springhead, Lees, Oldham. Resided in Lees. Enlisted at Milnsbridge.
1/7th Battalion DWR; killed in action 20 12 1915, aged 18.
Commemorated – Ypres (Menin Gate) Memorial, Belgium, J Fisher, page 107, and the **7 DWR Drill Hall WM panel 4, column 1.**

COOK, Harrison – 242276 Private.
Born at Shipley, Bradford, the son of George William and Clara Ellen Cook, of 29 Annie Street, Windhill, Shipley. Enlisted at Shipley.
1/7th Battalion DWR, C Company; killed in action 29 4 1918, aged 23 (German Spring Offensive).
Commemorated – Tyne Cot Memorial, Belgium, and the **7 DWR Drill Hall WM panel 6, column 1.**
CWGC & SDGW show number as 242726.

COOK, James Ratcliffe – 307588 Private.
Born and enlisted at Bradford.
2/7th Battalion DWR; killed in action 27 11 1917 (Battle of Cambrai).
Commemorated – Cambrai Memorial, Louverval, France, and the **7 DWR Drill Hall WM panel 3, column 2.**

CORDEN, Joseph – 2276 Private.
Resided at Binn House, Marsden. Enlisted at Milnsbridge in August, 1914. Embarked for France & Flanders, April 1915.
1/7th Battalion DWR; killed in action (shrapnel to head) on 03 7 1916, aged 28 (Battle of the Somme).
Commemorated – Thiepval Memorial, France; Marsden WM; M Stansfield, page 104, and the **7 DWR Drill Hall WM panel 4, column 3.**

CORNEY, Harry – 308117 Private.
Born at West Vale, Greetland, Halifax, the son of Arthur and Fanny Corney, of 12 Lambert Street, West Vale. Enlisted at Halifax.
2/7th Battalion DWR; killed in action 29 11 1917 (Battle of Cambrai).
Commemorated – Cambrai Memorial, Louverval, France; Greetland WM; St John's Church, West Vale, Halifax; West Vale Baptist Church; CWD, page 366, and the **7 DWR Drill Hall WM panel 7, column 3.**
Mentioned in the Halifax Courier 09 1 1918.

SDGW shows date of death as 28 11 1917.

COTTERILL, Edwin – 38559 Private.
Born in Sheffield, the son of William H and Alice Cotterill, of 29 Clarence Street, Sheffield. Resided and enlisted at Sheffield.
2/7th Battalion DWR; died of wounds 17 1 1918, aged 19.
Buried – Roclincourt Military Cemetery, France, 3, F, 2.
Commemorated - the **7 DWR Drill Hall WM panel 3, column 2.**

COTTRELL, Leonard – 306350 Private.
Born in Dobcross, the son of Dyson and Mary Hannah Cottrell, of 24 Royds Terrace, Marsden. Resided in Marsden, Huddersfield. Enlisted at Milnsbridge on 2 11 1915. Embarked for France & Flanders in February, 1916.
1/7th Battalion DWR, C Company; killed in action (shell fire) on 12 3 1918, aged 23 (German Spring Offensive).
Buried – Duhallow ADS Cemetery, Belgium, 9, C, 16.
Commemorated – Marsden WM; Marsden Liberal Club RoH; M Stansfield, page 105, and the **7 DWR Drill Hall WM panel 3, column 1.**
WM shows name as COTTRILL.
"REMEMBRANCE"

COULTON, David – 306722 Private.
Resided in Walsall. Enlisted at Birmingham.
2/7th Battalion DWR; killed in action 03 5 1917 (Battle of Bullecourt).
Commemorated – Arras Memorial, France, and the **7 DWR Drill Hall WM panel 2, column 1.**

COUPLAN, Maurice – 10917 Lance Corporal.
Born in Leeds, the son of Isaac and Esther Couplan, of 24 Ramsden Terrace, Leeds. Enlisted at Leeds.
1/7th Battalion DWR; died of wounds 03 5 1918, aged 22 (German Spring Offensive).
Buried – Boulogne Eastern Cemetery, France, 9, B, 42.
Commemorated – **7 DWR Drill Hall WM panel 2, column 2.**
WM shows COUPLAND.
"BELOVED SON OF ESTHER AND ISAAC COUPLAN OF LEEDS, ENGLAND"

COVERLEY, (John) William – 875 (later 305115) Private.
Born in Moldgreen, Huddersfield, on 28 2 1893, the son of John William and Mary Coverley, of 13 Garden Street, Lockwood, Huddersfield. Enlisted in 1910. Pre war local Territorial, mobilised on 05 8 1914. Embarked for France & Flanders in April, 1915. Demobilised on 03 2 1919.
1/7th Battalion DWR; died (pneumonia following influenza) at Royds Hall Military Hospital on 22 2 1919, age 24.
Buried – Huddersfield (Lockwood) Cemetery, C, 'C', 642.
Commemorated – St Stephen's Church, Rashcliffe; M Stansfield, page 105 and the **7 DWR Drill Hall WM panel 3, column 1.**
"IN SILENCE WE REMEMBER"

COX, Fred W – 1856 Private.
Born in Greenfield, the son of Robert and Mary Cox. Husband of Annie Swindells (formerly Cox), of 1354, Ashton Old Road, Higher Openshaw, Manchester. Resided in Stalybridge. Enlisted at Lees.
1/7th Battalion DWR; killed in action 08 8 1915, aged 24.
Buried – Colne Valley Cemetery, Belgium, D, 4 (Coll.)
Commemorated – Stalybridge WM and the **7 DWR Drill Hall WM panel 4, column 2.**
Mentioned in the Unit War Diary (killed in action) 08 8 1915.

CRABTREE, Richard – 2617 (later 307761) Private.
Born in Halifax. Enlisted at Halifax.
1/7th Battalion DWR; killed in action 29 4 1918 (German Spring Offensive).
Commemorated – Tyne Cot Memorial, Belgium; CWD, page 93, and the **7 DWR Drill Hall WM panel 6, column 3.**

CRAGG, Thomas – 13029 Private.
Born and enlisted at Sedbergh.
1/7th Battalion DWR; killed in action 14 4 1918 (German Spring Offensive).
Commemorated – Tyne Cot Memorial, Belgium, and the **7 DWR Drill Hall WM panel 2, column 3.**
Mentioned in CPGW, page 344 & website. Also served in the 10th Battalion, see -
tunstillsmen.blogspot.com (last accessed August, 2020).

CRAMPTON, Morris – 306012 Private, Military Medal.
Born in Golcar, Huddersfield, the son of David and Jane Crampton, of 115 Swallow Lane, Golcar.
Enlisted at Derby in March, 1915. Embarked for France & Flanders on 29 6 1915.
1/7th Battalion DWR; died of wounds (gas poisoning) at No 14 General Hospital, Wimereux, on 26 11 1917, aged 22.
Buried – Wimereux Communal Cemetery, France, 8, A, 1A.
Commemorated – St John's Church, Golcar RoH; M Stansfield, page 107, and the **7 DWR Drill Hall WM panel 7, column 2.**
Mentioned in the London Gazette (MM award) 28 1 1918, page 1383.
"ONE OF THE MANY TO ANSWER THE CALL, FOR THOSE HE LOVED, HE GAVE HIS ALL"

CRAVEN, Fred – 306064 Drummer.
Born and resided in Oldham, the son of John E and Elizabeth Craven, of 289 Featherstall Road North, Oldham. Enlisted at Thoresby Park, Nottingham.
2/7th Battalion DWR; died of wounds 11 4 1917, aged 22.
Buried – Achiet-Le-Grand Communal Cemetery, France, 1, B, 3.
Commemorated – the **7 DWR Drill Hall WM panel 1, column 2.**
"LOVINGLY HIS MEMORY LINGERS – MOTHER & FATHER"

CRAVEN, Harry H – 307041 Private.
Son of Hiram and Ann Craven, of 28, Soring Bank, Thornton, Bradford. Enlisted at Bradford.
2/7th Battalion DWR; died of wounds 14 5 1917, aged 33.
Buried – Mory Abbey Military Cemetery, Mory, 1, F, 6.
Commemorated – the **7 DWR Drill Hall WM panel 7, column 3.**
"TOO DEARLY LOVED TO BE FORGOTTEN"

CREUGHTON, W - see **CROUGHTON Wilfred.**
Commemorated – the **7 DWR Drill Hall WM panel 2, column 2.**

CRICK, Gordon – 1209 Private.
Born in Waterhead. Resided in Oldham. Enlisted at Lees.
1/7th Battalion DWR; killed in action 18 8 1915.
Commemorated – Ypres (Menin Gate) Memorial, Belgium, and the **7 DWR Drill Hall WM panel 4, column 2.**

CROOK, Clarence Gordon – 5433 Private.
Born at Wall Heath, Staffordshire, the son of Frederick and Maria Crook, of New Street, Wall Heath.
Enlisted at Brierley Hill.
1/7th Battalion DWR; killed in action 25 11 1916, aged 19 (Battle of the Somme).

Buried – Foncquevillers Military Cemetery, France, 1, H, 19.
Commemorated - the **7 DWR Drill Hall WM panel 5, column 1.**
WM shows name spelt as CROOKE.
"HE DID HIS DUTY"

CROSS, Samuel (Arthur) – 308880 L/Sergeant, Military Medal.
Born at Blackburn, the son of Arthur and Clara Cross of 5 Shakespeare Terrace, Burn Street, Leeds. Resided and enlisted at Barnoldswick.
1/7th Battalion DWR; killed in action 12 8 1915, aged 24 (Ypres Sector).
Buried – Leeds (Burmantofts) Cemetery, C, 12679.
Commemorated – the **7 DWR Drill Hall WM panel 3, column 2.**
Mentioned in the London Gazette (MID award) 24 5 1918, page 9096 & (MM award) 13 9 1918, page 10736.
"HE ANSWERED TO HIS COUNTRY'S CALL & DIED BELOVED BY ALL"

CROSSLEY, Norris H – 3548 (later 305856) Sergeant.
Born at Slaithwaite, the son of Hinchliffe and Elizabeth Crossley, of 46 Royd Street, Slaithwaite. Resided in Slaithwaite. Enlisted at Milnsbridge in November, 1914.
2/7th Battalion DWR; killed in action 03 5 1917, aged 24 (Battle of Bullecourt).
Commemorated – Arras Memorial, France; Carr Lane United Methodist Church RoH; St James's Church, Slaithwaite, RoH; Slaithwaite WM; CVA; M Stansfield, page 111, and the **7 DWR Drill Hall WM panel 1, column 3.**
Mentioned in the Huddersfield Examiner (wounded in action, casualty list) 6 1917 & (killed in action) 17 5 1917; the Colne Valley Almanac (killed in action) 10 10 1917.
WM shows initials as M H.

CROUGHTON, Wilfred – 25340 Private.
Born and enlisted at Bishop Auckland.
2/7th Battalion DWR; killed in action 26 11 1917.
Commemorated – Cambrai Memorial, Louverval, France, and the **7 DWR Drill Hall WM panel 2, column 2.**
WM shows surname spelt CREUGHTON and service number as 25346.

CROWTHER, Ralph L – 2513 Private.
Born in Stalybridge, the son of William and Hannah Crowther, of 113 Brierley Street, Stalybridge. Resided in Stalybridge. Enlisted at Mossley.
1/7th Battalion DWR; killed in action 21 9 1915, aged 18 (Ypres Sector).
Buried – Bard Cottage Cemetery, Belgium, 1, H, 21.
Commemorated – Stalybridge WM and the **7 DWR Drill Hall WM panel 4, column 3.**
"BLESSED ARE THEY THAT ARE PURE IN HEART FOR THEY SHALL SEE GOD"

CULLEY, James Cuthbert – 33732 Private.
Born at Dalston, London, the son of Mr and Mrs James Culley, of 18 Salisbury Street, Islington, London. Resided in Hoxton. Enlisted at Shoreditch.
1/7th Battalion DWR; died of wounds 13 10 1918, aged 18 (Advance to Victory).
Buried – Bucquoy Road Cemetery, Ficheux, France, 3, F, 4.
Commemorated – the **7 DWR Drill Hall WM panel 2, column 3.**

CUNNINGHAM, Michael – 240953 Private.
Born in Dewsbury, the son of William Cunningham and Catherine Hardy (formerly Cunningham), of 31 Balk Street, Batley. Resided in Batley. Enlisted at Mirfield.
1/7th Battalion DWR; killed in action 11 10 1918, aged 21 (Advance to Victory, Battle of Iwuy).

Buried – Wellington Cemetery, Rieux-En-Cambresis, France, 1, E, 3.
Commemorated - CWD, page 97, and the **7 DWR Drill Hall WM panel 1, column 3.**
Also shown as HONEYMAN. Formerly 639904 Pte, Labour Corps.

DAGLESS, Philip – 242457 Private.
Born in Aylsham, Norfolk, the son of Mrs J Dagless, of Queen's Square, Attleborough. Resided in Attleborough. Enlisted at Aylsham.
1/7th Battalion DWR; died of wounds 25 4 1918 (German Spring Offensive).
Buried – Grootebeek British Cemetery, Belgium, A, 10.
Commemorated – the **7 DWR Drill Hall WM panel 7, column 3.**

DALE, Clarence – 3055 (later 306092) Private.
Born in Oldham, the son of Thomas and Eda Dale, of Oldham. Resided in Oldham. Enlisted at Milnsbridge.
1/7th Battalion DWR, from 3/7th Battalion; died of wounds 12 4 1918, aged 20 (German Spring Offensive).
Buried – La Kreule Military Cemetery, France, 1, A, 38.
Commemorated – the **7 DWR Drill Hall WM panel 7, column 1.**
WM shows number as 306492.

DALEY, James – 306804 Private.
Enlisted at Halifax.
2/7th Battalion DWR; killed in action 26 3 1918 (German Spring Offensive).
Commemorated – Arras Memorial, France; CWD, page 98, and the **7 DWR Drill Hall WM panel 3, column 2.**

DALEY, John – 305919 Private.
Born in Oldham, the son of Mrs Dora Richardson, of 16 Hobson Street, Oldham. Resided in Oldham. Enlisted at Milnsbridge.
2/7th Battalion DWR; killed in action 03 5 1917, aged 20 (Battle of Bullecourt).
Commemorated – Arras Memorial, France, and the **7 DWR Drill Hall WM panel 3, column 2.**

DARTON, Bertram James – 325021 Private.
Born in Dewsbury, the son of Charles and Martha Darton. Husband of Rebecca Darton, of 8 Hanging Heaton, Batley.
1/7th Battalion DWR; died of wounds 27 4 1918, aged 23 (German Spring Offensive).
Buried – Boulogne Eastern Cemetery, France, 9, A, 54.
Commemorated – the **7 DWR Drill Hall WM panel 6, column 3.**
Formerly 204649 Private, York & Lancaster Regiment
"TO MEMORY EVER DEAR"

DARWENT, Sydney – 269059 Private.
Born in Sheffield, the son of Charles William and Eleanor Darwent, of Sheffield. Enlisted at Sheffield.
1/7th Battalion DWR; died of wounds 22 11 1917.
Buried – Lijssenthoek Military Cemetery, Belgium, 27, BB, 6.
Commemorated – the **7 DWR Drill Hall WM panel 7, column 1.**
"DEATH DIVIDES BUT MEMORY CLINGS"

DAVIDSON Alexander – 17147 Private.
Born, resided and enlisted at Aberdeen.
2/7th Battalion DWR; died of wounds 29 11 1917 (Battle of Cambrai).
Buried – Rocquigny-Equancourt Road British Cemetery, Manancourt, France, 5, B, 10.

Commemorated – The Scottish National War Memorial (Edinburgh Castle) and the **7 DWR Drill Hall WM panel 2, column 2.**
Formerly 126136 Pte, Army Service Corps.

DAVIES, Rudolph Ellis – 2nd Lieutenant.
Born in Taunton, the son of Rev A J Davies, of Taunton, Somerset. Resided in Cambridge, the husband of K Davies, of 29 Montague Road, Cambridge.
1/7th Battalion DWR; died of wounds 11 8 1917, aged 27 (Nieuport Sector).
Buried – Adinkerke Military Cemetery, Belgium, G, 3.
Commemorated – J Fisher, page 117, the **7 DWR Drill Hall WM panel 3, column 3.**
Mentioned in the Unit War Diary (wounded in action 03 9 1916) 04 9 1916, (raiding party 28 5 1917) 5 1917, (posted to 457 Field Company RE) 20 7 1917, (wounded, shellfire, head) 11 8 1917; the Huddersfield Examiner (died of wounds) 20 8 1917 & 23 8 1917; the HDH Album 7 DWR Volume 2 (wounded in action) page 15, (C Coy 7 DWR, Leipzig Salient) page 17, (wounded in action 10 8 1917, died of wounds 12 8 1917) page 25.

DEAN, Ernest – 307879 Sergeant.
Born in Morecambe. Enlisted at Leeds.
1/7th Battalion DWR; killed in action 03 6 1918, aged 23.
Buried – Hagle Dump Cemetery, Belgium, 1, B, 2.
Commemorated – the **7 DWR Drill Hall WM panel 6, column 1.**
Formerly 1365 Corporal, Army Cyclist Corps.
"REST IN PEACE"

DELANEY, George Henry – 1630 Private.
Born in 1896 in Mossley. Resided in Ashton-under-Lyne. Enlisted on 11 5 1914 at Mossley.
Embarked for France & Flanders on 15 4 1915.
1/7th Battalion DWR, F Company; killed in action 23 11 1915 (Ypres Salient).
Buried – Bard Cottage Cemetery, Belgium, 1, E, 4.
Commemorated – Albion United Reform Church WM, Ashton; St John the Baptist WM; Hazlehurst Sunday School RoH; R Vaughan, pages 24 & 42; and the **7 DWR Drill Hall WM panel 4, column 2.**

DENNETT, Charles William – 33870 Private.
Born in Faversham, Kent, the son of Charles Edward and Alice Dennett, of Cam Hill, Stockbury, Sittingbourne. Resided in Bredgar. Enlisted at Maidstone.
1/7th Battalion DWR; killed in action 11 10 1918, aged 19 (Advance to Victory, Battle of Iwuy).
Buried – Wellington Cemetery, Rieux-En-Cambresis, France, 3, B, 3.
Commemorated - the **7 DWR Drill Hall WM panel 2, column 2.**
"FOR GREATER LOVE HATH NO MAN THAN THIS"

DENNISON, Sam West – 29154 Private.
Born in Bradford, the son of W T and Mrs W Dennison, of 69 Wilberforce Street, Sticker Lane, Laisterdyke, Bradford. Enlisted at Bradford.
1/7th Battalion DWR; killed in action 29 4 1918 (German Spring Offensive).
Commemorated – Tyne Cot Memorial, Belgium, and the **7 DWR Drill Hall WM panel 2, column 2.**

DENT, Frank – 2123 Private.
Native of Springhead, Oldham, the son of Miriam Dent, of 92 Wrigley Street, Lees Road, Oldham. Resided in Lees. Enlisted at Uppermill.
1/7th Battalion DWR; killed in action 24 8 1918, aged 19 (Advance to Victory).
Buried – Bard Cottage Cemetery, Belgium 1, F, 30.
Commemorated – the **7 DWR Drill Hall WM panel 4, column 2.**

Mentioned in Unit War Diary (killed in action, shellfire on dugout) 24 8 1915.
"THY WILL, BE DONE"

DEWHURST, Ernest – 265031 Sergeant.
Born in Shipley. Husband of W Simpson (formerly Dewhurst), of 7, Chancery Lane, High Street, Skipton. Enlisted at Shipley.
2/7th Battalion DWR; died 18 5 1918, aged 30.
Buried – Bienvillers Military Cemetery, France, 16, D, 9.
Commemorated – CPGW, page 342, with photograph, and the **7 DWR Drill Hall WM Panel 3, column 1.**
WM shows name as DUEWHURST and number as 260031.

DICKINSON, Frank – 266478 Private, Military Medal.
Resided in Bradford. Enlisted at Skipton.
1/7th Battalion DWR; died of wounds 13 4 1918 (German Spring Offensive).
Buried – Longuenesse (St Omer) Souvenir Cemetery, France, 5, A, 30.
Commemorated – L Magnus, page 253, and the **7 DWR Drill Hall WM panel 7, column 2.**
Mentioned in S Barber (actions and MM award) 19/20 5 1917, pages 128/9.
Mentioned in the London Gazette (MM award) 18 7 1917, page 7278
WM shows number as 266474.

DIGNAM, Benjamin – 2380 Private.
Born in Waterhead, Oldham, the son of Henry and Sarah Dignam, of 28, Turner Street, Waterhead. Resided in Waterhead. Enlisted at Uppermill.
1/7th Battalion DWR; killed in action 03 9 1916, aged 19 (Battle of the Somme, Thiepval).
Commemorated – Thiepval Memorial, Somme, France, and the **7 DWR Drill Hall WM panel 5, column 2.**
Name spelt Digman on NA Roll.

DIXON Kenneth – 2nd Lieutenant.
Native of Leeds, the son of George Edward and Margaret Brewis Dixon, of 3 St Mark's Avenue, Leeds Road, Harrogate. Medical student, commissioned in Leeds University Officer Training Corps.
6th Battalion DWR; died of wounds 25 11 1916 aged 20 (Battle of the Somme).
Buried – Couin British Cemetery, France, 6, B, 15.
Commemorated – Leeds University RoH; J Fisher, page 103, and the **7 DWR Drill Hall WM panel 3, column 3.**
Mentioned in the Unit War Diary (died of wounds) 25 11 1916; the HDH Album 7 DWR Volume 2 (killed in action, Souastre) page 19.
"IN LOVING MEMORY"

DOGGETT, George Patrick – 2nd Lieutenant.
Son of George Henry and Mary Ann Doggett, of Abbey Lodge, Beche Road, Cambridge.
7th Battalion DWR; died 04 7 1917. aged 22.
Buried – Cambridge City Cemetery, B, 1802.
Commemorated – M Stansfield, page 163, and the **7 DWR Drill Hall WM panel 3, column 3.**
Formerly 2772 Corporal, Cambridge Regiment.
Mentioned in the Huddersfield Examiner (wrote to families of soldiers) 02 3 1917.

DOOSEY, John Henry – 241358 Private.
Born in Kirkgate, Huddersfield on 11 11 1896. Husband of Edith Doosey, of 5, Knight Street, Huddersfield. Enlisted at Huddersfield on 11 11 1914, aged 33.
1/7th Battalion DWR; killed in action 11 10 1918 (Advance to Victory, Battle of Iwuy).

Buried – Wellington Cemetery, Rieux-En-Cambresis, France, 2, C, 7.
Commemorated – M Stansfield, page 124, and the **7 DWR Drill Hall WM panel 1, column 1**.
Mentioned in Huddersfield Examiner (killed in action) 08 11 1918, (in memoriam) 11 10 1919.
WM, SDGW and first Huddersfield Examiner mention show name as DOSSEY.

DORSEY, Patrick – 805 Private.
Born in Manchester. Resided in Stalybridge. Enlisted at Micklehurst, Lancs.
1/7th Battalion DWR, F Company; died of wounds 17 11 1915 (Ypres Salient).
Buried – Lijssenthoek Military Cemetery, Belgium, 4, A, 4.
Commemorated – Stalybridge WM; R Vaughan, page 25, and the **7 DWR Drill Hall WM panel 4, column 3**.
Mentioned in Unit War Diary (wounded in action, shellfire on dug-out) 15 11 1915.

DOSSEY, J H – see **DOOSEY, John Henry**.
Commemorated – the **7 DWR Drill Hall WM panel 1, column 1**.

DOUGLAS Fred – 891 Private.
Resided in Oldham. Enlisted at Lees.
1/7th Battalion DWR; killed in action 28 2 1916.
Buried – Authuile Military Cemetery, France, C, 38.
Commemorated - the **7 DWR Drill Hall WM panel 4, column 3**.

DOWNEY, Thomas Crackett – 7105 (later 307960) Private.
Resided in Ashington, Northumberland. Enlisted at Alnwick.
1/7th Battalion DWR; killed in action 28 3 1918 (German Spring Offensive).
Buried – Belgian Battery Corner Cemetery, Belgium, 2, I, 14.
Commemorated - the **7 DWR Drill Hall WM panel 7, column 1**.
Formerly 2980 Private, Northumberland Fusiliers
CWGC and NA Roll show name as DOWNIE.

DOWNING, Arthur – 205103 Private.
Born in Leeds. Enlisted at Otley.
1/7th Battalion DWR; killed in action 11 10 1918 (Advance to Victory, Battle of Iwuy).
Buried – Wellington Cemetery, Rieux-En-Cambresis, France, 1, E, 8.
Commemorated - the **7 DWR Drill Hall WM panel 1, column 1**.

DRYDEN, J H - see **BRYDON, Joseph Henry**.
Commemorated - the **7 DWR Drill Hall WM panel 2, column 3**.

DRYSDALE, James – 7110 (later 307965) Corporal.
Born in North Seaton, Northumberland. Enlisted at Alnwick.
1/7th Battalion DWR; killed in action1 3 4 1918 (German Spring Offensive).
Commemorated – Tyne Cot Memorial, Belgium, and the **7 DWR Drill Hall WM panel 7, column 2**.
Formerly 3356 Pte, Northumberland Fusiliers.
WM shows number as 307967.

DUEWHURST, E, 260031 – see **DEWHURST, Ernest**.
Commemorated – the **7 DWR Drill Hall WM Panel 3, column 1**.

DUNN, Charles Edward – 306648 Private.
Enlisted at Bradford.
2/7th Battalion DWR; killed in action 26 11 1917 (Battle of Cambrai).

Commemorated – Cambrai Memorial, Louverval, France, and the **7 DWR Drill Hall WM panel 7, column 3.**

DUNN, James – 305764 Private.
Resided in Chadderton, Lancs. Enlisted at Uppermill.
1/7th Battalion DWR; killed in action 18 9 1916 (Battle of the Somme).
Buried – Bray Vale British Cemetery, Bray-Sur-Somme, France, 4, A, 20.
Commemorated – the **7 DWR Drill Hall WM panel 6, Column 1.**

DUNN, Joseph – 3074 Private.
Born in Stalybridge, the son of James H Dunn and Ann Kinsella (formerly Dunn), of 1 Forester's Court, Vaudrey Street, Stalybridge. Resided in Stalybridge. Enlisted at Milnsbridge.
1/7th Battalion DWR; killed in action 04 7 1916, aged 19 (Battle of the Somme).
Buried – Connaught Cemetery, Thiepval, France, 1, D, 1.
Commemorated – Stalybridge WM and the **7 DWR Drill Hall WM panel 4, Column 3.**

DYSON, George Henry – 2003 Private.
Born at Slaithwaite, the son of George and Eliza Dyson, of 11 Booth Banks, Slaithwaite. Enlisted at Slaithwaite on 31 8 1914. Embarked for France & Flanders in April 1915.
1/7th Battalion DWR; killed in action (gunshot to head) 24 6 1915, aged 28.
Buried – Rue-David Military Cemetery, Fleurbaix, France, 1, B, 9.
Commemorated – Slaithwaite WM; St James's Church, Slaithwaite; M Stansfield, page 131,and the **7 DWR Drill Hall WM panel 4, column 1.**

DYSON, H - see **POGSON Harry.**
Commemorated – the **7 DWR Drill Hall WM panel 4, column 2.**

EARL, Charles Rushworth – 265293 Corporal.
Born in Haworth, the son of Florence Earl, of 25 Elliott Street, Silsden, Keighley. Enlisted at Keighley
1/7th Battalion DWR; killed in action 29 4 1918, aged 18 (German Spring Offensive).
Commemorated – Tyne Cot Memorial, Belgium, CPGW, page 345 with photograph, and the **7 DWR Drill Hall WM panel 6, column 1.**

EARNSHAW, John Arthur – 305635 Lance Corporal.
Born at Thornton Lodge, Huddersfield, on 08 4 1896, the son of Benjamin and Mary Elizabeth Earnshaw, of 3 Crosland Street, Crosland Moor, Huddersfield. Enlisted at Milnsbridge on 11 9 1914.
2/7th Battalion DWR; killed in action 30 3 1918, aged 23 (German Spring Offensive).
Buried – St Amand British Cemetery, France, 1, C, 4.
Commemorated – Lockwood Cemetery Memorial; St Barnabas Church, Crosland Moor, RoH; M Stansfield, page 135, and the **7 DWR Drill Hall WM panel 1, column 1.**
CWGC & SDGW show rank as Lance Corporal.
"DEARLY LOVED SON OF Mr & MRS B EARNSHAW, CROSLAND MOOR, HUDDERSFIELD"

EASTICK, George – 33875 Private.
Born in Great Yarmouth, the son of James Alfred and Alice Maud Eastick, of 20 Norfolk Place, Boston. Resided in Boston. Enlisted at Spalding.
1/7th Battalion DWR; died (pneumonia) 30 6 1918, aged 19.
Buried – Longuenesse (St Omer) Souvenir Cemetery, France, 5, C, 22.
Commemorated – the **7 DWR Drill Hall WM panel 2, column 3.**
"REMEMBERED BY ALL AT HOME"

EASTWOOD, Fred – 2434 Private.
Born in Huddersfield, the son of Mr and Mrs George Eastwood, of Linthwaite. Resided in Linthwaite, Huddersfield, with his cousin, Mrs Mary Hannah Gledhill, of 9 Slantgate. Enlisted at Milnsbridge.
1/7th Battalion DWR; died of wounds (compound fracture of the skull) on 08 6 1915 at No 2 Canadian General Hospital, Etaples, France, aged 19.
Buried – Etaples Military Cemetery, France, 2, B, 5A.
Commemorated – Linthwaite RoH; M Stansfield, page 136, and the **7 DWR Drill Hall WM panel 4, column 1.**

EASTWOOD, Leonard – 3185 Private.
Born in Oldham, the son of Younger and Betty Eastwood of 86, Oldham Road, Springhead. Resided in Springhead. Enlisted at Greenfield.
1/7th Battalion DWR; died of wounds 29 9 1916, aged 20 (Battle of the Somme).
Buried – Boulogne Eastern Cemetery, France, 8, C, 159.
Commemorated – the **7 DWR Drill Hall WM panel 5, column 2.**
"HE DID HIS DUTY"

ELLIOTT, Frank Sidney – 26329 Private.
Born at Gussage, Wiltshire, the son of George and Annie Elizabeth Elliott, of 15 Highfield Lane, Highfield, Southampton. Enlisted at Southampton.
2/7th Battalion DWR; died of wounds 16 3 1918, aged 27 (German Spring Offensive).
Buried – Etaples Military Cemetery, France, 31, G, 12.
Commemorated – the **7 DWR Drill Hall WM panel 3, column 3.**
Formerly T4/065428 Driver, Army Service Corps.
WM shows number as 26239. NA Roll shows forename as Frederick.
"HIS LIFE FOR HIS COUNTRY HE GAVE"

ELLIS, Charles – 306549 Private.
Enlisted at Bradford.
2/7th Battalion DWR; killed in action 27 11 1917 (Battle of Cambrai).
Commemorated – Cambrai Memorial, Louverval, France, and the **7 DWR Drill Hall WM panel 3, column 2.**

ELLIS, Ernest – 6794 Private.
Born in Batley. Resided in Dewsbury. Enlisted at Strensall.
1/7th Battalion DWR; died of wounds 27 4 1918, aged 37 (German Spring Offensive).
Buried – Haringhe (Bandaghem) Military Cemetery, Belgium, 5, A, 10.
Commemorated the **7 DWR Drill Hall WM panel 5, column 3.**
"WE LIVE IN HOPES OF THE PROMISE GIVEN TO MEET AND PART NO MORE IN OUR HOME IN HEAVEN"

ELLISON, John – 268400 Private.
Enlisted at Leeds.
2/7th Battalion DWR; killed in action 27 11 1917 (Battle of Cambrai).
Commemorated – Cambrai Memorial, Louverval, France, and the **7 DWR Drill Hall WM panel 7, column 1.**

ELLISON, William – 267404 Private.
Born and resided in Eastburn, Keighley. Enlisted at Keighley.
2/7th Battalion DWR; killed in action 27 3 1918 (German Spring Offensive).
Buried – Pommier Communal Cemetery, France, 24.
Commemorated – the **7 DWR Drill Hall WM panel 7, column 2.**

Mentioned in Unit War Diary (wounded in action, shellfire) 14 8 1917.

ELVIDGE, Percy – 306510 Private.
Resided at 48, Lower Wade Street, Halifax. Enlisted at Halifax in March, 1916.
2/7th Battalion DWR; killed in action 03 5 1917, aged 30 (Battle of Bullecourt).
Commemorated – Arras Memorial; Halifax Civic Book of Remembrance; CWD, page 112, and the **7 DWR Drill Hall WM panel 1, column 1.**
Mentioned in Halifax Courier 24 5 1917 and Halifax Weekly Guardian 26 5 1917.

ENDERBY, Harry – 268433 Private.
Enlisted at Leeds.
2/7th Battalion DWR; killed in action 14 5 1917.
Commemorated – Arras Memorial, France, and the **7 DWR Drill Hall WM panel 2, column 1.**

ENGLAND, William – 1671 Corporal.
Born in Oldham, the son of Joseph and Margaret England, of 7 Stable Street, Huddersfield Road, Oldham. Resided in Oldham. Enlisted at Springhead, Oldham.
1/7th Battalion DWR; died of wounds 04 7 1916 (Battle of the Somme).
Buried – Bouzincourt Communal Cemetery Extension, France, 2, D, 11.
Commemorated – the **7 DWR Drill Hall WM panel 5, column 3.**

ESCOTT, Charles – 2231 (later 305643) Private.
Born in 1894 in Uppermill. Resided in Mossley. Enlisted at Milnsbridge. Embarked for France & Flanders on 15 4 1915.
1/7th Battalion DWR; killed in action 14 4 1918 (German Spring Offensive).
Commemorated – Tyne Cot Memorial, Belgium; Mossley Town Hall WM; Uppermill (Pots and Pans) WM; Uppermill (St Chad's Church) WM; St George's Church WM and R Vaughan, pages 16, 24 & 119, and the **7 DWR Drill Hall WM panel 6, column 3.**
Related to ESCOTT R, see Addenda, and ESCOTT W H, 2/6th Battalion DWR.

EVANS, Albert Edward – 33834 Private.
Born in Stoke-on-Trent, the son of George and Ann Elizabeth Evans of 'Hillside', Riseley Road, Hartshill. Resided in Stoke-on-Trent. Enlisted at Trentham.
1/7th Battalion DWR; Killed in action 11 10 1918, aged 19 (Advance to Victory, Battle of Iwuy).
Buried – Wellington Cemetery, Rieux-En-Cambresis, France, 3, B, 2.
Commemorated - the **7 DWR Drill Hall WM panel 2, column 1.**
"THY WILL, BE DONE"

EVERS, Thomas Leach – 38587 Lance Corporal.
Born in Leeds, the son of Ada Evers, of 79 Spencer Place, Leeds. Enlisted at Leeds.
2/7th Battalion DWR; killed in action 20 7 1918, aged 19 (Battle of Tardenois, Bligny).
Buried – Marfaux British Cemetery, France, Special Memorial 3.
Commemorated – the **7 DWR Drill Hall WM panel 2, Column 3.**
CWGC shows unit as 2/4th Battalion DWR. SDGW shows both units, pages 27 & 55.
"TOO DEARLY LOVED TO BE FORGOTTEN"

FAIRBANK, William (Willie) Harold – 306338 Private.
Born at Well House, Golcar. Resided in Marsden, the son of Sam Henry Fairbank, of 26, Grange Avenue, Marsden. Resided in Marsden. Enlisted at Milnsbridge November 1915. Embarked for France & Flanders in January 1916.
2/7th Battalion DWR; killed in action 03 5 1917 aged 23.

Commemorated – Arras Memorial, France; Marsden WM; M Stansfield, page 144, and the **7 DWR Drill Hall WM panel 1, column 3.**
Mentioned in the Huddersfield Examiner (killed in action, photograph) 24 5 1917 & 29 7 1917.

FARRAR, Kaye – 4380 Private.
Resided in Delph Hill, Rastrick, Brighouse. Enlisted at Halifax.
2/7th Battalion DWR; died at Henham Park, Suffolk, (in training) 16 7 1916, aged 33.
Buried – Rastrick (St Matthew's) Churchyard, Rastrick, Brighouse, Yorkshire (no grave location stated).
Commemorated – Brighouse WM; Rastrick WM; J Fisher, page 104; CWD, page 376, and the **7 DWR Drill Hall WM panel 5, column 1.**
Mentioned in Brighouse Echo 21 7 1916.

FAWCETT, James Albert – 1871 Private.
Born and resided in Marsden, the son of Mr and Mrs William Fawcett, of Netherleigh, Marsden, Huddersfield. Enlisted at Milnsbridge August, 1914.
1/7th Battalion DWR; died of wounds (to head) 21 11 1915, aged 22 (Ypres Sector).
Buried – Etaples Military Cemetery, France, 3, G, 7A.
Commemorated – Marsden WM; M Stansfield, page 146, and the **7 DWR Drill Hall WM panel 4, column 3.**

FELL, Cyrus – 126 (later 305018) Private.
Born at Marsden, the son of William and Ellen Fell, husband of Margaret Ann Fell, of 36 Wood's Avenue, Marsden.
1/7th Battalion DWR; died at home 29 8 1919, aged 39.
Buried – Marsden (St Bartholomew) Churchyard, Marsden, Yorkshire, South 32, 11.
Commemorated – Marsden WM; M Stansfield, page 146, and the **7 DWR Drill Hall WM panel 4, column 2.**
"THY WILL, BE DONE"

FELL, Frederick – 33166 Private.
Born in Sheffield, the son of William and Harriett Ann Fell, of 12 Spencer Road, Heeley, Sheffield. Resided and enlisted at Sheffield.
1/7th Battalion DWR; died of wounds 12 10 1918, aged 18 (Advance to Victory).
Buried – Bucquoy Road Cemetery, Ficheux, France, 3, G, 2.
Commemorated - the **7 DWR Drill Hall WM panel 2, column 1.**
"LOVED IN LIFE, REMEMBERED IN DEATH"

FIELD, Albert Edward Smith – 306157 Sergeant.
Resided at 20 Hardend Cottages, Marsden, Huddersfield. Enlisted at Milnsbridge in July, 1915. Embarked for France & Flanders in January 1917.
2/7th Battalion DWR; died of wounds, at No 49 Casualty Clearing Station, on 03 12 1917, aged 28.
Buried – Achiet-Le-Grand Communal Cemetery, France 2, A, 11.
Commemorated – Marsden WM, M Stansfield, page 147, and the **7 DWR Drill Hall WM panel 7, column 2.**

FIELDSEND, Robert – 203673 Sergeant.
Born in Morley, Leeds, the son of Joseph Fieldsend, of Bridge Street. Resided in Morley, the husband of Eva Fieldsend, of Church Street, Morley. Enlisted at Huddersfield.
1/7th Battalion DWR; killed in action 13 4 1918, aged 33 (German Spring Offensive).
Commemorated – Tyne Cot Memorial, Belgium; Morley WM and the **7 DWR Drill Hall WM panel 7, column 2.**

FIRTH, John Horace – 242841 Private.
Born in Bradford, the son of Luke and Esther Ann Firth. Husband of Jenny Firth, of 18 Peel Park Terrace, Idle Road, Undercliffe, Bradford. Enlisted at York.
1/7th Battalion DWR; died of wounds (gas) 22 10 1918, aged 32 (Advance to Victory).
Buried – Terlincthun British Cemetery, Wimille, France, 6, B, 15.
Commemorated – the **7 DWR Drill Hall WM panel 6, column 2.**
"DEARLY LOVED, DEEPLY MOURNED"

FISHER, Willie – 306644 Private.
Born in Leeds, the son of Harry and Mary Fisher, of 33, Raikes Lane, Birstall. Resided in Birstall. Enlisted at Liversedge
2/7th Battalion DWR; died of wounds 27 5 1917, aged 23.
Buried – St Sever Cemetery Extension, Rouen, France, P, 1, G, 6B.
Commemorated - the **7 DWR Drill Hall WM panel 1, column 1.**
"FOR EVER WITH THE LORD"

FISHER-BROWN, Kenneth Cuthbert – 2nd Lieutenant.
Son of the Rev John Fisher-Brown (Rector of Folkton), and Emily M Fisher-Brown, of Hill Rise, West Ayton, Yorks.
1/7th Battalion DWR; killed in action (shellfire) 13 11 1916, aged 23 (Battle of the Somme).
Buried – Foncquevillers Military Cemetery, France, 1, H, 3.
Commemorated – J Fisher, page 133, and the **7 DWR Drill Hall WM panel 4, column 1.**
Mentioned in 2/7th Battalion War Diary (transferred to 1/7th DWR, 1915). 1/7th Battalion War Diary (to UK, sick) 25 4 1916, (killed in action) 13 11 1916. HDH Album 7 DWR Volume 2, pages 2 column 2, 7, 9 19 & 44, with photos, and Volume 2, page 5.
"REQUIESCAT IN PACE"

FLETCHER, Arthur – 306174 Private.
Born in Springhead, Oldham, the son of Thomas and Elizabeth Ann Fletcher, of 100 Oldham Road, Springhead. Reside in Oldham. Enlisted at Greenfield.
1/7th Battalion DWR; died, pneumonia, 03 11 1918.
Buried – Etaples Military Cemetery, France, 49, A, 9.
Commemorated – the **7 DWR Drill Hall WM panel 1, column 3.**

FLETCHER, Leonard – 307255 Lance Corporal.
Born and enlisted at Sheffield.
1/7th Battalion DWR; died of wounds 30 7 1917 (Nieuport Sector).
Buried – Coxyde Military Cemetery, Belgium, 1, L, 46.
Commemorated – the **7 DWR Drill Hall WM panel 6, column 2.**

FLETCHER, Samuel Thomas – 5425 Lance Corporal.
Born and enlisted at Morley, Leeds.
1/7th Battalion DWR; killed in action 18 9 1916 (Battle of the Somme).
Commemorated – Thiepval Memorial, France; Morley WM and the **7 DWR Drill Hall WM panel 5, column 2.**

FLETCHER, Walter – 306504 Private.
Born in Halifax, the son of Helliwell and Emma Fletcher, of 76 Green Lane, West Vale, Halifax. Enlisted at Halifax.
2/7th Battalion DWR; killed in action 03 5 1917, aged 30 (Battle of Bullecourt).

Commemorated – Arras Memorial, France; Greetland WM; St John's Church, West Vale, Halifax; West Vale Baptist Church; Greetland Liberal Club RoH; CWD, page 378, and the **7 DWR Drill Hall WM panel 7, column 2.**
Mentioned in the Halifax Weekly Guardian 22 3 1919.

FLETCHER, William Robert – 3858 (later 306443) Private.
Born in Oakworth, Keighley, the son of John and Jane Fletcher, of 9 Brigg Street, Keighley. Enlisted at Bradford.
1/7th Battalion; died of wounds 28 4 1917, aged 20 (Hindenburg Line).
Buried – Merville Communal Cemetery Extension, France, 3, A, 13.
Commemorated – the **7 DWR Drill Hall WM panel 7, column 2.**

FLYNN, Frank – 306523 Private.
Born in Bradford, the son of Michael and Margaret Flynn, of 10 Many Gates, Manchester Road, Bradford. Enlisted at Bradford.
2/7th Battalion DWR; killed in action 05 5 1917 (Hindenburg Line).
Commemorated – Arras Memorial, France, and the **7 DWR Drill Hall WM panel 7, column 3.**

FOGGITT, Frank – 1660 Corporal.
Born in Kirkstall, Leeds, the son of Charlie and Mary Foggitt, of 18 Stansfield Row, Burley, Leeds. Enlisted at Leeds.
1/7th Battalion West Yorkshire Regiment; killed in action 14 7 1916, aged 21.
Commemorated – Thiepval Memorial, France, and the **7 DWR Drill Hall WM panel 5, column 3.**
WM & SDGW show name as FOGGETT. CWGC shows details as Frank FOGGITT, Lance Corporal, West Yorks Reg. Not DWR.

FOLEY, Leonard – 268402 Private.
Born in Leeds, the son of John H and Annie Foley, of 60 Salisbury Road, Armley, Leeds. Enlisted at Leeds.
2/7th Battalion DWR; killed in action 14 5 1917 (Hindenburg Line).
Commemorated – Arras Memorial, France, and the **7 DWR Drill Hall WM panel 3, column 2.**

FORSHAW, E H & T H - see **FORESHEW, Edward Horace & Thomas Hamer (Horner?).**
Commemorated – the **7 DWR Drill Hall WM panel 1, column 2 & the 7 DWR Drill Hall WM panel 2, column 1.**

FORSHEW, Edward Horace – 305235 Corporal.
Born in Golcar, Huddersfield, the son of William Richard and Mary Emma Forshew, of 90 Swallow Lane, Golcar. Resided in Golcar. Enlisted at Milnsbridge. Embarked for France & Flanders in December, 1916.
2/7th Battalion DWR, A Company; killed in action 14 5 1917 aged 21 (Hindenburg Line).
Commemorated – Arras Memorial, France; St John's Church, Golcar, RoH; CVA; M Stansfield, page 153, and the **7 DWR Drill Hall WM panel 1, column 2.**
Mentioned in the Huddersfield Examiner (reported missing) 05 6 1917 & 27 6 1917.
Brother of Thomas Hamer.
Some sources show surname spelt as FORSHAW.

FORSHEW, Thomas Hamer (Horner) – 306364 Private.
Born in Golcar, Huddersfield, the son of William Richard and Mary Emma Forshew, of 90 Swallow Lane, Golcar. Resided in Golcar. Enlisted at Milnsbridge. Reported missing, 03 5 1917.
2/7th Battalion DWR, A Company; presumed killed in action 14 5 1917, aged 22 (Hindenburg Line).

Commemorated – Arras Memorial, France; CVA; M Stansfield, page 152, and the **7 DWR Drill Hall WM panel 2, column 1.**
Mentioned in the Huddersfield Examiner (killed in action) 05 6 1917.
Brother of Edward Horace.
Some sources show surname spelt as FORSHAW.

FOSTER, Leonard – 306270 Private.
Resided in Springhead, Lees, Oldham, the husband of Annie Foster, of 196 Oldham Road, Springhead. Enlisted at Lees.
2/7th Battalion DWR; killed in action 27 11 1917, aged 32 (Battle of Cambrai).
Commemorated – Cambrai Memorial, Louverval, France; CWD, page 610, and the **7 DWR Drill Hall WM panel 7, column 1.**

FOWLES, Willie – 2170 Private.
Resided in Marsden, Huddersfield, the son of John and Elizabeth Ann Fowles, of Chain Road, Marsden. Enlisted at Milnsbridge in September, 1914.
1/7th Battalion DWR; killed in action (shot by sniper) 24 8 1915, aged 21 (Ypres Sector).
Buried – Bard Cottage Cemetery, Belgium, 1, F, 27.
Commemorated – Marsden WM; M Stansfield, page 154, and the **7 DWR Drill Hall WM panel 4, column 2.**
Mentioned in the Huddersfield Examiner (killed in action) 01 9 1915
"DEEPLY LOVED"

FRANCE, Wilfred Lawson - 2794 Private.
Born in Linthwaite, the son of Ellen France, resided at 53, Wood Top, Slaithwaite, Huddersfield. Enlisted at Milnsbridge in December, 1914. Embarked for France & Flanders in April, 1915.
1/7th Battalion DWR, attached to 147th Bde MGC; Killed in action 02 7 1916, aged 37 (Battle of the Somme).
Buried – Connaught Cemetery, Thiepval, France, 12, M, 1.
Commemorated – Slaithwaite WM; Carr Lane Methodist Church, Slaithwaite; St. James's Church, Slaithwaite; CVA, with photo; J Fisher, page 110; M Stansfield, page 156, and the **7 DWR Drill Hall WM panel 5, Column 1.**
Mentioned in the Huddersfield Examiner (killed in action) 13 7 1916.

FRANCES, Harry – 4780 Private.
Born in Saddleworth, the son of Charles and Emma Jane Frances. Husband of Alice Jane Frances, of 13 Hillside Avenue, Diggle, Dobcross, Oldham. Resided in Delph. Enlisted at Milnsbridge.
1/7th Battalion DWR; killed in action 02 7 1916, aged 25 (Battle of the Somme).
Commemorated – Thiepval Memorial, France, the 5 DWR Drill Hall WM, panel 4, column 4, and the **7 DWR Drill Hall WM panel 5, column 1.**
Mentioned in the Huddersfield Examiner (reported missing) 07 8 1916, (killed in action) 18 8 1916.
WM shows FRANCES J.

FRANCIS, Philip Edwin – 242469 Sergeant.
Born and resided at Belvedere, Kent. Enlisted at Sandwich.
1/7th Battalion DWR; killed in action 13 4 1918 (German Spring Offensive).
Buried – Trois Arbres Cemetery, Steenwerck, France, 2, L, 36.
Commemorated – the **7 DWR Drill Hall WM panel 7, Column 2.**
Formerly 24248 Private East Surrey Regiment.

FREEMAN, Thomas – 266190 Private.
Born in Skipton, the son of George and Mary Freeman, of 19 Devonshire Place, Skipton. Enlisted at Skipton.
2/7th Battalion DWR; died of pneumonia, 08 7 1918, aged 30.
Buried – Etaples Military Cemetery, France, 67, F, 32.
Commemorated – CPGW, page 355, with photograph, and the **7 DWR Drill Hall WM panel 3, column 1.**
"REST IN PEACE"

FROGGATT, Arthur – 5430 Private.
Born in Aston, Sheffield, the son of Tom and Caroline Froggatt, of 21 North Terrace, Waleswood, Sheffield. Enlisted at Sheffield.
1/7th DWR; killed in action 18 9 1916, aged 23 (Battle of the Somme).
Buried – Lonsdale Cemetery, Authuile, France, 8, F, 5.
Commemorated – the **7 DWR Drill Hall WM panel 5, column 3.**
Formerly 27251 Pte, King's Own Yorkshire Light Infantry.
WM shows name as FROGGART.

GAFFNEY, Charles Dawson – 325030 Private.
Born in Northam, Hampshire, the son of Mr and Mrs William Gaffney, of Southampton. Husband of Lucy Emma Gaffney, of 153 Priory Road, St Denys, Southampton. Resided in Woolston. Enlisted at Southampton.
1/7th Battalion DWR; killed in action 28 3 1918, aged 29 (German Spring Offensive).
Buried – Belgian Battery Corner Cemetery, Belgium, 2, H, 21.
Commemorated – the **7 DWR Drill Hall WM panel 7, column 1.**
Formerly SS/4770 Private, Army Service Corps; 300340 Private, Labour Corps.

GAMBLE, Walter – 307099 Private.
Born and enlisted at Bradford.
1/7th Battalion DWR; died of wounds 13 4 1918 (German Spring Offensive).
Buried – Haringhe (Bandaghem) Military Cemetery, Belgium, 2, B, 10.
Commemorated - the **7 DWR Drill Hall WM panel 7, column 3.**

GANT, Harry L – 242493 Private.
Resided in Lower Sydenham, London, the son of Ellen Gant, of 14 Watlington Grove, Sydenham. Enlisted at Camberwell.
1/7th Battalion DWR; died of wounds 16 4 1918, aged 21 (German Spring Offensive).
Buried – Longuenesse (St Omer) Souvenir Cemetery, France, 5, A, 54.
Commemorated – the **7 DWR Drill Hall WM panel 7, column 3.**
Formerly 5971 Private, Norfolk Regiment.

GARLICK, James – 3031 (later 306080) Lance Corporal, Military Medal.
Resided in Hey, Lees, the son of John and Annie Garlick, of, 10 Cambridge Street, Royton, Oldham. Enlisted at Milnsbridge.
1/7th Battalion DWR, B Company; killed in action 13 4 1918, aged 23 (German Spring Offensive).
Commemorated – Tyne Cot Memorial, Belgium, L Magnus, page 256, and the **7 DWR Drill Hall WM panel 7, column 2.**
Mentioned in the London Gazette (MM award) 22 1 1917, page 831. The Huddersfield Examiner (MM award) 11 1 1917.

GARSIDE, Edwin – 2410 Private.
Born in 1884 in Mossley. Husband of Margaret (nee Shaw). Enlisted on 02 11 1914, at Mossley.
1/7th Battalion DWR; killed in action, sniper, 10 7 1915 (Ypres Sector).
Buried – Ferme-Olivier Cemetery, Belgium, 2, C, 7.
Commemorated – St George's Church WM; St John the Baptist Church WM; R Vaughan, pages 20, 24 & 34, and the **7 DWR Drill Hall WM panel 4, column 2.**

GERRARD, George – 5006 Private.
Born in Nottingham, the brother of Charles H Gerrard, of 45 Grove Street, Derby. Enlisted at Derby.
1/7th Battalion DWR; killed in action 17 9 1916, aged 37 (Battle of the Somme, Leipzig Salient).
Buried – Bray Vale British Cemetery, Bray-Sur-Somme, France, 4, C, 11.
Commemorated – the **7 DWR Drill Hall WM panel 5, Column 1.**

GIBBONS, John – 306305 Private.
Resided in Royton, Lancs, the brother of James Gibbons, of 19 Tower Hill, Acrefair, Wrexham.
Enlisted at Milnsbridge.
2/7th Battalion DWR; killed in action 27 11 1917 (Battle of Cambrai).
Commemorated – Cambrai Memorial, Louverval, France, and the **7 DWR Drill Hall WM panel 3, column 2.**

GIBSON, Arthur Lionel – 2nd Lieutenant.
Resided in Harrogate, the son of Joseph and Mabel Gibson, of 'Winterton', 33 Ripon Road, Harrogate.
1/7th Battalion DWR; killed in action 08 8 1915, aged 24 (Ypres Sector).
Buried – Colne Valley Cemetery, Belgium, D, 5.
Commemorated – J Fisher, page 133, and the **7 DWR Drill Hall WM panel 4, column 1.**
Mentioned in the Unit War Diary (tour of trench instruction) 19 4 1916, (killed in action) 08 8 1915.
"DEVOTED SON, STAUNCH LOVER, TRUE FRIEND, AU REVOIR"

GIBSON, Ernest Alfred– 305494 Lance Corporal.
Born in Irthlingborough, Northants, the son of Mr and Mrs A J Gibson, of 34 High Street West, Irthlingborough. Resided with his cousin, Sergeant Gibson, at Hard End, Marsden. Enlisted at Milnsbridge in August, 1914. Had served for 4 years as a Territorial in the Northamptonshire Regiment.
1/7th Battalion DWR; died of wounds 26 7 1917, aged 24 (Nieuport Sector).
Buried – Coxyde Military Cemetery, Belgium, 1, L, 7.
Commemorated – Marsden War Memorial; M Stansfield, page 163, and the **7 DWR Drill Hall WM panel 6, column 1.**
Mentioned in the Huddersfield Examiner (died of wounds) 23 8 1917.
"HE DIED THAT WE MAY LIVE"

GIBSON, Fred Bamforth – 1929 Private.
Born in Slaithwaite, Huddersfield, the son of John William and Jane Gibson, of 7 Linfit Hall, Linthwaite. Enlisted at Slaithwaite in September, 1914.
1/7th Battalion DWR; killed in action 21 2 1917, aged 24 (Hindenburg Line).
Buried – Le Fermont Military Cemetery, Riviere, France, 2, E, 8.
Commemorated – Linthwaite WM; M Stansfield, page 163, and the **7 DWR Drill Hall WM panel 5, column 1.**
Mentioned in the Huddersfield Examiner (killed in action) 02 3 1917 & 22 3 1917. Howcroft, page 42.

GIBSON, John William – 1791 (later 11213) Corporal.
Born at Primrose Hill, Huddersfield. Resided at 12 Clough Lane, Paddock, Huddersfield. Enlisted at Milnsbridge.
1/7th Battalion DWR; killed in action 03 7 1916 (Battle of the Somme).

Commemorated – Thiepval Memorial, France; Paddock WM (held in Huddersfield Drill Hall); All Saints Church, Paddock, RoH; London and North Western Railway Company RoH; J Fisher, page 110; M Stansfield, page 163, and the **7 DWR Drill Hall WM panel 5, column 1.**
Mentioned in the Huddersfield Examiner (sympathy letter from HM King) 17 7 1916, (killed in action) 25 7 1916.

GIGGLE, Albert – 2205 Private.
Resided in Longwood, Huddersfield, the son of Mr and Mrs R Giggle, of 44 Scar Lane, Milnsbridge. Enlisted at Milnsbridge in August/September, 1914. Embarked for France & Flanders in May, 1916. Married Miss Walker of Lindley Street, Longwood, in May, 1916, whilst on home leave.
1/7th Battalion DWR; killed in action 17 9 1916 (Battle of the Somme, Leipzig Salient).
Commemorated – Thiepval Memorial, France; St Mark's Parish Church, Longwood, St John's Church, Golcar; J Fisher, page 113; M Stansfield, page 164, and the **7 DWR Drill Hall WM panel 5, column 3.**
Mentioned in the Huddersfield Examiner (killed in action) 10 8 1915, (killed in action) 13 10 1916 & 25 10 1916.

GILBERT, John – 306344 Private.
Resided in Dobcross. Enlisted at Milnsbridge.
2/7th Battalion DWR; killed in action 03 5 1917 (Battle of Bullecourt).
Commemorated – Arras Memorial, France, and the **7 DWR Drill Hall WM panel 2, column 1.**
Mentioned in the Huddersfield Examiner (reported missing) 27 6 1917.

GILL, Jack Eastwood – 2455 Sergeant.
Born in Windhill, Shipley, Yorkshire, the adopted son of Walter and Eliza Ann Gill, of 94 James Street, Golcar, Huddersfield. Resided in Golcar. Enlisted at Milnsbridge in October 1914. Embarked for France & Flanders in April, 1915.
1/7th Battalion DWR, attached to 147th Company Machine Gun Corps; killed in action 15 7 1916, aged 22 (Battle of the Somme).
Buried – Connaught Cemetery, Thiepval, France, 12, J, 6.
Commemorated – St John's Church, Golcar; M Stansfield, page 165, and the **7 DWR Drill Hall WM panel 5, Column 3.**

GLADWIN, James William – 5148 Private.
Born on Halifax, the son of Henry and Eliza Gladwin. Husband of Mary Gladwin, of 12 Clarence Square, Gibbet Street, Halifax. Resided 9 Back Shaw Lane, Halifax. Enlisted at Halifax in June, 1916.
3/7th Battalion DWR; died, pneumonia, 30 7 1916 at Clipston Camp, aged 22.
Buried – Halifax (Stoney Royd) Cemetery; Special Memorial.
Commemorated – Halifax Civic Book of Remembrance; J Fisher, page 104; CWD, page 129, and the **7 DWR Drill Hall WM panel 5, Column 1.**
Mentioned in The Halifax Courier 03 8 1916.

GLEDHILL, Augustus – 267649 Private.
Born in Bradford, the son of John Herbert Gledhill, of 105 Baird Street, Bradford. Husband of Maud Small (formerly Gledhill), of 15 Warwick Street, Leeds Road, Bradford. Enlisted at Bradford.
2/7th Battalion DWR; killed in action 31 8 1917, aged 31.
Buried – Favreuil British Cemetery, France, 1, D, 25.
Commemorated – the **7 DWR Drill Hall WM panel 7, column 1.**

GLEDHILL, Joe – 305068 Sergeant.
Born in Golcar, Huddersfield, the son of Charles and Amelia Gledhill, of Golcar. The husband of Mary A Gledhill, of 160 Leymoor Road, Golcar. Resided and enlisted at Golcar. Served eight years in the local Territorials.

2/7th Battalion DWR; killed in action (shellfire) 17 9 1917, aged 26.
Buried – Favreuil British Cemetery, France, 1, F, 20.
Commemorated – St John's Church, Golcar; CVA; M Stansfield, page 168, and the **7 DWR Drill Hall WM panel 7, column 1.**
Mentioned in the Unit War Diary (killed in action) 17 9 1917.
"HE GAVE HIS LIFE THAT OTHERS MIGHT LIVE"

GLEDHILL, Sam Gudger (known as Jack) – 2206 Private.
Born in Golcar on 09 3 1895. Resided in Lindley, Huddersfield, the son of Lena Gledhill, of 5 Thornhill Avenue, Lindley. Enlisted at Milnsbridge on 10 9 1914. Embarked for France & Flanders, April, 1915.
1/7th Battalion DWR, attached to 147th Company MGC; killed in action 03 9 1916, aged 21 (Battle of the Somme).
Buried – Connaught Cemetery, Thiepval, France, 12, M, 10.
Commemorated – Oakes Baptist Church; St Stephen's Church, Lindley; J Fisher, page 113; M Stansfield, page 167, and the **7 DWR Drill Hall WM panel 5, Column 1.**
"CUT DOWN AS A FLOWER, FRESH AND BEAUTIFUL"

GLEW, Sam – 7235 Private.
Resided in Belper, Derbyshire. Enlisted at Derby.
1/7th Battalion DWR; killed in action 17 9 1916 (Battle of the Somme, Leipzig Salient).
Commemorated – Thiepval Memorial, Somme, France, and the **7 DWR Drill Hall WM panel 5, column 2.**
WM spelling of surname can be mistaken for CLEW.

GODBER, Harold – 306948 Private.
Born in Nottingham, the son of Thomas and Elizabeth Godber, of 38 Noel Street, Nottingham. Enlisted at Nottingham.
2/7th Battalion DWR, C Company; killed in action 03 5 1917, aged 21 (Battle of Bullecourt).
Commemorated – Arras Memorial, France, and the **7 DWR Drill Hall WM panel 3, column 1.**

GODBER, Walter Owen – 306947 Private.
Born in Nottingham, the son of Walter and Annie Godber, of 29 Exeter Road, Sherwood Rise, Nottingham. Enlisted at Nottingham.
2/7th Battalion DWR, C Company; killed in action 11 4 1917, aged 20 (Hindenburg Line).
Buried – Ecoust Military Cemetery, Ecoust St Mein, France, 1, A, 11.
Commemorated – the **7 DWR Drill Hall WM panel 1, column 3.**
"HE WAS A LOVER OF PEACE"

GODDARD, Eric – 2nd Lieutenant.
Born in 1895 in Mossley, the son of Alfred and Betsy Goddard, of Clarendon House, Micklehurst, Mossley, Manchester. 1/7th Battalion DWR, attached Trench Mortar Battery; died 04 7 1916, aged 21 (Battle of the Somme).
Commemorated – Thiepval Memorial, France; Mossley Town Hall WM; All Saints Church WM; Micklehurst Conservative Club WM; Micklehurst Liberal Club WM; St George's Church WM; Abney Congregational Church RoH and window; family grave, St James' Church cemetery, Millbrook; R Vaughan, pages 19, 20, 24 51 & 154, and the **7 DWR Drill Hall WM panel 4, column 1.**
Mentioned in the Unit War Diary (From 3/7th Battalion) 29 5 1916, (Bde Liaison Officer, found dead, 04 7 1916). HDH Album 7 DWR Volume 2, pages 11-14. G Howcroft, page 60.
Some sources state missing in action from 01 7 1916 and killed in action 03 9 1916.

GODDARD, Percy – 1664 Private.
Born in 1896, the son of Harry and Ada Goddard, of 17 Merton Street, Copley, Stalybridge. Resided in Stalybridge. Enlisted at Mossley.
1/7th Battalion DWR, originally F Company; died of wounds 12 7 1916, aged 20.
Buried – St Sever Cemetery Extension, Rouen, France, A, 28, 19.
Commemorated – Stalybridge WM; R Vaughan, page 25, and the **7 DWR Drill Hall WM panel 5, column 2.**
"FOR HONOUR LIBERTY AND TRUTH HE SACRIFICED HIS GLORIOUS YOUTH"

GOLDEN, S – 306335 Private - see **GOULDER Stanley**.
Commemorated – 7 DWR Drill Hall WM panel 1, column 3.
WM shows name as GOLDEN, SDGW shows name as GOLDER.

GOODALL, Stanley – 5434 Private.
Born in Heckmondwike, Yorkshire. Resided in Dewsbury. Enlisted at Batley.
1/7th Battalion DWR; killed in action 17 9 1916 (Battle of the Somme, Leipzig Salient).
Commemorated – Thiepval Memorial, France, and the **7 DWR Drill Hall WM panel 5, column 1.**

GORMAN, Harry – 5546 Sergeant.
Born in Pontefract, the son of Mrs Elizabeth Jarvis, of 31 Chapel Street, Wheldon Lane, Castleford. Resided in Castleford. Enlisted at Pontefract.
1/7th Battalion DWR; killed in action 03 9 1916, aged 21 (Battle of the Somme, Thiepval).
Commemorated – Thiepval Memorial, France, and the **7 DWR Drill Hall WM panel 5, column 2.**
Formerly 11536, Private, King's Own Yorkshire Light Infantry.

GORMAN, H – 307348 Private.
No trace, by name or number, in CWGC or SDGW.
Possibly a duplicate of **GORMAN, Harry** – 5546, (above), possibly with the service number issued after the April 1917 re-numbering.
Commemorated – the **7 DWR Drill Hall WM panel 7, column 2.**

GORNALL, James Edgar Thomas – 3644 Private.
Born in Rimington, the son of John and Ellen Gornall, of Gisburn, near Clitheroe, Lancs. Resided in Gisburn. Enlisted at Halifax.
1/7th Battalion DWR; died 29 7 1916, aged 27 (Battle of the Somme).
Buried – Puchevillers British Cemetery, France, 2, C, 17.
Commemorated – CPGW, page 145 & website, and the **7 DWR Drill Hall WM panel 5, column 1.**
"REST IN PEACE"

GOULDER, Sydney – 306335 Private.
Resided in Marsden, the son of George Goulder of 5 Gladstone Buildings, Marsden, Huddersfield. Enlisted at Milnsbridge in 1916. Embarked for France & Flanders in December, 1916.
2/7th Battalion DWR; died of wounds at No 49 Casualty Clearing Station on 18 4 1917, aged 30 (Hindenburg Line).
Buried – Achiet-Le-Grand Communal Cemetery, France, 1, C, 9.
Commemorated – Marsden WM; M Stansfield, page 170, and the **7 DWR Drill Hall WM panel 1, column 3.**
Mentioned in the Huddersfield Examiner (died of wounds) 17 5 1917.
WM shows name as GOLDEN, SDGW shows name as GOLDER.

GOWERS, Wilfred- 307632 Private.
Born in Castle Howard, Yorkshire. Husband of A Gowers of 1 Prospect Street, Bingley. Resided in Bingley. Enlisted at Keighley.
1/7th Battalion DWR; died of wounds 30 7 1917, aged 24 (Nieuport Sector).
Buried – Coxyde Military Cemetery, Belgium, 1, L, 45.
Commemorated – the **7 DWR Drill Hall WM panel 6, column 3.**

GRAHAM, Harry Wilkinson – 269213 Private.
Born in Luddendenfoot, the son of Amos and Ann Elizabeth Graham, of Laurel Mount, Luddendenfoot. Resided in Rose Place, Luddendenfoot. Enlisted at Halifax.
1/7th Battalion DWR; died of wounds 15 4 1918, aged 29 (German Spring Offensive).
Buried – Haringhe (Bandaghem) Military Cemetery, Belgium, 2, E, 4.
Commemorated – Luddendenfoot Village WM; Halifax Civic Book of Remembrance; Todmorden Garden of Remembrance; CWD, page 527, and the **7 DWR Drill Hall WM panel 7, column 2.**
Mentioned in the Hebden Bridge Times 26 4 & 03 5 1918, with photograph. The Huddersfield Examiner (in memoriam) 03 5 1921.
"LOVING MEMORIES OF A DEAR SON, BROTHER & HUSBAND"

GRANT, William J – 17075 Private.
Born in Edinburgh, the son of William and Elizabeth Grant of, 80 Montgomery Street, Edinburgh.
2/7th Battalion DWR; died 27 3 1918, aged 23 (German Spring Offensive).
Buried – Pommier Communal Cemetery, France, 25.
Commemorated – the **7 DWR Drill Hall WM panel 2, column 1.**
Formerly 1597 Private, Royal Army Medical Corps.
WM shows name as BRANT.

GRAVES, Harold – 3907 Private.
Born and enlisted at Bradford.
1/7th Battalion DWR; killed in action 23 7 1916 (Battle of the Somme).
Commemorated – Thiepval Memorial, France, and the **7 DWR Drill Hall WM panel 5, column 3.**

GRAY, James – 305899 Lance Corporal.
Born in 1879 in Netherton, Northumberland. Husband of Amelia (nee Brennan) and resided in Mossley. Enlisted at Milnsbridge.
2/7th Battalion DWR, B Company; killed in action 03 5 1917 (Battle of Bullecourt).
Commemorated – Arras Memorial, France; Unitarian Church WM; St John the Baptist Church WM; R Vaughan, pages 74 & 175, and the **7 DWR Drill Hall WM panel 1, column 1.**

GRAY, John Thomas –18995 Private.
Born in Halton Holgate, Spilsby, Lincs, the son of Thomas and Elizabeth Gray, of 19, Albert Street, Brigg. Resided in Brigg, Lincs. Enlisted at Bradford.
1/7th Battalion DWR; killed in action 13 4 1918, aged 25 (German Spring Offensive).
Commemorated – Tyne Cot Memorial, Belgium, and the **7 DWR Drill Hall WM panel 2, column 1.**

GRAY, William Henry – 25206 Private.
Born and resided in Spalding, Lincs, the son of Mr W J and Mrs S A Gray, of Moulton Common, Spalding. Enlisted at Bourne.
2/7th Battalion DWR; killed in action 26 3 1918, aged 20 (German Spring Offensive).
Commemorated – Arras Memorial, France, and the **7 DWR Drill Hall WM panel 2, column 1.**
*Also served in the 10th Battalion, see - **tunstillsmen.blogspot.com** (last accessed August, 2020).*
GREENHALGH, James – 266981 Sergeant.

Son of Samuel and Jane Greenhalgh, of 47, Woodhey Road, Holcombe Brook, Ramsbottom, Manchester. Resided in Bury. Enlisted at Skipton.
2/7th Battalion DWR; killed in action 03 5 1917, aged 26 (Battle of Bullecourt).
Buried – Ecoust Military Cemetery, Ecoust-St-Mien, France, 2, A, 39.
Commemorated – the **7 DWR Drill Hall WM panel 1, column 1.**
WM shows rank as Private.
"WORTHY OF EVERLASTING LOVE"

GREENWAY, James William – 306730 Private.
Resided in Barnsley. Husband of Mrs I Greenway, of 105 Avenue Road, Wath-on-Dearne, Rotherham. Enlisted at Halifax.
2/7th Battalion DWR; killed in action 12 6 1918.
Buried – Bienvillers Military Cemetery, France, 21, C, 13.
Commemorated – the **7 DWR Drill Hall WM Panel 3, column 1.**
WM shows number as 307730.
"IN LOVING MEMORY OF MY SON JAMES, GONE BUT NOT FORGOTTEN, FATHER AND MOTHER"

GREENWOOD, Clifford – 1079 Private.
Born in Saddleworth, the son of John William, of 15 Halton Road, Wallasey, Cheshire, and Thyrza J P Greenwood (stepmother). Enlisted at Milnsbridge.
1/7th Battalion DWR; killed in action 17 9 1916, aged 23 (Battle of the Somme, Leipzig Salient).
Commemorated – Thiepval Memorial, France, and the **7 DWR Drill Hall WM panel 5, column 1.**

GREENWOOD, Fred – 241483.
Born in Rochdale, the son of John Robert Greenwood of 38 Victor Terrace, Manningham, Bradford. Enlisted at Bradford.
2/7th Battalion DWR; killed in action 09 4 1918, aged 27 (German Spring Offensive).
Buried – Bienvillers Military Cemetery, France, 9, B, 1.
Formerly 4839 Private, King's Own Yorkshire Light Infantry.
Commemorated – the **7 DWR Drill Hall WM Panel 7, column 2.**
Also served in the 10th Battalion, see - tunstillsmen.blogspot.com (last accessed August, 2020).

GREENWOOD, Harry – 3647 Private (later attached 1/5th King's Own Yorkshire Light Infantry from an Infantry Base Depot, Etaples).
Born and resided in Skipton, the son of Mr and Mrs Highton Greenwood. Enlisted at Keighley.
1/7th Battalion DWR (KOYLI on death); died of wounds, at 2nd West Riding Field Ambulance, 28 7 1916, aged 25 (Battle of the Somme).
Buried – Forceville Communal Cemetery and Extension, 2, D, 7.
Commemorated – the **7 DWR Drill Hall WM panel 5, column 1.**

GREENWOOD, Harry – 306877 Private.
Enlisted at Halifax.
2/7th Battalion DWR; killed in action 03 5 1917 (Battle of Bullecourt).
Commemorated – Arras Memorial, France; CWD, page 135, and the **7 DWR Drill Hall WM panel 2, column 3.**

GREENWOOD, Joseph – 306624 Private.
Resided in Baildon. Enlisted at Shipley.
2/7th Battalion DWR; killed in action 03 5 1917 (Battle of Bullecourt).
Commemorated – Arras Memorial, France, and the **7 DWR Drill Hall WM panel 2, column 3.**
GREENWOOD, Percy – 306132 Lance Corporal.

Resided in Stalybridge. Enlisted at Greenfield.
2/7th Battalion DWR; died of wounds; 25 5 1918 (German Spring Offensive)
Buried – Doullens Communal Cemetery Extension No 2. France, 2, C, 123.
Commemorated – Stalybridge WM and the **7 DWR Drill Hall WM panel 3, column 1.**

GRIFFIN, Arthur – 26674 Private.
Born and enlisted at Paisley, Scotland.
1/6th Battalion DWR; died of wounds in Germany as POW on 12 5 1918.
Buried – Cologne Southern Cemetery, Germany, 3, F, 38.
Commemorated – Arras Memorial, France; The Scottish National War Memorial (Edinburgh Castle) and the **7 DWR Drill Hall WM panel 2, column 2.**
Mentioned in S Barber, page 177.

GRIFFITHS, George Martin – 47344 Private.
Born in Easington. Resided in Wolverhampton. Enlisted at Walsall.
1/7th Battalion DWR; died of wounds 13 10 1918 (Advance to Victory).
Buried – Bucquoy Road Cemetery, Ficheux, France, 3, F, 9.
Commemorated - the **7 DWR Drill Hall WM panel 2, column 2.**
Formerly R/4/064241 Private, Army Service Corps.

GRIMSHAW, Thomas – 22146 Private.
Born and resided in Manchester, the son of Thomas Grimshaw. Husband of Clara Grimshaw, of 15 New Butler Street, Oldham Road, Manchester. Enlisted at Manchester.
2/7th Battalion DWR; killed in action 27 11 1917, aged 30 (Battle of Cambria).
Commemorated – Cambrai Memorial, Louverval, France, and the **7 DWR Drill Hall WM panel 2, column 2.**
Formerly S/2/11973 Private RASC.

GRUNDY, Harry – 2084 Private.
Born on 24 9 1895 at 91 South Street, Huddersfield, the son of Albert Edward and Mary Hannah Grundy, of 100 South Street, Huddersfield. Enlisted at Milnsbridge on 05 9 1914.
1/7th Battalion DWR; killed in action (shot by sniper) 16 12 1915, aged 20 (Ypres Sector).
Buried – Bard Cottage Cemetery, Belgium, 1, J, 13.
Commemorated – South Street Methodist Church; St Thomas's Church, Longroyd Bridge; M Stansfield ,page 176, and the **7 DWR Drill Hall WM panel 4, column 3.**
"TO MEMORY DEAR"

HAGAN, Thomas – 2527 Private.
Resided in Oldham. Enlisted at Milnsbridge.
1/7th Battalion DWR; died of wounds 13 7 1916 (Battle of the Somme).
Buried – Colchester Cemetery, Essex, P, 7, 24.
Commemorated – the **7 DWR Drill Hall WM panel 4, column 3.**

HAGGERTY W – 2810 Private.
7th Battalion DWR; died, at home, 29 11 1915.
Buried – Fulford Cemetery, York, A, 1.
Commemorated – the **7 DWR Drill Hall WM panel 4, column 3.**
Not in SDGW.

HAGUE, Samuel Ogden – 305711 Private.
Resided in Hey, Lancs. Enlisted at Uppermill.
2/7th Battalion DWR; killed in action 17 4 1917 (Hindenburg Line).

Commemorated – Arras Memorial, France, and the **7 DWR Drill Hall WM panel 1, column 1**.
WM shows surname spelt HAIGH.

HAIGH, Sidney – 5835 Private.
Resided and enlisted at Bradford into 6th Battalion (from Derby Scheme). Embarked for France & Flanders on 11 10 1916, unusually reaching 1/7th Battalion on the 12th, apparently, not having been to an Infantry Base Depot.
1/7th Battalion DWR; killed in action 17 11 1916 (Battle of the Somme).
Buried – Foncquevillers Military Cemetery, France, 1, H, 7.
Commemorated – the **7 DWR Drill Hall WM panel 5, column 3**.

HAIGH, S O – see **HAGUE, Samuel Ogden**.
CWGC & SDGW show surname spelt HAGUE.

HAIGH, Wilson – 1178 Private.
Born in 1890 in Mossley. Resided in Mossley. Enlisted at Slaithwaite. Embarked for France & Flanders on 15 4 1915.
1/7th Battalion DWR; killed in action 03 9 1916 (Battle of the Somme, Thiepval).
Commemorated – Thiepval Memorial, France; Lochnagar Crater walkway memorial plaque; France; Conservative Club RoH; St John the Baptist Church WM; R Vaughan, page 57, and the **7 DWR Drill Hall WM panel 5, column 3**.

HALEY, Frank – 306662 Corporal.
Son of Hardy and Mary Haley. Enlisted at Bradford.
2/7th Battalion DWR; killed in action 03 5 1917, aged 23 (Battle of Bullecourt).
Commemorated – Arras Memorial, France, and the **7 DWR Drill Hall WM panel 3, column 1**.

HALEY, Isaac – 5480 (later 7204 & 308051) Private.
Enlisted at Birstall.
1/7th Battalion DWR; killed in action 13 4 1918 (German Spring Offensive).
Commemorated – Tyne Cot Memorial, Belgium, and the **7 DWR Drill Hall WM panel 7, column 3**.

HALL, Robert – 7139 (later 307992) Private.
Born in Middleton, Northumberland, the son of Richard and Mary Hall, of High Street, Belford, Northumberland. Husband of E J Hall, of Green Close, Kirkbride, Cumberland. Enlisted at Alnwick.
1/7th Battalion DWR; killed in action 18 9 1916, aged 33 (Battle of the Somme).
Commemorated – Thiepval Memorial, France, and the **7 DWR Drill Hall WM panel 6, column 3**.
Formerly 3216 Private, Northumberland Fusiliers.

HALL, Thomas – 7151 Lance Corporal.
Resided in Ashington, Northumberland, the son of Charles and Mary Hall, of Ashington. Enlisted at Alnwick.
1/7th Battalion DWR; died of wounds 16 9 1916, aged 21 (Battle of the Somme).
Buried – Abbeville Communal Cemetery, France, 1, B, 7.
Commemorated – the **7 DWR Drill Hall WM panel 5, column 1**.
"MAY HIS REWARD BE AS GREAT AS HIS SACRIFICE"

HAMER, Frederick William – 24180 Private.
Born in Marylebone, London. Resided in Bedford, the husband of Florence Mary Hamer, of 45, Allhallows Lane, Bedford. Enlisted at London.
1/7th Battalion DWR; killed in action 25 4 1918, aged 30 (German Spring Offensive).
Buried – Mendinghem Military Cemetery, Belgium, 10, C, 27.

Commemorated – the **7 DWR Drill Hall WM panel 2, column 1.**
Formerly 109816 Private, Labour Corps.
"GONE BUT NOT FORGOTTEN"

HANKIN, William – 307038 Private.
Enlisted at Bradford.
2/7th Battalion DWR; killed in action 03 5 1917 (Battle of Bullecourt).
Buried – HAC Cemetery, Ecouste St Mien, France, 4, D, 18.
Commemorated – the **7 DWR Drill Hall WM panel 1, column 1.**

HANNAH, John Ogilvie – 3753 (later 204088) Sergeant.
Born on 13 10 1888 at 'The Glen', Innerleithen, Peebleshire, the son of Mr Hannah, of 'Braemar', 1 Fort Terrace, Bridlington. Resided in Rudston, Yorkshire, and Longley, Huddersfield. Enlisted at Huddersfield in December, 1914.
1/7th Battalion DWR; killed in action 29 4 1918 (German Spring Offensive).
Commemorated – Tyne Cot Memorial, Belgium; Almondbury WM; M Stansfield, page 190, and the **7 DWR Drill Hall WM panel 6, column 3.**

HANSOM, George Thomas – 305461 Private.
Son of Mrs Amanda Maria Hansom, of 21 Gate Head, Marsden, Huddersfield.
1/7th Battalion DWR; died 13 4 1918, aged 20 (German Spring Offensive).
Commemorated – Tyne Cot Memorial, Belgium; Marsden WM; M Stansfield, page 190, and the **7 DWR Drill Hall WM panel 7, column 3.**
WM shows name as HANSOM; M Stansfield shows his number as 30546.

HANSON, William Thomas – 2861 (11977 with 3 DWR) Private.
Born on 08 3 1884 at Manor House Farm, Crosland Hill, Huddersfield, the son of William and Eliza Hanson, of Starling End Farm, Lockwood. Enlisted 7 DWR at Milnsbridge on 27 8 1914 and posted to 3 DWR; discharged due to chronic medical condition on 07 11 1914. Re-enlisted on 19 1 1915.
2/7th Battalion DWR; died at home, kicked by mule, 09 6 1915, aged 31.
Buried – South Crosland (Holy Trinity) Churchyard, East of Church.
Commemorated – Emmanuel Church, Lockwood; Mount Pleasant Chapel, Lockwood; M Stansfield, page 192, and the **7 DWR Drill Hall WM panel 4, column 2.**
Mentioned in the Huddersfield Examiner (wounded) 06 5 1915.

HARDWICK, Leonard – 266714 Private.
Son of Mrs Eliza Hardwick, of 'Fern Royd', Tranmere Drive, Hawksworth, Guiseley.
1/7th Battalion DWR; died of wounds at home 19 10 1918.
Buried – Guiseley (St Oswald's) Churchyard, 458.
Commemorated – the **7 DWR Drill Hall WM panel 3, column 1.**
"AFTER WAR'S TUMULT, REST"

HARDWICK, Tom – 466 (later 3750) Private.
Born and enlisted at Bradford.
1/7th Battalion DWR; killed in action 03 9 1916 (Battle of the Somme, Thiepval).
Commemorated – Thiepval Memorial, France, and the **7 DWR Drill Hall WM panel 5, column 2.**
CWGC shows Battalion as 1/5th DWR.

HARDY, Willie – 306634 Private.
Enlisted at Bradford.
2/7th Battalion DWR; 16 4 1917 (Hindenburg Line).

Commemorated – Arras Memorial, France; R Vaughan, page 25, and the **7 DWR Drill Hall WM panel 1, column 1.**

HAREWOOD, Willie – 306744 Private.
Resided in Cleckheaton. Enlisted at Liversedge.
2/7th Battalion DWR; killed in action 03 5 1917 (Battle of Bullecourt).
Commemorated – Arras Memorial, France; Cleckheaton WM and the **7 DWR Drill Hall WM panel 1, column 1.**

HARGREAVES, George Arthur – 307267 Private.
Resided in Batley. Enlisted at Dewsbury.
1/7th Battalion DWR; died 26 2 1918.
Buried – Lijssenthoek Military Cemetery, Belgium, 27, E, 16.
Commemorated – the **7 DWR Drill Hall WM panel 7, column 2.**
Formerly 27057 Private, King's Own Yorkshire Light Infantry.

HARGREAVES, Wilfred – 307277 Private.
Born in Bingley, the son of Arthur and Sarah Ellen Hargreaves, of 6 Vulcan Road, Dewsbury. Resided in Dewsbury. Enlisted at Dewsbury.
1/7th Battalion DWR; killed in action 15 8 1917 (Nieuport Sector).
Buried – Coxyde Military Cemetery, Belgium, 2, H, 18.
Commemorated – the **7 DWR Drill Hall WM panel 6, column 2.**

HARRIS, Abel Farrer – 26386 Private.
Born in Shap, Cumberland. Enlisted at Stockport.
1/7th Battalion DWR; killed in action 11 10 1918 (Advance to Victory, Battle of Iwuy).
Buried – Wellington Cemetery, Rieux-En-Cambresis, France, 3, B, 7.
Commemorated - the **7 DWR Drill Hall WM panel 2, column 1.**
Formerly 67841 Pte, Liverpool Regiment & 44656 Pte, Labour Corps.

HARRIS, Charles – 305749 Private, Military Medal.
Born in 1893 in Mossley. Resided in Mossley. Enlisted at Uppermill.
1/7th Battalion DWR; died 22 11 1918 (Advance to Victory).
Buried – Douai British Cemetery, Cuincy, France, C, 13.
Commemorated – St George's Church WM; St John the Baptist Church WM; R Vaughan, pages 10, 24, 147 and the **7 DWR Drill Hall WM panel 1, column 1.**
Mentioned in the London Gazette (MM award) 23 7 1919, page 9374.

HARRIS, Edmund George – 2nd Lieutenant.
Son of Edmund Harris, of 119 Cowley Mill Road, Uxbridge, Middlesex.
2/7th Battalion DWR; died, accident, 26 6 1917, aged 26.
Buried – Achiet-Le-Grand Communal Cemetery, France 1, K, 5.
Commemorated – the **7 DWR Drill Hall WM panel 3, column 3.**
Formerly 2340 CSgt, 8 Middlesex Regiment.
Mentioned in the Unit War Diary (appointed Adjutant) 01 12 1916, (wounded, bomb accident) 25 6 1917.

HARRISON, John Irvin – 307772 Private.
Son of John and Martha Harrison, of 1 Back Green, Outlane, Huddersfield. Enlisted at Huddersfield.
1/7th Battalion DWR; died of wounds 11 5 1918, aged 29 (German Spring Offensive).
Buried – Boulogne Eastern Cemetery, France, 9, B, 69.
Commemorated – M Stansfield, page 196, and **7 DWR Drill Hall WM panel 6, column 2.**
Mentioned in the Huddersfield Examiner (gassed, in Canadian General Hospital) 07 8 1917.

WM shown initials J A.

HARRISON, John William – 268411 Private.
Enlisted at Leeds.
2/7th Battalion DWR; died of wounds 21 11 1917, Battle of Cambrai).
Buried – Grevillers British Cemetery, France, 7, D, 3.
Commemorated – the **7 DWR Drill Hall WM panel 7, column 2.**

HARROD, Herbert George – 306924 Lance Corporal.
Enlisted at Nottingham.
2/7th Battalion DWR; killed in action 28 3 1918 (German Spring Offensive).
Buried – Pommier Communal Cemetery, France, 2.
Commemorated – the **7 DWR Drill Hall WM panel 2, column 3.**

HARROP, Herbert – 1858 Lance Corporal.
Born and resided in Lees, Oldham. Husband of Charlotte Harrop, of 3 Rhodes Hill, Lees. Enlisted at Lees.
1/7th Battalion DWR; killed in action 03 9 1916, aged 37 (Battle of the Somme, Thiepval).
Commemorated – Thiepval Memorial, France, and the **7 DWR Drill Hall WM panel 5, column 2.**

HARTLEY, Dennis – 3939 Private.
Born and resided in Birstall, Leeds, the son of George and Emma Hartley, of 13 Industrial Avenue, Birstall. Enlisted at Birstall.
1/7th Battalion DWR; killed in action 03 9 1916, aged 25 (Battle of the Somme).
Commemorated – Thiepval Memorial, France, and the **7 DWR Drill Hall WM panel 5, column 1.**

HAWKINS, Cecil Stephen – 24387 Private.
Born and resided in West Hartlepool, the son of E and Mary Ann Hawkins, of 5 Lister Street, West Hartlepool.
2/7th Battalion DWR; died of wounds 02 12 1917, aged 22.
Buried – Red Cross Corner Cemetery, Beugny, France, 1, F, 9.
Commemorated – the **7 DWR Drill Hall WM panel 2, column 2.**
Formerly 766 Pte, Durham Light Infantry.
"FOR OTHERS"

HAWORTH, Harry – 266206 Lance Corporal.
Son of John and Frances Ellen Haworth; husband of Florence Jane Haworth, of 15, Clifford Street, Barnoldswick, Yorks.
2/7th Battalion DWR; died 09 4 1918, aged 30.
Buried – Bienvillers Military Cemetery, 9, B, 2.
Commemorated – Barnoldswick WM; CPGW, page 341, with photograph, and the **7 DWR Drill Hall WM panel 1, column 1.**
WM shows HOWARTH H.
"WORTHY OF EVERLASTING LOVE"

HAYES, Edward Dyson – 628 Sergeant.
Born at Slaithwaite, Huddersfield, the son of John and Emily Hayes, of 13 Waterside, Slaithwaite. Enlisted at Slaithwaite in August, 1914.
1/7th Battalion DWR, B Company; killed in action 22 10 1915, aged 27 (Ypres Salient).
Buried – Talana Farm Cemetery, Belgium, 4, C, 16.
Commemorated – Slaithwaite WM; Carr Lane Methodist Church; St James's Church, Slaithwaite; M Stansfield, page 199, and the **7 DWR Drill Hall WM panel 4, column 1.**

Mentioned in the Unit War Diary (killed in action) 22 10 1915; The Huddersfield Examiner (Machine Gun Section, killed in action) 28 4 1915, 28 10 1915 & 10 1 1916.

HEALD, Albert – 3591 Private.
Son of Mrs Heald, of 9 Pymroyd, Milnsbridge. Enlisted at Milnsbridge in October, 1915. Embarked for France & Flanders in April, 1916.
1/7th Battalion DWR; killed in action 03 9 1916, aged 25 (Battle of the Somme, Thiepval).
Commemorated - Thiepval Memorial, France; M Stansfield, page 200, and the **7 DWR Drill Hall WM panel 4, column 3.**

HEALD, Edgar – 306235 Drummer.
Resided in Barnoldswick. Enlisted at Skipton.
2/7th Battalion DWR; killed in action 03 5 1917 (Battle of Bullecourt).
Commemorated – Arras Memorial, France; Barnoldswick WM; CPGW, page 240, and the **7 DWR Drill Hall WM panel 3, column 1.**

HELLEWELL, Richard – 307185 Private.
Born in Blackpool, 1884. Resided, with spouse, Elizabeth Hellewell, Gregory Cottage, Grassington, Yorks. Enlisted at Bradford.
1/7th Battalion DWR; died of wounds 30 4 1918, aged 34 (German Spring Offensive).
Buried – Boulogne Eastern Cemetery, 9, B, 8.
Commemorated – the **7 DWR Drill Hall WM panel 6, column 2.**
"THY WILL, BE DONE"

HEMINGWAY, Harry – 307278 Private.
Born in Ossett, the son of William and Eliza Hemingway. Enlisted at Ossett.
1/7th Battalion DWR; killed in action 18 9 1916 (Battle of the Somme).
Commemorated – Thiepval Memorial, France, and the **7 DWR Drill Hall WM panel 6, column 2.**
Formerly 27767 Private, King's Own Yorkshire Light Infantry.
WM shows number as 307378.

HEMSLEY, Sam – 307187 Private.
Born and resided at Hebden Bridge, the son of James Hemsley, of 22 Balmoral Street, Hebden Bridge. Enlisted at Hebden Bridge in October, 1916.
1/7th Battalion DWR; killed in action (shellfire) 03 8 1917, aged 21, (Nieuport Sector).
Buried – Coxyde Military Cemetery, Belgium, 2, D, 4.
Commemorated – Hebden Bridge Methodist Church; J Fisher, page 115; CWD, page 539, and the **7 DWR Drill Hall WM panel 6, column 2.**
Mentioned in the Hebden Bridge Times 17 8 1917 & 09 8 1918
"UNTIL THE DAY BREAKS"

HENNIGAN, Anthony – 306214 Private.
Resided in Shipley. Enlisted at Skipton.
2/7th Battalion DWR; died of wounds 25 6 1917.
Buried – Achiet-Le-Grand Communal Cemetery, France, 1, M, 17.
Commemorated – the **7 DWR Drill Hall WM panel 1, column 3.**

HENSON, Sidney – 4702 Private.
Resided in Nottingham. Enlisted at Newark.
1/7th Battalion DWR; killed in action 03 9 1916 (Battle of the Somme, Thiepval).
Commemorated – Thiepval Memorial, France, and the **7 DWR Drill Hall WM panel 5, column 2.**

HETT, Harold – 2836 (later 305961) Private, Distinguished Conduct Medal.
Resided in Oldham, the son of Mr and Mrs Wright Hett, of 125 Wellyhole Street, Salem, Oldham. Enlisted at Milnsbridge.
1/7th Battalion DWR, D Company; killed in action 29 4 1918, aged 22 (German Spring Offensive).
Commemorated – Tyne Cot Memorial, Belgium, and the **7 DWR Drill Hall WM panel 6, column 1.**
Mentioned in the London Gazette (DCM award) 03 10 1918, page 11672. L Magnus (MM (sic) award) page 256.

HEY, Charlie – 306809 Private.
Resided in Ripponden, Halifax, the son of Fred Hey, of Mount Pleasant, Ripponden. Enlisted at Halifax.
2/7th Battalion DWR; killed in action 27 11 1917, aged 24 (Battle of Cambrai).
Commemorated – Cambrai Memorial, Louverval, France; Barkisland Village WM; St Bartholomew's Church, Ripponden; Ripponden Remembers, page 5; CWD, page 540, and the **7 DWR Drill Hall WM panel 3, column 2.**
Mentioned in the Halifax Courier 02 1 1918, with photograph.

HEY, Herbert – 1912 Private.
Born on 02 11 1887 at Thomas Street, Lindley, the son of Joseph and Alice Ann Hey of 51 Thomas Street, Lindley, Huddersfield. Enlisted at Milnsbridge on 04 9 1914.
1/7th Battalion DWR; died of wounds, at 15th CCS, on 20 8 1915, aged 27 (Ypres Sector).
Buried – Hazebrouck Communal Cemetery, France, 1, G, 13
Commemorated – St Stephen's Church, Lindley; Lindley Zion Wesleyan Church; M Stansfield, page 207, and the **7 DWR Drill Hall WM panel 4, column 2.**
Mentioned in the Huddersfield Examiner (died of wounds) 23 8 1915.

HEY, Lawrence – 306910 Lance Corporal.
The son of John Hey, of Keighley. Husband of Lilian Chandler (formerly Hey), of 82 Main Street, Cononley, Keighley. Resided in Carleton, Skipton. Enlisted at Keighley.
2/7th Battalion DWR; killed in action 03 5 1917, aged 28 (Battle of Bullecourt).
Commemorated – Arras Memorial, France; CPGW, website, and the **7 DWR Drill Hall WM panel 3, column 2.**

HICKEN, Mark – 306704 Private.
The son of Thomas and Fanny Hickin, of 86 Himley Road, Lower Gornal, Dudley. Resided in Dudley, Worcestershire. Enlisted at Sedgley.
2/5th Battalion DWR; died of wounds 24 5 1917, aged 25.
Buried – St Sever Cemetery Extension, Rouen, France, P, 1, G, 11B.
Commemorated – the **7 DWR Drill Hall WM panel 1, column 2.**
CWGC & SDGW show name spelt as HICKIN
"WHO DIED FOR RIGHT AND DID HIS SHARE SHALL THE VICTOR'S LAUREL WEAR"

HIGGINBOTTOM, Thomas Hastings – 306978 Private.
Son of Joseph and Mary Higgingbottom, of 8 King James Street, Sheffield. Enlisted at Sheffield
2/7th Battalion DWR; killed in action 02 12 1917. aged 21.
Commemorated – Cambrai Memorial, Louverval, France, and the **7 DWR Drill Hall WM panel 5, column 2.**

HIGHLEY, John Joseph – 6652 Private.
Son of James and Ann Highley, of 3 Victoria Square, Haley Hill, Halifax. Enlisted at Halifax.
1/7th Battalion DWR; killed in action 19 1 1917, aged 34.
Buried – Berles New Military Cemetery, France, 1, C, 1.

Commemorated – Sacred Heart & St Bernard's Church, Halifax; Halifax Civic Book of Remembrance; CWD, page 157, and the **7 DWR Drill Hall WM panel 6, Column 1.**
Mentioned in the Halifax Weekly Guardian 17 2 1917.
WM shows initials as H H.
"REST IN PEACE"

HIGHT, Samuel Edward – 2472 Lance Sergeant.
Born in 1886 in Mossley. Husband of Lily Rose Hight (nee Powell), of 22 Vernon Street, Mossley. Enlisted at Mossley. Embarked for France & Flanders on 15 4 1915.
1/7th Battalion DWR; died of wounds (shellfire, 26 11 1915) at 10 Casualty Clearing Station on 30 11 1915 (Ypres Salient).
Buried – Lijssenthoek Military Cemetery, Belgium, 2, C, 6A.
Commemorated – All Saints Church WM; St George's Church WM; St John the Baptist Church WM; Micklehurst Conservative Club WM; R Vaughan, pages 23 & 43, and the **7 DWR Drill Hall WM panel 4, column 1.**

HILL, Albert – 306977 Private.
Son of John William and Rose Hannah Hill, of 35 Court, 2 House, Solly Street, Sheffield. Enlisted at Sheffield.
2/7th Battalion DWR, D Company; killed in action 28 11 1917, aged 20 (Battle of Cambrai).
Commemorated – Cambrai Memorial, Louverval, France, and the **7 DWR Drill Hall WM panel 3, column 2.**

HILL, Ernest Hatton – Captain.
Born 14 1 1861 in Halifax, the son of John Edwards Hill and Phoebe Anne Hill. Husband of Anis Hill, of 2 Whinney Field, Halifax.
7th Battalion DWR; died 11 4 1918 at the Military Hospital, Yorks, aged 57.
Buried – Halifax (All Saints) Churchyard, Sect. 2.34P/30.
Commemorated – the **7 DWR Drill Hall WM panel 3, column 3.**

HILL, Frank – 3068 (later 6657) Private.
Resided in Holmfirth, brother of Ethel Hill, of 62, Woodhead Road, Holmfirth. Enlisted at Huddersfield in October, 1914. Embarked for France & Flanders on April, 1915.
1/7th Battalion DWR; killed in action (head and chest) at No. 7 CCS on 15 3 1917, aged 24.
Buried – Merville Communal Cemetery Extension, France, 1, B, 21.
Commemorated – Memorial Hospital (Upperthong plaque) WM; M Stansfield, page 209, and the **7 DWR Drill Hall WM panel 6, column 1.**
"HE GAVE HIS RICHEST GIFT, HIS LIFE"

HILL, Francis William – 308054 Lance Corporal.
Born in Wolverhampton, the son of James Henry and Martha Hill, of 43 Bilston Road, Wolverhampton. Enlisted at Wolverhampton.
1/7th Battalion DWR; died of wounds 30 4 1918, aged 21 (German Spring Offensive).
Buried – Boulogne Eastern Cemetery, France, 9, B, 29.
Commemorated – the **7 DWR Drill Hall WM panel 7, column 1.**
"EVER REMEMBERED BY FATHER, MOTHER, AND BROTHERS OF WOLVERHAMPTON"

HILL, George – 307059 Private.
Born in Nottingham, the son of Sarah Ann Hill, of 27 Oldham Street, Carlton Road, Nottingham. Enlisted at Nottingham.
1/7th Battalion DWR, D Company; died of wounds 12 10 1918, aged 21 (Advance to Victory).
Buried – Queant Communal Cemetery British Extension, France, D, 52.

Commemorated – the **7 DWR Drill Hall WM panel 6, column 1.**
WM shows Corporal HILLS.

HILL, James – 29248 Private.
Son of Mr W H Hill, of 69 Thursby Road, Harin Street, Leeds Road, Bradford. Enlisted at Bradford.
2/7th Battalion DWR; killed in action 10 4 1918 (German Spring Offensive).
Buried – Bienvillers Military Cemetery, France, 9, B, 8.
Commemorated – the **7 DWR Drill Hall WM panel 2, column 3.**
CWGC & SDGW show rank as Lance Corporal.

HILLS, G – 307059 Private - See **Hill G**.
Commemorated – the **7 DWR Drill Hall WM panel 6, column 1.**
CWGC & SDGW show surname spelt as HILL, and rank as Corporal

HILTON, George – 7141 (later 307994) Private.
Born and resided in Wigtoft, Boston, Lincs, the son of Mr and Mrs J Hilton, of Wigtoft. Enlisted at Spalding.
1/7th Battalion DWR; killed in action 03 5 1917 (Battle of Bullecourt).
Buried – St Vaast Post Military Cemetery, France, 4, G, 4.
Commemorated – the **7 DWR Drill Hall WM panel 6, column 1.**
Formerly 4078 Pte Northumberland Fusiliers.
"NEVER FORGOTTEN"

HINTON, Percy – 2448 Private.
Resided in Oldham, the son of John and Emma Hinton, of Oldham. Enlisted at Uppermill.
1/7th Battalion DWR, C Company; died of wounds 18 11 1916, aged 21 (Battle of the Somme).
Buried –Warlincourt Halte British Cemetery, France, 4, C, 4.
Commemorated – the **7 DWR Drill Hall WM panel 5, column 1.**
"ASLEEP IN JESUS, THY WILL BE DONE O LORD"

HIRST, Albert – 267303 Private, Brighouse Tribute Medal.
Born in Rastrick. Resided at 73 Thornhill Road, Rastrick, Brighouse. Enlisted at Halifax in March, 1916.
2/7th Battalion DWR; killed in action 24 9 1917, aged 22.
Buried – Favreuil British Cemetery, 2, A, 2.
Commemorated – Brighouse WM; Rastrick WM; CWD, page 393, and the **7 DWR Drill Hall WM panel 7, column 1.**
Mentioned in the Brighouse Echo 12 10 1917, with photograph; the Huddersfield Examiner (killed in action) 29 10 1917.

HIRST, Harold – 6655 Private.
Born in Meltham, Huddersfield, the son of Charles Richard and Annie Hirst, of School Hill, Meltham. Resided in Huddersfield. Enlisted at Halifax.
1/7th Battalion DWR; killed in action 19 1 1917, aged 23.
Buried – Berles New Military Cemetery, France, 1, C, 3.
Commemorated – 7 DWR Drill Hall WM panel 6, Column 1.
"ONLY GOOD NIGHT BELOVED, NOT FAREWELL"

HIRST, Henry – 307747 Sergeant, Military Medal & Meritorious Service Medal.
Resided in Holmbridge, Huddersfield, the son of Mary Hannah Hirst, of 158 Woodhead Road, Holmbridge. Pre war local Territorial, F (Holmfirth) Company. Embarked for France & Flanders with

1/5th DWR in April, 1915. Discharged 'time expired' in 1916. Re-enlisted later that year and posted to 1/7th DWR.
1/7th Battalion DWR; killed in action 29 4 1918, aged 28 (German Spring Offensive).
Commemorated –Tyne Cot Memorial, Belgium; Memorial Hospital (Holme and Holmbridge plaque) WM; L Magnus, page 255; M Stansfield, page 217, and the **7 DWR Drill Hall WM panel 6, column 1.**
Mentioned in the London Gazette (MM award) 07 10 1918 & (MSM award) 17 6 1918.

HITCHIN, Herbert – 4373 Private.
Resided in Sandbed Villas, Eastwood, Todmorden. Enlisted at Halifax.
2/7th Battalion DWR; died (of pneumonia) at Lark Hill, Wiltshire 17 4 1916, aged 39.
Buried – Cross Stone (St Paul) Church Cemetery, Todmorden, Yorks, New part 9, 41.
Commemorated – Todmorden Municipal Memorial; Centre Vale Park; CWD, page 672, and the **7 DWR Drill Hall WM panel 4, Column 3.**
Mentioned in the Todmorden Advertiser 21 4 1916 & Hebden Bridge Times 28 4 1916.
WM shows surname HITCHEN.

HITCHMAN, Fred – 1038 (later 305140) Private, Military Medal.
Born in 1892 in Denton, the son of Harry E and Jane E, of 1 Woodend View, Mossley. Resided in Uppermill. Enlisted at Uppermill. Embarked for France & Flanders on 15 4 1915.
1/7th Battalion DWR; killed in action 10 8 1917, aged 26 (Nieuport Sector).
Buried – Coxyde Military Cemetery, Belgium, 2, F, 16.
Commemorated – Mossley Town Hall WM; Abney Congregational Church RoH and window; St John the Baptist Church WM; Calico Printers Association RoH; R Vaughan, pages 59 & 91, and the **7 DWR Drill Hall WM panel 6, column 2.**
Mentioned in the London Gazette (MM award) 16 11 1916, page 1140. HDH Album 7 DWR Volume 2, (MM award) page 17 & (killed in action) page 25.
CWGC & SDGW show rank as Sergeant.
"FREE FROM THE WORLD'S TEMPTATIONS"

HODGSON, Harry – 306456 Sergeant.
Born and Enlisted at Bradford.
2/7th Battalion DWR; killed in action 27 3 1918 (German Spring Offensive).
Buried – Pommier Communal Cemetery, France, 26.
Commemorated – the **7 DWR Drill Hall WM panel 2, column 3.**

HODGSON, Barton Horace – 300066 Private.
Son of John Hodgson, of 19 Priestley Street, Bradford. Enlisted at Bradford.
2/7th Battalion DWR; killed in action 21 11 1917, aged 21.
Commemorated – Cambrai Memorial, Louverval, France, and the **7 DWR Drill Hall WM panel 7, column 1.**
WM shows names as HODGSON H B.

HOGAN, Thomas – 307586 Private.
Enlisted at Keighley.
2/7th Battalion DWR; died of wounds 28 11 1917 (Battle of Cambrai).
Buried – Achiet-Le-Grand Communal Cemetery Extension, France 1, Q, 13.
Commemorated – the **7 DWR Drill Hall WM panel 3, column 2.**

HOLDEN, Harry – 954 Private.
Born in 1894 in Mossley, the son of William and Eliza Holden, of 118 Roaches, Mossley. Resided in Mossley. Enlisted at Micklehurst.
1/7th Battalion DWR; killed in action 29 10 1915, aged 21 (Ypres Sector).

Buried – Talana Farm Cemetery, Belgium, 3, D, 7, (originally buried at Ashwell Cemetery).
Commemorated – St John the Baptist Church WM; R Vaughan, pages 24, 25, & 42, and the **7 DWR Drill Hall WM panel 4, column 2.**
"SON OF WILLIAM AND ELIZA HOLDEN, 118 ROACHES, MOSSLEY, TRUST IN THE LORD"

HOLLINGWORTH, Colin – 2248 Private.
Resided in Diggle, the son of Ingham and Alice Hollingworth, of 19 Hill View, Diggle, Dobcross, Oldham. Enlisted at Milnsbridge.
1/7th Battalion DWR; died of wounds 22 11 1915, aged 22 (Ypres Sector).
Buried – Lijssenthoek Military Cemetery, Belgium, 4, A, 17A.
Commemorated – the **7 DWR Drill Hall WM panel 4, column 3.**
Mentioned in the Unit War Diary (died of wounds) 17 11 1915.
WM shows number as 2240.
"BENEATH THE CROSS OF JESUS I FAIN WOULD TAKE MY STAND"

HOLT, Clarke – 307773 Private.
Son of Mrs Annie Holt, of 8 Cross Hills, Halifax. Resided at Halifax. Enlisted at Halifax.
1/7th Battalion DWR; reported missing, believed died of wounds 14 4 1918, aged 30 (German Spring Offensive).
Commemorated – Tyne Cot Memorial, Belgium; Halifax Civic Book of Remembrance; CWD, page 163, and the **7 DWR Drill Hall WM panel 3, column 2.**
Mentioned in the Halifax Weekly Guardian 27 4 1918 & 18 1 1919; the Halifax Courier 14 4 1919.

HONEYMAN, M - see CUNNINGHAM, Michael.
Commemorated - the **7 DWR Drill Hall WM panel 1, column 3.**

HOOLE, Ernest – 16138 (later 308152) Private.
Enlisted at Chesterfield.
2/7th Battalion DWR; killed in action 04 2 1918.
Buried – Roclincourt Military Cemetery, France 4, A, 1.
Commemorated – the **7 DWR Drill Hall WM panel 3, column 2.**

HOPKINSON, George Ernest – 306577 Private.
Son of Mr T G Hopkinson, of 18 St George's Terrace, Bentley Road, Doncaster. Resided at 8 Studleigh Terrace, Hove Edge, Brighouse. Enlisted at Shipley.
2/7th Battalion DWR; killed in action 26 5 1918 aged 23.
Buried – Bienvillers Military Cemetery, France, 10, C, 13.
Commemorated – Brighouse WM; Hove Edge Conservative and Bowling Club RoH; CWD, page 397, and the **7 DWR Drill Hall WM panel 7, column 2.**
"CHERISHED MEMORIES OF ONE SO DEAR ARE OFT RECALLED BY A SILENT TEAR"

HOPKINSON, James – 2290 Private.
Son of Mrs Buckley, of 39 St Paul's Street. Resided in Huddersfield. Enlisted at Milnsbridge.
1/7th Battalion DWR; died of wounds (shellfire) 20 12 1915, aged 21 (Ypres Sector).
Buried – Lijssenthoek Military Cemetery, Belgium, 2, D, 23A.
Commemorated – M Stansfield, page 229, and the **7 DWR Drill Hall WM panel 4, column 2.**
"DEATH DOES NOT DIVIDE"

HOPWOOD, Walter – 269360 Private.
Born in 1889 in Stalybridge. Resided in Stalybridge. Husband of Annie (nee Derwent). Enlisted at Rugeley Camp, Staffs.
1/7th Battalion DWR; killed in action 11 10 1918 (Advance to Victory, Battle of Iwuy).

Buried – Wellington Cemetery, Rieux-En-Cambresis, France, 1, E, 1.
Commemorated – All Saints Church WM; St James' School, Carrbrook, WM; Micklehurst Liberal Club WM; Mossley Working Men's Club WM; R Vaughan, pages 24, 25 & 140, and the **7 DWR Drill Hall WM panel 1, column 1.**

HORSFALL, Albert – 205558 Private.
Son of Mr and Mrs T Horsfall. Born and resided in Bradford, the husband of Lucy Horsfall, of 304 Moorside Road, Eccleshill, Bradford. Enlisted at Bradford.
1/7th Battalion DWR, C Company; died of wounds 15 10 1918, aged 31 (Advance to Victory).
Buried – Bucquoy Road Cemetery, Ficheux, France, 4, H, 8.
Commemorated – the **7 DWR Drill Hall WM panel 6, column 2.**
WM shows number as 205508.

HORSFALL, Fred – 389 (later 305042) Private.
Son of Mr and Mrs Horsfall, of 78 Albert Street, Lockwood. Enlisted at Milnsbridge in 1909. Pre war local Territorial, mobilised on 05 4 1914.
1/7th Battalion DWR; killed in action 29 4 1918 (German Spring Offensive).
Commemorated – Tyne Cot Memorial, Belgium; Emmanuel Church, Lockwood; M Stansfield, page 230, and the **7 DWR Drill Hall WM panel 6, column 3.**
Mentioned in the Huddersfield Examiner (reported missing) 07 6 1917.

HOWARD, Albert – 1951 Private.
Born in 1883 in Mossley. Resided in Mossley. Husband of Alice Howard, of 7 Rodney Street, Mossley. Enlisted at Mossley. Embarked for France & Flanders on 15 4 1915.
1/7th Battalion DWR; died of wounds 24 11 1915, aged 32 (Ypres Sector).
Buried – Hospital Farm Cemetery, Belgium, D, 12.
Commemorated – St George's Church WM; Micklehurst Conservative Club WM; Yorkshire Ward Conservative Club WM; R Vaughan, pages 24 & 42, and the **7 DWR Drill Hall WM panel 4, column 2.**
"IN REMEMBRANCE"

HOWARD, Herbert Arthur – 268420 Private.
Enlisted at Leeds.
2/7th Battalion DWR; died of wounds 09 5 1917.
Buried – Mont Huon Military Cemetery, Le Treport, France 4, H, 11A.
Commemorated - the **7 DWR Drill Hall WM panel 1, column 3.**

HOWARTH, Harry – 266206 – see **HAWORTH Harry**.
Commemorated – the **7 DWR Drill Hall WM panel 1, column 1.**
CWGC and CPGW show name spelt HAWORTH.

HOYLE, Ernest Albert – 203711 Lance Corporal.
Born on 28 8 1896 at Intake Farm, Stainland, Halifax, the son of John T and Clara Hoyle, of 64 Holly Bank Road, Lindley, Huddersfield. Enlisted at Huddersfield on 16 2 1916.
1/7th Battalion DWR; died of wounds (shrapnel) at the General Hospital, Boulogne, on 18 11 1918, aged 22 (Advance to Victory).
Buried – Terlincthun British Cemetery, Wimille, France, 9, B, 34.
Commemorated – St Stephen's Church, Lindley, Bethel United Methodist Church, Outlane; M Stansfield, page 233, and the **7 DWR Drill Hall WM panel 1, column 2.**
Mentioned in the Huddersfield Examiner (wounded, in hospital) 15 11 1918 & (died of wounds) 21 11 1918.
WM shows rank as Private.

"IN OUR HOME YOU ARE EVER REMEMBERED, IN OUR HEARTS YOU ARE EVER DEAR"

HUGHES, Vincent – 307214 Private.
Born at Bradford. Husband of E H Hepworth (formerly Hughes), of 39 Annie Street, Bradford. Enlisted at Bradford.
1/7th Battalion DWR; died of wounds 15 8 1917, aged 30 (Nieuport Sector).
Buried – Adinkerke Military Cemetery, Belgium, C, 17.
Commemorated - the **7 DWR Drill Hall WM panel 6, column 3.**

HUNTER, Abraham – 306432 Private.
Born in Bentham, Lancs. Husband of Ethel Hunter, of 5 North Avenue, Barnoldswick. Enlisted at Barnoldswick.
1/7th Battalion DWR; died of wounds 29 4 1918, aged 28 (German Spring Offensive).
Buried – Boulogne Eastern Cemetery, France, 9, B, 2.
Commemorated – Barnoldswick WM, CPGW, page 343, with photograph, and the **7 DWR Drill Hall WM panel 7, column 3.**
"EVER REMEMBERED BY HIS DEAR WIFE, ETHEL"

HUNTON, John William – 23795 Private.
Born, resided and enlisted at Newcastle-on-Tyne.
2/7th Battalion DWR; killed in action 30 11 1917 (Battle of Cambrai).
Commemorated – Cambrai Memorial, Louverval, France, and the **Hall WM panel 2, column 3.**
Formerly 29042 Private, Northumberland Fusiliers.
WM shows name as HUNTER.

HUTCHINSON, John – 16056 Private.
Born at Hetton-le-Hole, County Durham, the son of Thomas and Christina Wemyss Hutchinson, of 52 Caroline Street, Hetton-le-Hole. Enlisted at Houghton-le-Spring.
1/7th Battalion DWR; died of wounds 02 5 1918, aged 21 (German Spring Offensive).
Buried – Boulogne Eastern Cemetery, France, 9, B, 15.
Commemorated – the **7 DWR Drill Hall WM panel 7, column 2.**
WM shows HUTCHKINSON.
"ARM HER SOLDIERS WITH THE CROSS, BRAVE TO SUFFER TOIL OR LOSS"

HUTCHINSON, Thomas – 7134 (later 307988) Private.
Born and resided in Appleby, Lincolnshire, the son of Thomas and Maria Hutchinson, of Appleby. Enlisted at Hull.
1/7th Battalion DWR; killed in action 13 4 1918, aged 37 (German Spring Offensive).
Buried - Cabaret-Rouge British Cemetery, Souchez, France, 20, D, 26.
Formerly 4011 Private, Northumberland Fusiliers.
Commemorated – the **7 DWR Drill Hall WM panel 7, column 2.**

HUTCHKINSON, J – see **HUTCHINSON, John.**
CWGC & SDGW show surname as HUTCHINSON.

HUTLEY, Horace Abrey – 2nd Lieutenant.
Son of William King and Edith Hutley.
7th Battalion DWR; died 12 4 1918, aged 23 (German Spring Offensive).
Buried – Le Grand Beaumart British Cemetery, Steenwerck, France, 3, C, 5.
Commemorated – the **7 DWR Drill Hall WM panel 3, column 3.**
Mentioned in the Unit War Diary (joined the Battalion) 29 10 1917, (killed in action) 12 4 1918.
HDH Album 7 DWR Volume 2, (joined the Battalion) page 29, (killed in action) page 33.

Formerly 2403 Private, Essex Yeomanry.
"KILLED IN ACTION E OF BAILLEUL, FIGHTING FOR KING AND COUNTRY"

HUTTON, Ralph Boyd – 307098 Private.
Born at Idle, Bradford. Resided in Bradford. Enlisted at Shipley.
1/7th Battalion DWR; died 11 1 1918.
Buried – Lijssenthoek Military Cemetery, Belgium, 24, C, 18A.
Commemorated – the **7 DWR Drill Hall WM panel 7, column 1.**

INGHAM, Walter – 2393 Private.
The son of James and Ann Ingham, of 29 Glodwick Road, Oldham. Formerly resided Cain Lane, Southowram, Halifax. Resided in Oldham. Enlisted at Uppermill in 1914.
1/7th Battalion DWR; killed in action 18 9 1916, aged 22.
Commemorated – Thiepval Memorial, France; Southowram WM; St Anne's-in-the Grove Church, Southowram; Halifax Civic Book of Remembrance; CWD, pages 170 & 400, and the **7 DWR Drill Hall WM panel 5, column 1.**
Mentioned in Brighouse Echo 17 11 1916.

IREDALE, John William - 1777 Lance Corporal.
Born in Slaithwaite, Huddersfield, the son of Richard and Clara Eliza Iredale, of 26 Grove Street, Hill Top, Slaithwaite. Resided in Slaithwaite, Huddersfield. Re-enlisted at Milnsbridge, had been a previous member of the 7th Battalion for four years. Embarked for France & Flanders in April, 1915.
1/7th Battalion DWR; killed in action 09 5 1915, aged 25 (Ypres Sector).
Buried – Rue-David Military Cemetery, Fleurbaix France, 1, H, 7.
Commemorated – Slaithwaite WM; St James's Church, Slaithwaite; M Stansfield, page 241, and the **7 DWR Drill Hall WM panel 4, column 1.**
Mentioned in the Huddersfield Examiner (killed in action) 17 5 1915.

JACKSON, Fred – 307804 Private.
Born in Jagger Green, Halifax. Resided in Holme Villas, Marsden. Enlisted at Huddersfield.
1/7th Battalion DWR; killed in action 28 3 1918, aged 28 (German Spring Offensive).
Buried – Belgium Battery Corner Cemetery, Belgium, 2, I, 14.
Commemorated – Marsden WM; Jagger Green Baptist Sunday School RoH; Salendine Nook Chapelyard, 23E; CVA; M Stansfield, page 242, and the **7 DWR Drill Hall WM panel 7, column 3.**

JACKSON, George – 4704 Private.
Resided and enlisted at Nottingham.
1/7th Battalion DWR; killed in action 17 9 1916 (Battle of the Somme, Leipzig Salient).
Buried – Lonsdale Cemetery, Authuile, France, 9, F, 10.
Commemorated – the **7 DWR Drill Hall WM panel 5, column 2.**

JACKSON, George W – 305256 Lance Corporal.
Born on 20 8 1897, the son of Mr and Mrs Ann Jackson, at Albion Street, Nottingham, later of 30, Hawthorne Terrace, Crosland Moor. Resided in Huddersfield. Enlisted at Milnsbridge in 1913. Pre war local Territorial, mobilised on 05 4 1914.
2/7th Battalion DWR; killed in action (machine gun fire) 27 11 1917, aged 20 (Battle of Cambrai).
Commemorated – Cambrai Memorial, Louverval, France: St Barnabas Church, Crosland Moor; M Stansfield, page 242, and the **7 DWR Drill Hall WM panel 6, column 2.**

JACKSON, Harry – 2nd Lieutenant.
Son of Annie A Stebbing (formerly Jackson), of 'Normandale', Bradford Road, Wakefield, and the late William Jackson,

1/7th Battalion DWR, D Company; killed in action 09 10 1917 (3rd Battle of Ypres, Passchendaele).
Commemorated – Tyne Cot Memorial, Belgium and the **7 DWR Drill Hall WM panel 3, column 3.**
Mentioned in HDH Album 7 DWR Volume 2, page 27.
No record in SDGW.

JACKSON, Robert – 6/5434 (later 7209) Private.
Born and resided in Menston, Leeds. Enlisted at Keighley.
1/7th Battalion DWR; killed in action 18 9 1916 (Battle of the Somme).
Commemorated – Thiepval Memorial, France, and the **7 DWR Drill Hall WM panel 5, column 1.**
Originally 6th Battalion.

JACKSON, Samuel – 2391 Private.
Resided in Mumps, Oldham, the son of Albert Edward and Mary Jackson, of 1, Dale Street, Mumps. Enlisted at Uppermill.
1/7th Battalion DWR, B Company; killed in action 15 10 1915, aged 21 (Ypres Salient).
Buried – Talana Farm Cemetery, Belgium, 4, C, 11.
Commemorated – the **7 DWR Drill Hall WM panel 4, column 2.**
Mentioned in the Unit War Diary (killed in action) 14 10 1915.
"HE PLACED ON THE ALTAR OF DUTY HIS RICHEST & NOBLEST GIFT, HIS LIFE"

JAGGER, Zina – 307638 Private.
The son of Marshall and Susannah Jagger, of 94, Rochdale Road, Greetland, Halifax. Resided in Greetland. Enlisted at Elland.
1/7th Battalion DWR; died of wounds at No 2 General Hospital, France, on 18 4 1918, aged 25 (German Spring Offensive).
Buried – Ste Marie Cemetery, Le Havre, France, Div. 62, 3, E.
Commemorated – Greetland WM; CWD, page 402, and the **7 DWR Drill Hall WM panel 7, column 3.**
Mentioned in Brighouse Echo 03 5 1918.
"DUTY NOBLY DONE"

JENNINGS, William Henry – 269160 Private.
Born at Hipping Hall, Kirkby Lonsdale, Westmorland, the son of Annie Jennings, of 'Duxbury', Tunstall, Resided in Kirkby Lonsdale. Enlisted at Lancaster.
1/7th Battalion DWR; killed in action 14 4 1918, aged 25 (Geman Spring Offensive).
Buried – Le Grand Beaumart British Cemetery, Steenwerck, France, 3, F, 5.
Commemorated – the **7 DWR Drill Hall WM panel 3, column 1.**
"A LOVING SON, THOUGHTFUL AND KIND, A BEAUTIFUL MEMORY LEFT BEHIND"

JESSOP, Tom – 203041 Private.
Enlisted at Shipley, Yorkshire.
2/7th Battalion DWR; died of wounds 17 3 1918 (German Spring Offensive).
Buried – Roclincourt Military Cemetery, France, 6, A, 19.
Commemorated - the **7 DWR Drill Hall WM panel 2, column 1.**

JOHNSON, Arthur – 7154 Private.
Born in London, the son of Mrs Ann Masters Johnson, of 41 Hedgehope Terrace, Chivington Drift, Morpeth. Enlisted at Alnwick.
1/7th Battalion DWR, B Company; killed in action 17 9 1916, aged 23 (Battle of the Somme, Leipzig Salient).
Commemorated – Thiepval Memorial, France, and the **7 DWR Drill Hall WM panel 5, column 2.**

7th Battalion, The Duke of Wellington's (West Riding Regiment)

World War One War Memorial Tablets

Originally unveiled on 3rd December, 1921 at Milnsbridge Drill Hall,

Headquarters of the Colne Valley Territorials

Centre Panel Finial

1914 - Roll of Honour - 1919

305462 CPL. F. SYKES	305235 CPL. H. FORSHAW	305294 PTE. W. TOWNSEND
305711 PTE. S. O. HAIGH	305953 PTE. S. MANSLEY	306140 PTE. C. SINGLETON
305899 L-CPL. J. GRAY	306064 DRMR. F. CRAVEN	306335 PTE. S. GOLDEN
306108 PTE. J. WALSH	306496 PTE. J. W. BROWN	306338 PTE. W. FAIRBANK
306532 PTE. T. WALSH	306510 PTE. P. ELVIDGE	306592 PTE. S. PLEASANT
306520 PTE. F. MORGAN	306574 L-CPL. H. BRIGGS	306629 L-CPL. J. W. SYKES
306622 PTE. F. SHARP	306635 PTE. E. MORTIMER	306618 PTE. M. RAISBECK
306561 PTE. A. BLAND	306538 PTE. F. CLAYTON	306913 PTE. G. SUTCLIFFE
306633 PTE. M. BURNS	306593 PTE. C. MAUGHAN	306947 PTE. W. O. GODBER
306634 PTE. W. HARDY	306754 PTE. J. R. BYRON	268420 PTE. H. A. HOWARD
306644 PTE. W. FISHER	307045 PTE. J. W. TAYLOR	306214 PTE. A. HENNIGAN
308115 PTE. G. A. BERRY	308098 PTE. J. W. ROGERS	306790 PTE. W. COCKCROFT
308166 PTE. G. MADDER	308122 PTE. F. ABBOTTS	306247 CPL. T. PURSLOVE
306999 PTE. A. BLADES	325028 PTE. A. CLAYDON	305334 PTE. C. PARTRIDGE
205103 PTE. A. DOWNIG	307825 PTE. A. PICKLES	305856 SGT. M. H. CROSSLEY
241358 PTE. J. DOSSEY	305262 PTE. E. ROBINSON	240953 PTE. M. HONEYMAN
242126 SGT. H. E. BIRCH	203232 PTE. A. ALLISON	307697 PTE. H. J. BRENNAN
269360 PTE. W. HOPWOOD	306552 PTE. G. W. BATES	367053 L-SGT. H. ANDERSON
265543 PTE. J. OTLEY	267108 PTE. W. BARBER	203213 PTE. J. BRUMBELL
307874 PTE. M. BODDY	203711 PTE. E. A. HOYLE	306174 PTE. A. FLETCHER
305749 PTE. C. HARRIS	306692 PTE. S. MARTIN	306956 PTE. H. SUTCLIFFE
235329 PTE. J. AINLEY	306704 PTE. M. HICKEN	306649 PTE. P. O. PROCTOR
306647 PTE. E. OATES	306902 PTE. T. LYONS	306767 PTE. S. N. NAYLOR
306795 PTE. A. BROOK	306796 PTE. H. J. SMITH	306652 PTE. G. NAYLOR
307038 PTE. W. HANKIN	308096 PTE. S. TURNER	267305 PTE. C. BEDFORD
306915 PTE. W. SMITH	306345 PTE. J. S. O'HARA	306050 PTE. T. SKELDON
307791 L-CPL. A. STEPHENSON		
203785 PTE. H. SWITHENBANK		
306820 PTE. B. WARRINGTON		
307031 PTE. C. R. ROLLINSON		
266981 PTE. J. GREENHALGH		
305635 PTE. J. A. EARNSHAW		
201593 PTE. T. LANGHORN		
166106 L-CPL. H. HOWARTH		
306744 PTE. W. HAREWOOD		
34648 PTE. A. H. BROADLEY		
305279 PTE. G. H. WHARTON		
23868 PTE. T. N. BOTTOMLEY		

Tablet 1

1914 ROLL OF HONOUR 1919

34825 Pte. F. Rowley	33806 Pte. C.H. Theobald	33732 Pte. J.C. Culley
33166 Pte. F. Fell	33850 Pte. C.E. Battams	11689 Pte. T. Watson
47336 Pte. A. Allan	26674 Pte. A. Griffin	23799 Pte. C. Tidswell
17150 Pte. F. Pope	47344 Pte. C.M. Griffiths	23795 Pte. J.W. Hunter
11861 Pte. F. Wood	22146 Pte. T. Grimshaw	14225 Pte. F. Whiteley
12336 Pte. J.A. Castle	24387 Pte. C.S. Hawkins	24517 Pte. J. Clough
13184 Pte. J. Bailey	17147 Pte. A. Davidson	26430 Pte. G. Sharpe
16799 Pte. A. Taylor	25346 Pte. W. Creughton	26741 Pte. T. Joy
17202 Pte. J. Mohan	16357 Pte. M. Walsh	29009 Pte. W. Pedley
24834 Pte. P. Redman	26358 Pte. F.W. Woodrow	29445 Pte. H.M. Smith
30621 Pte. O. Peel	23518 Pte. W. Stephenson	13207 Pte. D. Smith
16333 Pte. F.B. Lane	24795 Cpl. A. Warrington	13029 Pte. T. Cragg
20635 Pte. S. Steele	25458 Pte. J.R. Ainscough	33430 Pte. F. Summers
16909 Sgt. J. Brown	15384 Cpl. E.A. Spachman	26152 Pte. A.S. Sherwood
26686 Pte. J. Lynch	29499 Sgt. A.D. Wheeler	13603 Pte. W. Thomas
29983 Pte. R.H. Kaye	26649 Pte. C.E. Woodcock	33815 Pte. S. Carey
26693 Pte. C.S. Sims	10917 L-Cpl. M. Coupland	34089 Pte. E. Caseman
24180 Pte. F.W. Hamer	23189 Pte. B. Littlewood	34069 Pte. H. Bell
18955 Pte. J.T. Gray	33870 Pte. C.W. Dennett	34647 Pte. J. Brannan
33834 Pte. A. Evans	34080 Pte. W. Buterworth	34661 Pte. J.H. Dryden
306364 Pte. T.H. Forshaw	306917 Pte. E. Sunderland	307645 Pte. J.C. Mortimer
306344 Pte. J. Gilbert	308129 Pte. F.W.R. Barratt	205158 Pte. A.T. Lindley
307024 Pte. E. Townsend	305878 L-Sgt. R. Buckley	308173 Pte. H.G. Williams
306274 Pte. L. Wrigley	306249 Pte. A. Singleton	306870 Pte. A. Beaumont
306722 Pte. D. Coulton	306034 Pte. F. Whitworth	306895 Pte. H. Tidswell
306500 Pte. A. Kershaw	306602 Pte. F. Thompson	306878 Pte. E. Robinson
306131 Pte. F. Kimpton	306527 Pte. F.B.F. Bartle	306877 Pte. H. Greenwood
306958 Pte. W.E. Breeze	306667 Pte. C. Wilkinson	306624 Pte. J. Greenwood
306933 Pte. H. Langton	305254 L-Sgt. R.G. Metcalf	306813 Pte. J.W. Clayton
306501 Pte. W.M. Walker	306268 Pte. E. McDermott	306777 Pte. A. Wimpenny
268433 Pte. H. Enderby	308026 Cpl. R. Richardson	306924 L-Cpl. C. Harrod
203041 Pte. T. Jessop	307808 Pte. F. Lichtfowler	306456 Sgt. H. Hodgson
17075 Pte. W. Brant	22447 Pte. W. Peakman	29986 Pte. J.E. Taylor
24086 Pte. J.E. Scott	22445 Pte. J.A. Parsons	26416 Pte. E.A. Bumell
15121 Pte. W. Newell	38577 Pte. G. McManus	38574 Pte. E. Linney
18865 Pte. C. Moore	22492 Pte. W.S. Porter	33875 Pte. G. Eastick
25491 Pte. C. Norton	26370 Pte. A. Anderson	33907 Pte. C.E. Nossiter
34091 Pte. S. Chapman	23865 Pte. H. Adams	38587 L-Cpl. T.L. Evers
16524 Pte. F. Walker	24028 Pte. W.H. Roberts	26641 Pte. F. Taylor
20708 Cpl. A. Bowyer	22301 Pte. A. Revill	17004 Pte. J.L. Kelly
26386 Pte. A.F. Harris	34825 Pte. J.F. Mullany	22305 Pte. W.H. Squire
15206 Pte. W.H. Gray	29154 Pte. S.W. Dennison	29248 Pte. J. Hill
	16056 Pte. J. Hutchkinson	
	30342 Pte. W.H. Newsholme	
	29643 Pte. E.C. Priestley	

Tablet 2

1914 - ROLL OF HONOUR - 1919

267237 L-Cpl. W. Sanderson	235098 Pte. D. Sykes	
266452 Pte. H. Liddimore	268629 Pte. F. W. Ball	
306926 Pte. A. Spendlove	305544 Sgt. H. Allan	
260031 Sgt. E. Duewhurst	307612 Pte. H. Stead	**Officers**
306132 L-Cpl. P. Greenwood	306306 Pte. W. Knight	2nd Lt. G. W. Barraclough
306637 Pte. A. Brambini	306305 Pte. J. Gibbons	2nd Lt. C. P. Doggett
307730 Pte. J. Greenway	307773 Pte. C. Holt	2nd Lt. J. L. Berry
201889 Pte. J. Stenton	307720 Pte. D. Masham	2nd Lt. T. P. Bradbury
269160 Pte. W. H. Jennings	305954 Pte. J. Carey	2nd Lt. A. A. Chapman
307737 Pte. W. Whittaker	306298 Pte. A. Morgan	2nd Lt. R. E. Davies
307608 Pte. G. F. Kirby	306836 Pte. L. Turner	2nd Lt. E. C. Harris
266190 Pte. T. Freeman	306619 L-Cpl. L. Wright	2nd Lt. H. A. Hutley
307325 Pte. P. Staniforth	306709 Pte. R. Moore	2nd Lt. B. C. Johnson
241496 Pte. W. H. Turret	267379 Pte. T. Brown	2nd Lt. E. P. Kaye
242218 Pte. H. Stansfield	308880 L-Sgt. S. Cross	2nd Lt. J. Mallilieu
306576 Pte. T. Balmforth	305971 L-Sgt. H. Orr	2nd Lt. J. C. D. Moore
305925 Cpl. L. W. Champkin	308090 Pte. W. Noble	2nd Lt. J. E. Thorpe
305115 Pte. W. Coverley	306851 Pte. W. Lumb	2nd Lt. F. A. Booth
266714 Pte. L. Hardwick	306752 Pte. C. Neale	2nd Lt. H. Price
202216 Pte. A. Roebuck	306566 Pte. F. Berry	2nd Lt. W. Swift
305913 Pte. J. A. Kiddy	306972 Pte. T. C. Plews	Lt. J. H. Beaumont
305383 Pte. J. S. Bill	307592 Pte. S. McHugh	Lt. J. H. Parkinson
306662 Cpl. F. Haley	306572 Pte. F. Brown	Lt. W. D. Parsons
307617 Pte. S. Booth	268432 Pte. J. Smith	Lt. J. Radcliffe
267644 Pte. H. Baxter	268402 Pte. L. Foley	Lt. H. K. Bagshaw
267821 Pte. J. Turner	306910 L-Cpl. L. Hey	Capt. H. Whitwam
306550 Pte. S. Smith	306675 Pte. F. Land	Capt. E. H. Hill
306643 Pte. T. Whitham	306804 Pte. J. Daley	Capt. & Qtr. Mtr.
306051 Pte. H. Wrigley	305919 Pte. J. Daley	W. McFarlane
306821 Pte. J. W. Brown	307588 Pte. J. R. Cook	Capt. J. S. Pearson
306350 Pte. L. Cottrill	242019 Pte. W. Smith	Lt. R. A. Lyon
306750 Pte. H. Barker	306809 Pte. C. Hey	Lt. Col. D. F. Campbell
307591 Pte. W. H. Kaye	306549 Pte. C. Ellis	2nd Lt. K. Dixon
306993 Pte. P. Clarke	307586 Pte. T. Hogan	2nd Lt. H. Jackson
306945 Pte. A. Making	306868 Pte. F. Nixon	
306948 Pte. H. Codber	268429 Pte. R. Lowe	
307039 Pte. J. Oakley	306977 Pte. A. Hill	
306235 Drm. E. Heald	306768 Pte. J. Ross	
307609 Pte. L. Redman	308152 Pte. E. Hoole	R.S.M. R. H. Robb
308103 Pte. J. F. Lucas	308135 Pte. J. Oakes	
33008 Pte. J. Chew	12764 Pte. W. Shaw	
10585 Pte. W. B. Bray	33901 Pte. C. Minn	26239 Pte. F. Elliott
	26406 Pte. J. Thornborrow	
	38559 Pte. E. Cotterill	
	34074 Pte. A. J. Bramhall	

Tablet 3

7th Battalion Duke of Wellington's West Riding Regiment

"Greater love hath no man than this, that a man lay down his life for his friends."

1914 – Roll of Honour – 1919

Officers

- Lt. L. M. Tetlow
- 2nd Lt. R. Rapp
- 2nd Lt. A. L. Gibson
- 2nd Lt. W. Preston
- 2nd Lt. E. Goddard
- 2nd Lt. G. W. Q. Walker
- 2nd Lt. A. Nicholl
- 2nd Lt. A. A. Nuttall
- 2nd Lt. K. C. Fisher-Brown
- 2nd Lt. C. B. Newman
- 2nd Lt. F. Quarmby
- 2nd Lt. J. S. Quarmby
- Lt. S. Ruff

N.C.O's & Men

- 1777 Cpl. J. W. Iredale
- 1853 Cpl. S. Uttley
- 1147 Cpl. J. W. Wagstaff
- 2774 Cpl. J. W. Pogson
- 2026 L-Cpl. G. Shaw
- 1033 L-Cpl. T. Shaw
- 1174 L-Sgt. J. Varley
- 1302 L-Cpl. J. Spencer
- 1387 Cpl. C. H. Nield
- 1908 Sgt. N. Whitwam
- 480 L-Sgt. H. Shaw
- 1044 Sgt. N. Sykes
- 151 Sgt. S. W. Kinder
- 813 Sgt. J. Webb
- 2472 L-Sgt. S. E. Hight
- 852 L-Cpl. W. Robinson
- 1278 L-Cpl. J. Walker
- 628 Sgt. E. D. Hayes
- 3101 L-Cpl. H. Connor
- 1737 Pte. T. Cartwright
- 2434 Pte. F. Eastwood
- 2003 Pte. G. H. Dyson
- 2240 Pte. H. L. Broadbent
- 1913 Pte. F. Clough
- 2506 Pte. H. Schofield
- 2191 Pte. H. Pogson
- 2861 Pte. W. Hanson
- 2410 Pte. E. Garside
- 1748 Pte. W. Brixton
- 1856 Pte. F. Cox
- 1596 Pte. W. Pickup
- 2221 Pte. L. Carter
- 2123 Pte. F. Dent
- 2360 Pte. T. Buckley
- 2170 Pte. W. Fowles
- 1912 Pte. H. Hey
- 1209 Pte. G. Crick
- 986 Pte. T. Oliver
- 2832 Pte. A. Carter
- 2604 Pte. T. Buckley
- 1201 Pte. W. Bennett
- 1309 Pte. A. W. Newby
- 1575 Pte. G. Stewart
- 1343 Pte. P. Bradbury
- 1415 Pte. H. Matthews
- 2567 Pte. H. Marshall
- 2095 Pte. F. Milliard
- 790 Pte. J. T. Taylor
- 1110 Pte. H. Beswick
- 954 Pte. H. Holden
- 2296 Pte. J. Mullarky
- 2391 Pte. S. Jackson
- 1939 Pte. W. Wharf
- 1630 Pte. G. H. Delany
- 1951 Pte. A. Howard
- 1335 Pte. J. O'Brien
- 1789 Pte. J. Blakey
- 2317 Pte. O. Schofield
- 2316 Pte. D. Sykes
- 2290 Pte. J. Hopkinson
- 2286 Pte. J. Wareing
- 936 Pte. G. Burke
- 3024 L-Cpl. J. T. Bower
- 305018 Pte. C. Fell
- 2082 Pte. G. Cartwright
- 1341 Pte. R. Whittaker
- 2165 Pte. E. Butterworth
- 1781 Pte. W. H. Richardson
- 882 Drm. W. Shuttleworth
- 1871 Pte. J. A. Fawcett
- 2464 Pte. A. Smith
- 891 Pte. F. Douglas
- 2810 Pte. W. Haggerty
- 2084 Pte. H. Grundy
- 3476 Pte. J. Burns
- 3499 Pte. F. G. Woodward
- 2240 Pte. C. Hollingworth
- 947 Pte. A. Buckley
- 2595 Pte. G. Barlow
- 5636 Pte. H. Waite
- 3074 Pte. J. Dunn
- 930 Pte. F. Wright
- 5571 Pte. J. M. Neesham
- 1270 Pte. J. Maker
- 4373 Pte. H. Hitchen
- 2466 Pte. F. Wood
- 5467 Pte. J. Longstaff
- 101 Drm. H. Beardsall
- 884 Sgt. J. Philibin
- 2314 Pte. L. E. Booth
- 1257 L-Cpl. F. E. Tomlinson
- 1655 Pte. E. W. Nugent
- 2513 Pte. R. Crowther
- 2007 Pte. J. Walker
- 805 Pte. P. Dorsey
- 1420 Pte. J. Sullivan
- 2746 Pte. E. Sykes
- 1378 Pte. J. Woolman
- 3591 Pte. A. Heald
- 3527 Pte. H. Surtees
- 5581 Pte. E. Mudd
- 2276 Pte. J. Corden
- 2527 Pte. T. Hagan

Tablet 4

1914 - ROLL OF HONOUR - 1919

2162 Pte. O. Brierley
2191 Pte. H. Dyson
2238 Pte. F. Berry
2448 Pte. P. Hinton
2794 Pte. W. L. France
1791 Cpl. J. W. Gibson
3668 Pte. S. Swift
5555 Pte. H. Johnson
5534 Pte. T. Wood
5583 Pte. F. Myers
5600 Pte. A. Robinson
2705 Pte. G. Collier
2897 Pte. S. Walker
3647 Pte. H. Greenwood
3644 Pte. J. E. T. Cornall
5493 Pte. H. Petty
3691 Pte. J. Lee
1650 Pte. H. Snell
2206 Pte. S. G. Gledhill
3806 Pte. S. Scott
3939 Pte. D. Hartley
5539 Pte. R. Walford
394 Pte. W. Brierley
1079 Pte. G. Greenwood
1790 Pte. G. Lord
2393 Pte. W. Ingham
2884 Sgt. C. Kent
3742 Pte. H. Pickles
5006 Pte. G. Gerrard
5434 Pte. S. Goodall
5615 Pte. A. Smith
7223 Pte. E. Weaver
2213 Pte. H. Metcalfe
7151 L-Cpl. T. Hall
5148 Pte. J. Gladwin
4780 Pte. J. Frances
5433 Pte. C. G. Crooke
7074 Pte. A. Rollond
4879 Pte. S. Carter
7209 Pte. R. Jackson
4380 Pte. K. Farrar
1929 Pte. F. B. Gibson

2569 Pte. A. Brooks
3750 Pte. T. Hardwick
5245 Pte. G. Beaumont
5500 Pte. W. Rogers
2953 Pte. J. T. Nield
3835 Pte. H. Richardson
5515 Pte. S. Steer
5537 Pte. W. R. Watson
3971 Pte. H. Sykes
1664 Pte. P. Goddard
5565 Pte. R. Magee
362 Pte. G. Pownall
5624 Pte. F. Stevenson
3683 Pte. H. Wigglesworth
3815 Pte. H. Chappell
3776 Pte. C. Sheard
1858 L-Cpl. H. Harrop
1839 Sgt. W. W. Buckley
2380 Pte. B. Dignam
3836 Pte. H. Rushworth
4702 Pte. S. Henson
5546 Sgt. H. Gorman
1616 Pte. E. Wood
1434 Pte. F. Williams
2179 L-Cpl. E. Littlewood
2507 Pte. E. Morrissey
3356 Pte. F. King
4704 Pte. G. Jackson
5425 Pte. S. T. Fletcher
5480 Pte. T. Mallinder
7154 Pte. A. Johnson
7235 Pte. S. Glew
3185 Pte. L. Eastwood
341 Sgt. J. Webster
5047 Pte. W. H. Cherry
2774 Cpl. J. Wadsworth
4455 Pte. H. Wood
4176 Pte. W. Boffey
5776 Pte. C. Shaw
6057 Pte. A. Lambert
2828 Pte. H. Savage
4289 Pte. F. Margerison

5540 Pte. H. Winkle
5571 Pte. J. M. Meeghan
5835 Pte. S. Haigh
6530 Pte. E. M. Mellor
417 Sgt. G. Warwick
2118 Pte. S. Shaw
2343 Pte. T. Lax
2455 Sgt. J. E. Gill
2331 L-Sgt. J. W. Shaw
3907 Pte. H. Graves
3780 Pte. H. Stoney
1671 Cpl. W. England
1645 Sgt. F. Lockwood
2436 Pte. W. Wright
3700 Pte. P. Smith
5098 Pte. J. Allen
1178 Pte. W. Haigh
1967 Cpl. P. Methurst
3291 Pte. J. Winterbottom
3894 Pte. F. Kershaw
4838 Pte. A. Larrison
5576 Pte. J. Milnes
865 Pte. E. Chapman
1614 L-Cpl. H. Slater
2205 Pte. A. Giggle
2846 Pte. H. Booth
3551 Pte. J. Shorrocks
4957 Pte. F. A. Berry
5430 Pte. A. Froggatt
5522 Pte. F. Seward
7180 L-Cpl. T. Smith
1485 Pte. E. Williams
7059 Pte. J. F. Marshall
4785 Pte. W. Blakey
1166 Pte. F. Bacon
1660 L-Cpl. F. Foggett
3839 Pte. G. Rafter
3949 Pte. A. Knowles
5575 Pte. P. Miller
4802 Pte. J. Lowford
5968 Pte. E. Bottomley
6794 Pte. E. Ellis

306978 Pte. T. H. Higginbottom
306909 Pte. J. H. Bintcliffe
305846 L-Cpl. P. Biltcliffe

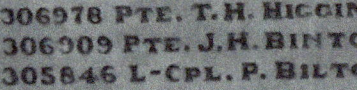

Tablet 5

1914 - ROLL OF HONOUR - 1919

306453 Pte. H. Smith	306416 Pte. J.H. Barrett	307641 Pte. A. Lawley
305484 L-Cpl. G.E. Cater	307074 Pte. W.H. Marshall	307112 Pte. A. Birch
305731 Pte. J. Taylor	305058 Pte. W. Slater	305643 Pte. C. Escott
306415 Pte. P. Clarke	307185 Pte. R. Hellewell	325021 Pte. B.J. Darton
6652 Pte. H.H. Highley	307824 Pte. A. Peace	307749 Pte. W. Ainley
6655 Pte. H. Hirst	307666 Pte. R. Lofthouse	7000 Pte. S. Waring
6657 Pte. F. Hill	307693 Pte. A. Barran	7051 Pte. J. Myers
307924 Pte. J. Agnew	7190 L-Cpl. W.H. Williams	308057 Pte. S. Price
307994 Pte. G. Hilton	7226 Pte. G. Waterhouse	307992 Pte. R. Hall
305764 Pte. J. Dunn	307113 Pte. H. Pickbourne	305673 Sgt. A. Shaw
307347 Pte. E. Youle	306931 Pte. W.H. Western	307844 Pte. J.W. Stott
306451 Pte. J. McGathan	307378 Pte. H. Hemingway	305319 Pte. J. Leslie
307934 Pte. J.W. Brooks	306241 Pte. J. Broadbent	305420 Cpl. G.T. Smith
306461 Pte. N. Sugden	305503 L-Cpl. J. Taylor	204297 Pte. A. Pratt
305494 L-Cpl. E. Gibson	307388 Pte. J.W. Rushworth	307632 Pte. W. Gowers
308068 Pte. A. Woodall	307255 L-Cpl. L. Fletcher	307672 Pte. W. Sharp
3723 Pte. D.M. Wishart	307759 Pte. H. Brook	307938 Pte. H.M. Bean
305892 Pte. T. Barker	307187 Pte. S. Hemsley	307214 Pte. V. Hughes
305637 Pte. J. Palmer	305140 Pte. F. Hitchman	307810 Pte. H. Lumb
305834 Pte. T. Rydhalgh	307751 Pte. H. Beaumont	307089 Pte. N. Shaw
307185 Pte. R. Swann	307277 Pte. W. Hargreaves	307195 Pte. G. Sugden
305197 Sgt. H. Brook	204303 Pte. H. Metcalfe	305801 Pte. T. Barker
308058 Pte. W. Stanton	305780 Pte. T. Schofield	205120 Pte. S. Ashurst
307915 Pte. A. Steggles	269227 Pte. J.E. Midgeley	307567 Pte. A.E. Towler
307712 Pte. A. Clayton	266267 Pte. W.J. Williamson	241939 Pte. L. Barrett
268048 Cpl. E. Clark	305256 L-Cpl. G. Jackson	242927 Pte. R. Tucker
307155 Pte. R. Wrigley	29113 Pte. T.L. Lightfoot	306302 Pte. E. Smith
242276 Pte. H. Cook	307580 Pte. J. Waterworth	305042 Pte. F. Horsfall
241680 Pte. J.W. Whiles	307772 Pte. J.A. Harrison	267363 Cpl. C. Lowe
305161 Cpl. A. Pemberton	268586 Pte. J.J. Woodhouse	204088 Sgt. J. Hannah
265293 Cpl. C.R. Earl	266625 Pte. H. Longfellow	306567 Pte. A. Worsnop
307747 Sgt. H. Hirst	268588 Pte. L. Bottomley	307761 Pte. R. Crabtree
307121 Pte. G. Martin	308047 Cpl. J.T. Thompson	307419 Pte. A. Wright
305961 Pte. H. Hett	307785 Pte. S. Robinson	306147 Pte. A. Sands
307879 Sgt. E. Dean	308028 Pte. D. Rogerson	202312 Pte. R. Caden
204481 Pte. A. Ramsden	207644 Pte. C.R. Mellor	268193 Pte. G. Brown
269176 Pte. W. Shaw	240283 Pte. J. Berry	267078 Pte. C. Wild
307059 Pte. G. Hills	205508 Pte. A. Horsfall	202304 Pte. J. Bagley
240756 Pte. J. Pickles	267803 Pte. N. Boyes	268358 Pte. A. Oddy
307890 Pte. F. Wharam	305192 L-Sgt. H. Morton	268418 Pte. J.P. Moran
235538 Pte. J. Naylor	242841 Pte. J.H. Firth	306015 L-Sgt. F. Baxter
307486 Pte. A. Spicer	205104 Pte. A.L. Appleby	306516 Pte. J. Lewis

306935 Pte. A.W.H. Wakefield
306959 Pte. W.H. Laddington
307613 L-Cpl. E. Parkinson

1914 - ROLL OF HONOUR - 1919

305298 Pte. E. Kiddy	300096 Pte. R.A. Marshall	307365 Pte. G. Mason
269059 Pte. S. Darwent	307816 Pte. H. Macfarlane	307052 Pte. W. Clarke
205110 Pte. W. Bingham	306012 Pte. M. Crampton	307288 Pte. T. Long
307390 Pte. W. Scargill	307856 Pte. Joe Wimpenny	307249 Pte. J. Coll
307803 Pte. E. Judson	305189 Pte. J. Wimpenny	307152 Pte. F. Bostock
307098 Pte. R.B. Hutton	307477 Pte. J.O. Tattersall	305867 Pte. H. Wrigley
306431 Pte. T.H. Riley	306314 L-Cpl. J. Lindley	307540 Pte. T.E. Smith
307831 Pte. E. Redman	307267 Pte. C.A. Hargreaves	268472 L-Cpl. J. Smith
269163 Pte. S.T. Payne	306201 Pte. W. Townley	307804 Pte. F. Jackson
307960 Pte. T.C. Downey	307830 Pte. T. Rawlinson	242493 Pte. H. Gant
325030 Pte. C.D. Gaffney	266474 Pte. F. Dickinson	307099 Pte. W. Gamble
205105 Pte. W. Rusling	269213 Pte. H.W. Graham	307638 Pte. Z. Jagger
307789 Pte. C.A. Shaw	203673 Sgt. R. Fieldsend	242818 Pte. H. Mellor
306492 Pte. C. Dale	241541 Pte. L.T. Schofield	242457 Pte. P. Dagless
203918 Pte. C.E. Waller	242469 Sgt. P.E. Francis	202247 Pte. J. Spencer
328004 Pte. N.H. Lund	307837 Pte. J.A. Schofield	203023 Pte. T. Ramsden
308027 Cpl. R. Ross	307312 Pte. W. Poucher	205414 Pte. E. Walker
325033 Pte. J. Brown	306080 L-Cpl. J. Garlick	306432 Pte. A. Hunter
305472 Cpl. G. Wood	265400 Pte. W. Lonsdale	307333 Pte. W. Taylor
307931 Pte. T. Betts	269184 Pte. H. Boothroyd	308051 Pte. I. Haley
269858 Pte. F. Bland	265737 Pte. T.H. Bailey	307191 Pte. G. Binks
308054 L-Cpl. F.W. Hill	307988 Pte. T. Hutchinson	305461 Pte. G. Hanson
306483 Pte. H. Ripley	307967 Cpl. J. Drysdale	307002 Pte. C. Rukin
306410 Cpl. W. Collins	307753 Pte. O. Bottomley	305612 Cpl. D. Shaw
267649 Pte. A. Gledhill	308190 Pte. T.H. Sutcliffe	306427 Pte. A. Oddy
305068 Sgt. J. Gledhill	308826 Pte. W.K. Whitehead	307593 Pte. F.G. Nimmo
306688 L-Cpl. H. West	306707 Pte. H.M. Collins	306600 Pte. J.H. Biddles
267303 Pte. A. Hirst	305660 Pte. J. Tunnacliffe	306523 Pte. F. Flynn
308116 Pte. A. Simpson	268411 Pte. J.W. Harrison	306351 Pte. F. Lawton
300066 Pte. H.B. Hodgson	306157 Sgt. A.E.S. Field	306856 Cpl. H. Speak
268400 Pte. J. Ellison	306979 A-Sgt. B. Barton	305775 Pte. W. Mills
306787 Pte. W. Lumb	305810 Pte. J.J. Whiteman	306300 Pte. J. Walsh
303002 Pte. D. Naigle	306443 Pte. W.R. Fletcher	307041 Pte. H. Craven
305517 Pte. A. Benson	307241 Pte. C.A. Beaumont	306678 Pte. L. Wood
306753 Pte. S. Swaine	307348 Pte. H. Gorman	306688 Pte. E. Ward
306650 Pte. J. Walker	267404 Pte. W. Ellison	306582 Pte. H. Sykes
242012 Pte. S. Mellor	306640 Pte. A. Akeroyd	307155 Pte. N. Bland
201682 Pte. F. White	307594 Pte. L. Ratcliffe	306361 Pte. T. Allan
308087 Pte. W. Reading	306504 Pte. W. Fletcher	306710 Pte. C.J. Read
268389 Pte. H.J. Whiting	306526 Pte. R. Wilkinson	386912 Pte. S. Carter
306270 Pte. L. Foster	305936 Pte. W. Bottomley	306648 Pte. C.E. Dunn
305599 Pte. C. Perry	241483 Pte. F. Greenwood	308117 Pte. H. Corney
	307196 Pte. T.H. Shackleton	
	306577 Pte. G.E. Hopkinson	
	34080 Pte. W. Butterworth	

GEORGE IREDALE SCULP.

Tablet 7

JOHNSON, Bernard Copestake – 2nd Lieutenant.
Resided in Holmfirth. Enlisted at Holmfirth on 02 10 1914. Commissioned in September, 1915, joined 1/7th Battalion in Jan 1916.
2/7th Battalion DWR, A Company; died 14 5 1917, aged 37.
Buried – Ecoust Military Cemetery, Ecoust-St-Mien, France 2, A, 38.
Commemorated – Memorial Hospital (Holmfirth plaque) WM; M Stansfield, page 247, and the **7 DWR Drill Hall WM panel 3, column 3.**
Previously wounded on 30 6 1916 by a British shell.
Mentioned in the Unit War Diary, 12 1915 & 13 5 1915; the HDH Album 7 DWR Volume 2, pages 9, 11 & 13.
CWGC & M Stansfield show rank as Lieutenant.

JOHNSON, Harry – 5555 Private.
Born and resided in Bingley, the son of Charles Johnson, of 28, Belgrave Road, Bingley. Enlisted at Bingley.
1/7th Battalion DWR; killed in action 03 9 1916, aged 19 (Battle of the Somme, Thiepval).
Buried – Authuile Military Cemetery, France, F, 3.
Commemorated - the **7 DWR Drill Hall WM panel 5, column 1.**

JOY, Tom – 26741 Private.
Born in Silsden, Keighley, the son of Joseph and Sarah Joy, of 26 Chatsworth Street, Keighley. Resided and enlisted at Keighley.
2/7th Battalion DWR; died of wounds 28 11 1917, aged 21 (Battle of Cambrai).
Buried – Achiet-Le-Grand Communal Cemetery Extension, France, 1, Q, 15.
Commemorated – the **7 DWR Drill Hall WM panel 2, column 3.**
"IN THE MIDST OF LIFE WE ARE IN DEATH"

JUDSON, Ernest – 307803 Private.
Resided at 2 Whitehall Cottages, Heptonstall, Hebden Bridge. Enlisted at Halifax in August, 1916. Embarked for France & Flanders in December, 1916.
1/7th Battalion DWR; killed in action 26 11 1917, aged 37 (3rd Battle of Ypres, Passchendaele).
Buried – Dochy Farm New British Cemetery, Belgium, 3, B, 30.
Commemorated – Heptonstall Methodist Church; CWD, page 549, and the **7 DWR Drill Hall WM panel 7, column 1.**
Mentioned in Hebden Bridge Times 07 & 14 12 1917, with photograph, & 28 11 1919, with photograph.

KAY, William Henry – 307591 Private.
Born and enlisted at Bradford.
2/7th Battalion DWR; killed in action 27 11 1917 (Battle of Cambrai).
Commemorated – Cambrai Memorial, Louverval, France, and the **7 DWR Drill Hall WM panel 3, column 1.**

KAYE, Eric Priestley – 2nd Lieutenant.
Son of Joseph James and Ellen Kaye, of 2 Manor House Street, Peterborough.
7th Battalion DWR; killed in action 03 5 1917, aged 22 (Battle of Bullecourt).
Commemorated – Arras Memorial, France, and the **7 DWR Drill Hall WM panel 3, column 3.**
Formerly 4675 Private, Inns of Court Officers' Training Corps.
Mentioned in the Unit War Diary (joined the Battalion) 05 4 1917; the 62nd Division History (killed in action), page 186.

KAYE, Robert Hedley – 29983 Private.
Born in Barnsley, the son of Walter and Priscilla Kaye of Barnsley. Husband of Noel Mary Kaye, of 4 Whetley Terrace, Manningham, Bradford. Enlisted at Bradford.
1/7th Battalion DWR; died of wounds 04 5 1918, aged 27 (German Spring Offensive).
Buried – Boulogne Eastern Cemetery, France, 9, B, 40.
Commemorated – the **7 DWR Drill Hall WM panel 2, column 1.**
"UNTIL WE MEET AGAIN, FROM HIS LOVING WIFE"

KAYE, W H – see **Kay, William Henry**.
Commemorated – the **7 DWR Drill Hall WM panel 3, column 1.**
CWGC & SDGW show name as KAY.

KELLY, Joseph Leo – 17044 Private.
Resided in Paisley, Scotland. Enlisted at Glasgow.
1/7th Battalion DWR; killed in action 29 4 1918 (German Spring Offensive).
Commemorated – Tyne Cot Memorial, Belgium, and the **7 DWR Drill Hall WM panel 2, column 3.**
Formerly 3/404 Private, Army Service Corps.
WM shows number as 17004.

KENT, Charles – 2884 Sergeant.
Born in Brightside, Sheffield. Resided in Oxenhope, the husband of Ethel Kent, of 6 Uppertown, Oxenhope, Keighley. Enlisted at Slaithwaite.
1/7th Battalion DWR; killed in action 17 9 1916, aged 32 (Battle of the Somme, Leipzig Salient).
Commemorated – Thiepval Memorial, Somme, France, Slaithwaite WM; St James's Church, Slaithwaite, RoH; J Fisher, page 114; CVA; M Stansfield, page 265, and the **7 DWR Drill Hall WM panel 5, column 1.**
Mentioned in the Huddersfield Examiner (killed in action) 25 10 1916, (wife and child moved to Oxenhope) 27 10 1916.

KERSHAW, Arthur – 306500 Private.
Son of John and Mary Ann Kershaw, of 8 Montrose Place, Mountain, Queensbury, Bradford. Enlisted at Bradford.
2/7th Battalion DWR; killed in action 03 5 1917, aged 30 (Battle of Bullecourt).
Commemorated – Arras Memorial, France; Queensbury WM; Holy Trinity Church, Queensbury, RoH and the **7 DWR Drill Hall WM panel 2, column 1.**

KERSHAW, Fred – 3894 Private.
Born, resided and enlisted at Bradford.
1/7th Battalion DWR; killed in action 03 9 1916 (Battle of the Somme, Thiepval).
Commemorated – Thiepval Memorial, France, and the **7 DWR Drill Hall WM panel 5, column 3.**

KIDDY, John Allen – 305913 Private.
Born in 1891 in Stalybridge, the son of John and Margaret Ann Kiddy, of 9 Hollingworth Place, Stalybridge. Resided in Stalybridge, the husband of Alice Kiddy, of 65 Forester Street, Stalybridge. Enlisted at Milnsbridge.
2/7th Battalion DWR; killed in action 14 5 1917.
Commemorated – Arras Memorial, France; Stalybridge WM and the **7 DWR Drill Hall WM panel 3, column 1.**

KIDDY, William Edward – 1440 (later 305298) Private.
Born in Stalybridge, the son of John and Margaret Ann Kiddy, of 9 Hollingworth Place, Stalybridge. Resided in Stalybridge. Enlisted at Mossley in May, 1914. Pre war local Territorial, mobilised on 05 4 1914.
1/7th Battalion DWR, originally F Company; killed in action 03 9 1916 (Battle of the Somme, Thiepval).
Commemorated – Thiepval Memorial, France; Stalybridge WM; R Vaughan, page 25, and the **7 DWR Drill Hall WM panel 7, column 1.**

KIMPTON, Frederick – 306137 Private.
Resided in Lees. Enlisted at Greenfield.
2/7th Battalion DWR; killed in action 03 5 1917 (Battle of Bullecourt).
Commemorated – Arras Memorial, France, and **7 DWR Drill Hall WM panel 2, column 1.**
WM shows number as 306131.

KINDER, Stuart Whitehead – 151 Sergeant.
Born in Marsden, Huddersfield, the son of Mr and Mrs Samuel Kinder of The Grove, Marsden. Husband of Elsie Kinder, of Rough Lea, Marsden. Enlisted at Marsden. Local Territorial since 1908. Embarked for France & Flanders in April, 1915.
1/7th Battalion DWR; died of wounds at No. 17 CCS on 28 10 1915, aged 27 (Ypres Salient).
Buried – Lijssenthoek Military Cemetery, Belgium, 1, B, 36A.
Commemorated – Marsden WM; M Stansfield, page 269, and the **7 DWR Drill Hall WM panel 4, column 1.**
Mentioned in the Unit War Diary (killed in action) 23 10 1915; the Huddersfield Examiner (died of wounds, 10 CCS) 01 11 1915, HDH Album 7 DWR Volume 2, page 4, with photograph.
"DEARLY LOVED"

KING, Fred – 3356 Private.
Resided in Oldham. Enlisted at Lees.
1/7th Battalion DWR; killed in action 18 9 1916 (Battle of the Somme).
Buried – Lonsdale Cemetery, Authuile, France, 5, T, 1.
Commemorated – the **7 DWR Drill Hall WM panel 5, column 2.**

KIRBY, George Fletcher – 307608 Private.
Born in Leeds, the son of Ralph and Sarah Eliza Kirby. Husband of Emily Kirby, of 9 Bowker Street, Great Horton, Bradford. Enlisted at Bradford.
2/7th Battalion DWR, B Company; died of wounds 26 5 1918, aged 37 (German Spring Offensive).
Buried – Doullens Communal Cemetery Extension No 2, France, 2, C, 29.
Commemorated – the **7 DWR Drill Hall WM panel 3, column 1.**
Served in the South African Campaign, 6057 Pte, 1st Battalion DWR.

KNIGHT, William – 306306 Private.
Resided in Oldham. Enlisted at Milnsbridge.
2/7th Battalion DWR; killed in action 27 11 1917.
Commemorated – Cambrai Memorial, Louverval and the **7 DWR Drill Hall WM panel 3, column 2.**

KNOWLES, Sam – 3949 Private.
Born and resided in Liversedge, the son of Arthur and Jane Knowles. Enlisted at Heckmondwike.
1/7th Battalion DWR; killed in action 10 10 1916, aged 24 (Battle of the Somme).
Buried – Foncquevillers Military Cemetery, France, 1, J, 11.
Commemorated – Cleckheaton WM and the **7 DWR Drill Hall WM panel 5, column 3.**
WM shows initial A.
"EVER REMEMBERED, ONE BELOVED BY ALL"

LADDINGTON, W H – see SADDINGTON, William Henry – 306959.
Commemorated – the 7 DWR Drill Hall WM panel 6, column 2.
CWGC & SDGW show surname as SADDINGTON.

LAMBERT, Arthur – 6057 Private.
Resided in Skipton, the son of Mr and Mrs A Lambert, of 12 Cowper Street, Skipton.
1/7th Battalion DWR; killed in action 28 11 1916, aged 27 (Battle of the Somme).
Buried – Foncquevillers Military Cemetery, France, 1, H, 21.
Commemorated - CPGW, page 193 and website, and the **7 DWR Drill Hall WM panel 5, column 2.**
"HE BRAVELY ANSWERED DUTY'S CALL, HIS LIFE HE GAVE FOR ONE AND ALL. R.I.P"

LAND, Fred – 306675 Private.
Brother of Miss Eva Land, of 103 Great Horton Road, Bradford. Enlisted at Bradford.
2/7th Battalion DWR; killed in action 03 5 1917, aged 25 (Battle of Bullecourt).
Commemorated – Arras Memorial, France, and the **7 DWR Drill Hall WM panel 3, column 2.**
CWGC shows rank as Lance Corporal.

LANE, Francis Benson – 16333 Private.
Born and resided in Hanley, Stoke-on-Trent, Staffordshire, the son of Francis Patrick and Mary Ann Lane, of 37 Mayer Street, Hanley. Enlisted at Stoke-on-Trent.
1/7th Battalion DWR; killed in action 23 2 1918, aged 19.
Buried – Duhallow ADS Cemetery, Belgium, 9, C, 12.
Commemorated – the 7 DWR Drill Hall WM panel 2, column 1.
Formerly 8447 Private, North Staffordshire Regiment.
"TILL WE MEET AGAIN"

LANGHORN, Thomas – 3861 (later 201593) Corporal.
Resided at 16, Victoria Terrace, Halifax. Enlisted at Halifax.
2/7th Battalion DWR; killed in action 15 4 1918 aged 26.
Buried – Gommecourt British Cemetery No. 2, Hebuterne, France, 5, J, 2.
Commemorated – Halifax Civic Book of Remembrance; CWD, page 180, and the **7 DWR Drill Hall WM panel 1, column 1.**
Mentioned in Halifax Courier (wounded) 24 5 1917.
CWGC shows name spelt LANGHORNE; SDGW shows number as 201933.

LANGTON, Harold – 306933 Private.
Enlisted at Nottingham.
2/7th Battalion DWR; killed in action 03 5 1917 (Battle of Bullecourt).
Commemorated – Arras Memorial, France, and the **7 DWR Drill Hall WM panel 2, column 1.**

LARRISON, A - see LORRISON Arthur.
Commemorated – and the **7 DWR Drill Hall WM panel 5, column 3.**
CWGC & SDGW show name spelt LORRISON.

LAWFORD, Joseph – 4802 Private.
Born at Bradford. Enlisted at Leeds.
1/7th Battalion DWR; died of wounds 27 11 1916 (Battle of the Somme).
Buried – Foncquevillers Military Cemetery, France, 1, H, 20.
Commemorated - the **7 DWR Drill Hall WM panel 5, column 3.**
WM shows spelling as LOWFORD.

LAWLEY, Arthur – 307641 Private.
Born and enlisted at Bradford.
1/7th Battalion DWR; died of wounds 30 4 1918 (German Spring Offensive).
Buried – Esquelbecq Military Cemetery. France, 2, A, 4.
Commemorated – the **7 DWR Drill Hall WM panel 6, column 3.**

LAWTON, Francis – 306351 Private.
Born in Millbrook, Stalybridge. Resided in Mossley, the son of James Lawton. Husband of Mary Lawton, of 1 Block, New Bridge Hotel, Micklehurst Road, Mossley. Enlisted Milnsbridge.
2/7th Battalion DWR, F Company; died of wounds 21 11 1917, aged 39 (Battle of Cambrai).
Buried – Rocquigny-Equancourt Road British Cemetery, Manancourt, 2, F, 11.
Commemorated - St George's Church WM; Micklehurst Conservative Club WM; R Vaughan, pages 25, 104, 156 & 164, and the **7 DWR Drill Hall WM panel 7, column 3.**
"IN LOVING MEMORY OF MY DEAR HUSBAND GONE TO REST, WIFE & FAMILY"

LAX, Thomas – 2343 Private.
Born in 1894 in Ashton under Lyne. Resided in Luzley. Enlisted at Milnsbridge.
1/7th Battalion DWR; died of wounds 10 7 1916 (Battle of the Somme).
Buried – Puchevillers British Cemetery, France, 1, D, 11.
Commemorated – St George's Church WM; Albion United Reform Church, Ashton, WM; Hazlehurst Sunday School RoH; R Vaughan, pages 159 & 163, and the **7 DWR Drill Hall WM panel 5, column 3.**

LEE, John – 3691 Private.
Born in Bradford, the son of Richard Henry and Christina Lee, of 25 Buller Street, Sticker Lane, Bradford. Enlisted at Bradford.
1/7th Battalion DWR; died of wounds 09 9 1916, aged 24 (Battle of the Somme).
Buried – Puchevillers British Cemetery, France, 4, B, 35.
Commemorated – the **7 DWR Drill Hall WM panel 5, column 1.**
"UNTIL THE DAY BREAKS AND THE SHADOWS FLEE AWAY"

LESLIE, James – 305319 Private.
Born in 1895 in Edinburgh, the son of Robert and Agnes Leslie, of 2 Quickwood Cottage, Mossley. Enlisted at Mossley. Embarked for France & Flanders on 15 4 1915.
1/7th Battalion DWR, F Company; killed in action 13 10 1916, aged 21 (Battle of the Somme).
Buried – Gommecourt British Cemetery No 2, Hebuterne, France, 5, F, 28.
Commemorated – All Saints Church WM; St George's Church WM; R Vaughan, pages 24, 25 & 64, and the **7 DWR Drill Hall WM panel 6, column 3.**

LEWIS, John – 306516 Private.
Husband of Florrie Tingle (formerly Lewis), of 411 Little Horton Lane, Bradford. Enlisted at Bradford.
1/7th Battalion DWR, F Company; killed in action 13 4 1917, aged 27 (German Spring Offensive).
Commemorated – Loos Memorial, France; R Vaughan, pages 25, and the **7 DWR Drill Hall WM panel 6, column 3.**

LIDDEMORE, Harry Wolsey – 266452 Private.
Resided in Keighley, the son of Mrs R Liddemore, of 35 Barcroft, Cross Roads, Keighley. Enlisted at Skipton.
2/7th Battalion DWR; killed in action 09 4 1918, aged 19 (German Spring Offesive).
Buried – Bienvillers Military Cemetery, 9, C, 12.
Commemorated – the **7 DWR Drill Hall WM panel 3, column 1.**
WM shows spelling LIDDIMORE.

"THERE IS NO DEATH, WHAT SEEMS SO, IS TRANSITION"

LIDDIMORE, H – see **LIDDEMORE, Harry Wolsey**.
Commemorated – the **7 DWR Drill Hall WM panel 3, column 1**.
CWGC & SDGW show name as LIDDEMORE and middle name of Wooley.

LIGHTFOOT, Thomas Lawson – 29113 Private.
Born in Dalston, Carlisle, the son of Thomas and Elizabeth Lightfoot, of The Lodge, Grimstone Manor, Gilling East, Yorkshire and Healey House, Netherton. Resided in Netherton. Enlisted at Huddersfield in August, 1916.
1/7th Battalion DWR; killed in action 13 4 1918, aged 19 (German Spring Offensive).
Commemorated – Tyne Cot Memorial, Belgium; South Crosland & Netherton WM; M Stansfield, page 277, and the **7 DWR Drill Hall WM panel 6, column 2**.

LIGHTOWLER, Fred – 307808 Private.
Born in Bradford, the son of David and Sarah Jane Lightowler, of Low Moor, Bradford. Husband of Florrie Lightowler, of 25 Worthing Head Road, Wyke, Bradford. Resided in Wyke. Enlisted at Bradford.
1/7th Battalion DWR; died of wounds 17 3 1918, aged 24 (German Spring Offensive).
Buried – Lijssenthoek Military Cemetery, Belgium, 26, E, 2.
Commemorated – the **7 DWR Drill Hall WM panel 2, column 2**.
WM shows Lightfowler.
"HE RESTS IN GOD'S BEAUTIFUL GARDEN IN THE SUNSHINE OF A PERFECT DAY"

LINDLEY, Arnold Thomas – 205158 Private.
Born and resided in Sheffield, the son of Bernard and Gertrude Eliza Lindley, of 7 Derbyshire Lane, Sheffield. Enlisted at Sheffield.
1/7th Battalion DWR; died of wounds 14 12 1917, aged 19 (3rd Battle of Ypres, Passchendaele).
Buried – Dochy Farm New British Cemetery, 8, A, 16.
Commemorated - the **7 DWR Drill Hall WM panel 2, column 3**.
"HE LIVED WELL AND DIED BRAVELY, EVER REMEMBERED BY THOSE WHO LOVED HIM"

LINDLEY, John – 306314 Lance Corporal.
Born in Marsden, the son of Sam and Mary Ann Lindley, of 1 Grange Avenue, Marsden. Enlisted at Milnsbridge in October, 1915. Embarked for France & Flanders in February, 1916.
1/7th Battalion DWR; killed in action 10 10 1917, aged 22 (3rd Battle of Ypres, Passchendaele).
Commemorated – Tyne Cot Memorial, Belgium; Marsden WM; M Stansfield, page 278, and the **7 DWR Drill Hall WM panel 7, column 2**.

LINNEY, Ernest – 38574 Private.
Son of Charles Ernest and Mary Elizabeth Linney, of 4 Bankfoot Terrace, Hebden Bridge, later 3 White Houses, Mytholmroyd. Resided in Hebden Bridge. Enlisted at Halifax.
2/7th Battalion DWR; killed in action 24 5 1918, aged 19 (German Spring Offensive).
Buried – Bienvillers Military Cemetery, France, 20, B, 2.
Commemorated – Slack Baptist Churchyard, Heptonstall; Hebden Bridge Methodist Church; CWD, page 553, and the **7 DWR Drill Hall WM Panel 2, column 3**.
Formerly 30166 Trooper, the Yorkshire Dragoons.
Mentioned in the Todmorden Advertiser 24 5 1919; Hebden Bridge Times 07 & 14 6 1918, with photograph.

LITTLEWOOD, Ben – 23189 Private.
Born and resided in Honley, Huddersfield, the son of Mrs Littlewood, of Moor Bottom. Enlisted at Huddersfield.
1/7th Battalion DWR; killed in action 12 4 1918, aged 30 (German Spring Offensive).
Buried – Cabaret-Rouge British Cemetery, Souchez, France, 20, C, 11.
Commemorated – Honley WM; C Ford, page 24; M Stansfield, page 279, and the **7 DWR Drill Hall WM panel 2, column 2.**

LITTLEWOOD, Ernest – 2179 Lance Corporal.
Resided at 126 Woodhead Road, Hinchliffe Mill, Holmbridge. Enlisted at Milnsbridge in August, 1914.
1/7th Battalion DWR; reported missing (killed in action) 18 9 1916, aged 22 (Battle of the Somme).
Commemorated – Thiepval Memorial, France; (Memorial Hospital (Holme and Holmbridge plaque) WM; M Stansfield, page 280, and the **7 DWR Drill Hall WM panel 5, column 2.**

LOCKWOOD, Fred – 1645 Sergeant.
Born in Meltham, Huddersfield. Resided in Oxenhope. Enlisted at Slaithwaite in June, 1914. Pre war local Territorial, mobilised on 05 4 1914.
1/7th Battalion DWR; died of wounds 23 7 1916 (Battle of the Somme).
Buried – Worloy-Baillon Communal Cemetery Extension, France, 5, C, 22.
Commemorated – Slaithwaite WM; St James's Church, Slaithwaite; CVA; M Stansfield, page 282, and the **7 DWR Drill Hall WM panel 5, column 3.**

LOFTHOUSE, Ralph – 307666 Private.
Resided at 886 Jubilee Terrace, Portsmouth, Todmorden. Enlisted at Todmorden in August, 1916.
1/7th Battalion DWR; killed in action 07 4 1917, aged 26 (German Spring Offensive).
Buried – St Vaast Post Military Cemetery, France, 4, F, 7.
Commemorated – Municipal War Memorial, Centre Vale Park; Cornholme Ward WM, at Vale Baptist Churchyard, Todmorden; Todmorden Garden of Remembrance; CWD, page 683, and the **7 DWR Drill Hall WM panel 6, column 2.** Mentioned in the Halifax Weekly Guardian 21 4 1917 & Todmorden Advertiser 20 & 27 4 1917, with photograph.

LONG, Thomas – 307288 Private.
Son of Joseph and Mary Ann Long, of Bradford. Husband of May Carter (formerly Long), of 6 Rawson Road, Bradford. Enlisted at Bradford.
1/7th Battalion DWR; died of wounds 02 1 1918, aged 27.
Buried – Lijssenthoek Military Cemetery, Belgium, 26, D, 15A.
Commemorated – the **7 DWR Drill Hall WM panel 7, column 3.**
Formerly 27675 Private, Kings Own Yorkshire Light Infantry.
"REST IN PEACE"

LONGFELLOW, Harry – 266625 Private.
Son of Mr and Mrs A Longfellow, of 11 Lombard Street, Rawdon, Leeds. Resided in Little London, Yeadon, Leeds. Enlisted at Skipton.
1/7th Battalion DWR; killed in action 29 4 1918, aged 21 (German Spring Offensive).
Buried – La Clytte Military Cemetery, Belgium, 5, C, 10.
Commemorated – the **7 DWR Drill Hall WM panel 6, column 2.**
SDGW shows number as 266265.
"DEARLY LOVED AND NOT FORGOTTEN, ALWAYS IN OUR MEMORY, FROM FAMILY"

LONGSTAFF, Joseph – 5467 Private.
Born in Dewsbury, the son of William and Sarah Longstaff, of 36 Whitley Street, Dewsbury. Enlisted at Dewsbury.

1/7th Battalion DWR; killed in action 03 7 1916, aged 19 (Battle of Bullecourt).
Commemorated – Thiepval Memorial, France, and the **7 DWR Drill Hall WM panel 4, column 3.**

LONSDALE, William (Willie) – 2138 (later 265400) Private.
Born and enlisted at Keighley.
1/7th Battalion DWR; died of wounds 29 4 1918 (German Spring Offensive).
Buried – Lijssenthoek Military Cemetery, Belgium, 28, E, 11A.
Commemorated – Morley WM; the **7 DWR Drill Hall WM panel 7, column 2.**
Mentioned in the 1/6th DWR Unit War Diary (D Company, suffering from gas poisoning) 05 8 1917; Renumbered in 1/6th Battalion Part 2 Order, dated 20 4 1917, page 1.

LORD, Charlie – 1790 Private.
Born on 13 9 1893 in Longwood, Huddersfield, the son of Edgar and Elizabeth Lord, of Longwood, Huddersfield. Resided in Fartown, Huddersfield. Enlisted at Milnsbridge. Pre-war local Territorial. Embarked for France & Flanders in April, 1915.
1/7th Battalion DWR; killed in action 17 9 1916, aged 23 (Battle of the Somme, Leipzig Salient).
Commemorated – Thiepval Memorial, France; Fartown and Birkby WM; Christ Church, Woodhouse Hill; M Stansfield, page 286, and the **7 DWR Drill Hall WM panel 5, column 1.**
Mentioned in the Huddersfield Examiner (killed in action) 11 10 1916.

LORRISON, Arthur – 4838 Private.
Born and enlisted at Bradford.
1/7th Battalion DWR; killed in action 03 9 1916 (Battle of the Somme, Thiepval).
Commemorated – Thiepval Memorial, France, and the **7 DWR Drill Hall WM panel 5, column 3.**
WM shows name spelt LARRISON.

LOWE, Christopher Donald – 267363 Corporal.
Resided in Kingswinford, Staffs, the son of Richard and Alice Low, of 36 High Street, Kingswinford. Enlisted at Brierley Hill.
1/7th Battalion DWR; killed in action 29 4 1918, aged 21 (German Spring Offensive).
Commemorated – Tyne Cot Memorial, Belgium, and the **7 DWR Drill Hall WM panel 6, column 3.**
SDGW shows middle name Donald.

LOWE, Richard – 268429 Private.
Husband of Malinda Smithson (formerly Lowe), of 8 Bowness Terrace, Holbeck, Leeds. Enlisted at Leeds.
2/7th Battalion DWR; died of wounds 20 1 1918, aged 23.
Buried – St Sever Cemetery Extension, Rouen, France, P, 6, E, 1B.
Commemorated - the **7 DWR Drill Hall WM panel 3, column 2.**
"TIME AND FRIENDS MAY CHANGE, BUT LOVE LIVES ON FOR EVER"

LOWFORD, J - see LAWFORD, Joseph.
Commemorated - the **7 DWR Drill Hall WM panel 5, column 3.**
CWGC & SDGW show name spelt LAWFORD.

LUCAS, John Frederick – 16024 (later 308103) Private.
Enlisted at Wolverhampton.
2/7th Battalion DWR; killed in action 03 5 1917 (Battle of Bullecourt).
Commemorated – Arras Memorial, France, and the **7 DWR Drill Hall WM panel 3, column 1.**

LUMB, H - see LUNN, Herbert.
Commemorated – the **7 DWR Drill Hall WM panel 6, column 3.**

CWGC & SDGW show surname as LUNN.

LUMB, Walter – 306787 Private.
Resided in Little London Farm, Mill Bank, Triangle, Halifax. Enlisted at Halifax in March, 1916.
2/7th Battalion DWR; killed in action (shellfire) 26 11 1917, aged 32 (Battle of Cambrai).
Commemorated – Cambrai Memorial, Louverval, France; St Peter's Church, Sowerby; Mill Bank Wesleyan Methodist Church; St Mary's Church, Cottonstones, Ripponden; CWD, page 555, and the **7 DWR Drill Hall WM panel 7, column 1.**
Mentioned in Hebden Bridge Times 18 1 1918 & Halifax Courier 16 1 1918.

LUMB, Willie – 306851 Private.
Son of Sam and Lucy Lumb. Resided at Chapel House, Moor End Road, Halifax. Enlisted at Halifax in March, 1916.
2/7th Battalion DWR; killed in action 03 5 1917, aged 39 (Battle of Bullecourt).
Commemorated – Arras Memorial, France; Halifax Civic Book of Remembrance; CWD, page 187, and the **7 DWR Drill Hall WM panel 3, column 2.**
Mentioned in Halifax Courier 04 7 1917.

LUND, M Henry – 4310 (later 328004) Private.
Resided in Hellifield. Enlisted at Skipton.
1/7th Battalion DWR; killed in action 25 4 1918 (German Spring Offensive).
Commemorated – Tyne Cot Memorial, Belgium, and the **7 DWR Drill Hall WM panel 7, column 1.**
WM shows initials as N H.

LUNN, Herbert – 307810 Private.
Born in Milnsbridge, Huddersfield, the son of William Henry and Hannah Lunn, of Milnsbridge. Husband of Clara Lunn, of 132 Brierley Road, Manchester Road, Huddersfield. Enlisted at Huddersfield.
1/7th Battalion DWR; killed in action 14 8 1917, aged 29 (Nieuport Sector).
Buried – Coxyde Military Cemetery, Belgium, 2, H, 21.
Commemorated – M Stansfield, Page 288, and the **7 DWR Drill Hall WM panel 6, column 3.**
Mentioned in the Huddersfield Examiner (killed in action) 17 9 1917 & 12 12 1917.
WM shows spelling as LUMB.
"WORTHY OF EVERLASTING LOVE FROM THOSE HE HAS LEFT BEHIND"

LYNCH, James – 26686 Private.
Born at Glenluce, Wigtownshire, Scotland, the son of Robert and Elizabeth Lynch of Glenluce. Resided in Stranraer. Enlisted at Ayr.
1/7th Battalion DWR; died of wounds 11 4 1918, aged 28 (German Spring Offensive).
Buried – La Kreule Military Cemetery, France, 1, A, 35A.
Commemorated – The Scottish National War Memorial (Edinburgh Castle); Glenluce WM, and the **7 DWR Drill Hall WM panel 2, column 1.**
Formerly 27605 Private, King's Own Scottish Borderers, 39895 Private, Royal Scots.
CWGC & SDGW show rank as Sergeant.
"THY WILL, BE DONE"

LYON, Reginald Anthony – Lieutenant.
Son of Thomas and Margaret Lyon. Husband of Emily Ann Lyon, of 73 Naunton Crescent, Cheltenham.
Army Cyclist Corps, attached 6th (Cyclist) Battalion, Norfolk Regiment, attached DWR.
1/7th Battalion DWR; killed in action (raid) 13 8 1917, aged 27 (Nieuport Sector).
Buried – Coxyde Military Cemetery, Belgium, 1, H, 17.

Commemorated – the **7 DWR Drill Hall WM panel 3, column 3.**
Mentioned in the Unit War Diary (raid action) 30 7 1917, (killed in action) 14 8 1917; HDH Album 7 DWR Volume 2, (killed during relief after raid on enemy trench) page 25.
"DULCE ET DECORUM EST PRO PATRIA MORI"

LYONS, Timothy – 306902 Private.
Enlisted at Halifax.
2/7th Battalion DWR; died 03 4 1917.
Buried – Varennes Military Cemetery, France, 1, J, 65.
Commemorated – Sacred Heart & St Bernard's Church, Halifax; Halifax Civic Book of Remembrance; CWD, page 188, and the **7 DWR Drill Hall WM panel 1, column 2.**

MACFARLANE, Harry – 307816 Private.
Born in Bradford, the son of Samuel and Sarah Hannah Macfarlane, of 49 Primrose Terrace, Manningham, Bradford. Enlisted at Bradford.
1/7th Battalion DWR; killed in action 21 11 1917, aged 32 (3rd Battle of Ypres, Passchendaele).
Buried – Dochy Farm New British Cemetery, Belgium, 3, B, 22.
Commemorated - the **7 DWR Drill Hall WM panel 7, column 1.**
"REST IN PEACE"

MADDER, George – 16592 (later 308166) Private.
Born in Kirby Muxloe, Leicester, the son of E Madder. Husband of F Ida L Madder, of Gartree Hill Farm, Dalby, Melton Mowbray. Enlisted at Leicester.
2/7th Battalion DWR; killed in action 17 3 1917, aged 28 (Hindenburg Line).
Buried – Queens Cemetery, Bucquoy, France, 4, A, 1.
Commemorated - the **7 DWR Drill Hall WM panel 1, column 1.**
Formerly 32866 Private, Leicestershire Regiment.
"IN MEMORY EVER DEAR"

MAGEE, Robert – 5565 Private.
Born in Bingley, the son of Richardson and Henriette Magee, of 43 Lane End, Gilstead, Bingley. Resided in Bingley. Enlisted at Keighley.
1/7th Battalion DWR; killed in action 06 7 1916, aged 19 (Battle of the Somme).
Commemorated – Thiepval Memorial, France, and **7 DWR Drill Hall WM panel 5, column 2.**

MAHER, Joseph – 1270 Private.
Born at Moate, County Meath, Ireland. Resided in Oldham. Enlisted at Uppermill.
1/7th Battalion DWR; killed in action 03 7 1916 (Battel of the Somme).
Commemorated – Thiepval Memorial and the **7 DWR Drill Hall WM panel 4, column 3.**
WM shows name as MAKER.

MAKIN, Albert – 306945 Private.
Enlisted at Nottingham.
2/7th Battalion DWR; killed in action 22 11 1917 (Battle of Cambrai).
Commemorated – Cambrai Memorial, Louverval, France, and the **7 DWR Drill Hall WM panel 3, column 1.**
WM shows name as MAKING.

MALLALIEU, Joseph – 2nd Lieutenant.
1/7th Battalion; died of wounds 05 11 1918 (Advance to Victory).
Buried – Calais Southern Cemetery, France, B, 15.

Commemorated – St Georges' Church RoH; Abney Congregational Church RoH and window; Stamford Golf Club WM and RoH; R Vaughan, pages 19, 24, 102, 154, 164, and the **7 DWR Drill Hall WM panel 3, column 3.**
Formerly 6158 Private, London Regiment & Artists Rifles; from 3/7th Battalion DWR 11 1916. Mentioned in the Unit War Diary (joined Battalion) 25 11 1916, (wounded in action) 24 1917; HDH Album 7 DWR Volume 2, pages 19, 20 & 21, with photograph.
WD shows MALLILIEU.

MALLENDER, Thomas – 5480 Private.
Born in Everton the son of Walter and Polly Mallender, of Woodlands View, Scaftworth, Bawtry. Enlisted at Doncaster.
1/7th Battalion DWR; killed in action 17 9 1916, aged 22 (Battle of the Somme, Leipzig Salient).
Commemorated – Thiepval Memorial, France, and the **7 DWR Drill Hall WM panel 5 column 2.**
Formerly 26939 Private, King's Own Yorkshire Light Infantry.
WM shows name as MALLINDER.

MANGAN, Cornelius – 306593 Private.
Resided in Saltaire, Shipley. Enlisted at Shipley.
2/7th Battalion DWR; died 20 3 1917 (Hindenburg Line).
Buried – Aveluy Communal Cemetery Extension, France, M, 9.
Commemorated - the **7 DWR Drill Hall WM panel 1, column 2.**
WM shows surname as MAUGHAN.

MANSLEY, Stephen – 305953 Private.
Resided in Oldham. Enlisted at Milnsbridge.
2/7th Battalion DWR; killed in action 03 5 1917 (Battle of Bullecourt).
Commemorated – Arras Memorial, France, the **7 DWR Drill Hall WM panel 1, column 2.**

MARGERISON, Fred – 4289 Private.
Son of Marshall and Annie Margerison, of Wibsey, Bradford. Husband of Sarah Ellen Margerison, of 2 Marsland Place, Thornbury, Bradford. Enlisted at Bradford.
2/7th Battalion DWR; died of wounds 15 2 1917.
Buried – Varennes Military Cemetery, France, 1, D, 32.
Commemorated – the **7 DWR Drill Hall WM panel 5, column 2.**
"GREATER LOVE HATH NO MAN THAN THIS"

MARSHALL, Harry – 2567 Private.
Born in 1896, in Barnsley. Resided in Stalybridge, the son of George and Ann Marshall, of 20 Carr Cottages, Carrbrook, Stalybridge. Enlisted at Stalybridge. Embarked for France & Flanders on 15 4 1915.
1/7th Battalion DWR; died of wounds (fractured pelvis) 11 12 1915, aged 20 (Ypres Sector).
Buried – Lijssenthoek Military Cemetery, Belgium, 4, C, 25A.
Commemorated – St Joseph's School, Carrbrook, WM; R Vaughan, pages 16, 24, 44, 163, and the **7 DWR Drill Hall WM panel 4, column 2.**
"BENEATH THE SOIL IN SWEET REPOSE IS LAID A MOTHER'S DEAREST PRIDE"

MARSHALL, Joseph Frederick – 7059 (later 307918) Private.
Born at Nottingham, the son of George Henry and Mary Ann Marshall, of Old Basford, Nottingham. Enlisted at Nottingham.
1/7th Battalion DWR; died of wounds 23 9 1916, aged 21 (Battle of the Somme).
Buried – Puchevillers British Cemetery, France, 4, D, 36.
Commemorated – the **7 DWR Drill Hall WM panel 5, column 3.**

Formerly 5773 & 39283 Private, Northumberland Fusiliers.

MARSHALL, Robert Albert – 300096 Private.
Born in Bradford, the son of Mrs S E Houghton, of 'Westlands', Francis Avenue, Colwyn Bay, Denbighshire. Resided and Enlisted at Bradford.
9th Battalion DWR; died of wounds 11 11 1917, aged 28.
Buried – Dozingham Military Cemetery, Belgium, 15, B, 20.
Commemorated – the **7 DWR Drill Hall WM panel 7, column 2.**
"THY WILL, BE DONE"

MARSHALL, William Henry – 307074 Private.
Born and resided in Walkley, Sheffield, the son of William Henry and Mary Marshall, of 10 Parsonage Crescent, Walkley. Enlisted at Walkley.
1/7th Battalion DWR; killed in action 13 4 1918, aged 22 (German Spring Offensive).
Commemorated – Tyne Cot Memorial, Belgium, and the **7 DWR Drill Hall WM panel 6, column 2.**

MARTIN, George – 307121 Private.
Born in Nottingham, the son of George and Elizabeth Martin, of 64 Carlton Road, Nottingham. Enlisted at Nottingham.
1/7th Battalion DWR; killed in action 29 4 1918, aged 21 (German Spring Offensive).
Buried – Perth Cemetery (China Wall), Belgium, 4, D, 3.
Commemorated – the **7 DWR Drill Hall WM panel 6, column 1.**
CWGC shows rank as Lance Corporal.
"HE DIED THAT WE MIGHT LIVE: REST IN PEACE"

MARTIN, Samuel – 306692 Private.
Enlisted at West Bromwich.
2/7th Battalion DWR; killed in action 03 5 1917 (Battle of Bullecourt).
Commemorated – Arras Memorial, France, and the **7 DWR Drill Hall WM panel 1, column 2.**

MASHAM, D - see MESSHAM, David.
Commemorated – the **7 DWR Drill Hall WM panel 3, column 2.**
CWGC & SDGW show surname as MESSHAM.

MASON, George – 307365 Private, Military Medal.
Born and resided in Caton, Lancs. Enlisted at Keighley.
1/7th Battalion DWR; killed in action 14 12 1917.
Commemorated – Tyne Cot Memorial, Belgium, Caton WM, and the **7 DWR Drill Hall WM panel 7, column 3.**
Mentioned in the London Gazette (MM award) 28 1 191, page 1329. L Magnus (MM award) page 256.

MATTHEWS, Harry Pyke – 1415 Private.
Born in Uppermill, the son of Mr and Mrs Matthews, of Calf Hey, Denshaw, Delph. Resided in Delph. Enlisted at Uppermill in May, 1913. Pre war local Territorial, mobilised on 05 8 1914.
1/7th Battalion DWR, D Company; died of wounds 19 8 1915, aged 23 (Ypres Salient).
Buried – Hazebrouck Communal Cemetery, France, 2, G, 12.
Commemorated – the **7 DWR Drill Hall WM panel 4, column 2.**
CWGC show additional middle name of Pyke.
"THE MIDNIGHT STARS SHINE O'ER HIS GRAVE OF ONE WE LOVED AND COULD NOT SAVE"

MAUGHAN, C - see MANGAN, Cornelius.
Commemorated - the **7 DWR Drill Hall WM panel 1, column 2.**

CWGC and SDGW shows name as MANGAN.

McDERMOTT, Edward – 306268 Private.
Resided in Oldham. Enlisted at Mossley.
2/7th Battalion DWR; died 18 3 1918 (German Spring Offensive).
Buried – St Sever Cemetery Extension, Rouen, France), P, 4, B, 6A.
Commemorated - the **7 DWR Drill Hall WM panel 2, column 2.**

McFARLANE, William – Captain (Quartermaster).
Born in Valetta, Malta, the son of William and Ellen McFarlane, of 75, Vyner Street, York,
7th Battalion DWR; died 01 1 1919, aged 44.
Buried – Cairo War Memorial Cemetery, Egypt, Q, 232.
Commemorated – J Fisher, page 56, with photograph, and **7 DWR Drill Hall WM panel 3, column 3.**
Formerly 527 Staff Quartermaster Sergeant, Army Pay Corps.
"HE DIED FOR FREEDOM AND HONOUR"

McGATHAN, John – 306451 Private.
Born in Wolviston, Durham, the son of David and Elizabeth McGathan, of Thorn Tree House, Grimstone, Gilling East, York. Resided in Malton. Enlisted at Huddersfield.
1/7th Battalion DWR; killed in action 18 9 1916, aged 26 (Battle of the Somme).
Buried – Lonsdale Cemetery, Authuile, France, 5, O, 1.
Comemmorated – the **7 DWR Drill Hall WM panel 6, column 1.**
WM shows name as McGATHEN.
"NEARER MY GOD TO THEE, NEARER TO THEE"

McHUGH, Stephen – 307592 Private.
Born in Huddersfield. Enlisted at Keighley.
2/7th Battalion DWR; killed in action 03 5 1917 (Battle of Bullecourt).
Commemorated – Arras Memorial, France, and the **7 DWR Drill Hall WM panel 3, column 2.**

McMANUS, George – 38577 Private.
Born at Leeds, the brother of Percy McManus, of 5 Goxhill Street, Buslingthorpe Lane, Leeds. Enlisted at Leeds.
2/7th Battalion DWR; died of wounds 23 4 1918, aged 20 (German Spring Offensive).
Buried – Doullens Communal Cemetery Extension No 1, France, 6, B, 54.
Commemorated – the **7 DWR Drill Hall WM panel 2, column 2.**
Formerly 30117 Trooper, Dragoons.
"SLEEP ON BROTHER. R.I.P."

MEEGHAN, J M - see MEEHAN James Matthew.
Commemorated – the **7 DWR Drill Hall WM panel 5, column 3.**
CWGC and SDGW shows name as MEEHAN.

MEEHAN, James Matthew – 5571 Private.
Born in Bradford, the son of Mrs F Meehan, of 17 Greenhill Place, Bradford. Enlisted at Bradford.
1/7th Battalion DWR; killed 03 5 1917, aged 19 (Battle of Bullecourt)
Buried – Authuile Military Cemetery, France, F, 2.
Commemorated – the **7 DWR Drill Hall WM panel 5, column 3.**
WM shows name as MEEGHAN.
"IN THE MIDST OF LIFE WE ARE IN DEATH. R.I.P."

MELLOR, Cyril Rhodes – 307644 Lance Corporal.
Born and resided in Honley, Huddersfield, the son of Mr and Mrs Hallas Mellor, of Far End, Honley. Enlisted at Halifax.
1/7th Battalion DWR; killed in action 04 7 1918, aged 37, (Battle of the Somme).
Commemorated – Tyne Cot Memorial, Belgium; Honley WM; C Ford, page 24; M Stansfield page, 298, and the **7 DWR Drill Hall WM panel 6, column 2.**
WM shows 207644 Private.

MELLOR, Edgar Mercer – 6530 Private.
Son of Stephen C and Betsy Mellor, of Bramley, Leeds.
1/4th Battalion KOYLI; died 09 9 1916, aged 20 (Battle of the Somme).
Buried – Varennes Military Cemetery, France, 1, A, 38.
Commemorated – the **7 DWR Drill Hall WM panel 5, column 3.**
"TOO DEARLY LOVED TO BE FORGOTTEN, DEEPLY MOURNED BY ALL WHO LOVED HIM"

MELLOR, Herbert – 242818 Private.
Born at Linthwaite, the son of Henry Mellor, of Slaithwaite, Huddersfield. Husband of Eva Mellor, of 11 Hollins Glen, Slaithwaite. Resided at Linthwaite. Enlisted at Huddersfield.
1/7th Battalion DWR, D Company; killed in action 25 4 1918, aged 35 (German Spring Offensive).
Buried – Poperinghe New Military Cemetery, Belgium, 2, K, 5.
Commemorated – Slaithwaite WM; Linthwaite WM; Milnsbridge WM; St James's Church, Slaithwaite; M Stansfield, page 299, and the **7 DWR Drill Hall WM panel 7, column 3.**

MELLOR, Stanley – 242012 Private.
Son of Willie and A M Mellor of, 22, Hill Top, Salendine Nook, Huddersfield. Enlisted at Huddersfield.
2/7th Battalion DWR; killed in action 15 4 1918, aged 21 (German Spring Offensive).
Buried – Gommecourt British Cemetery No 2, Hebuterne, France, 5, J, 1.
Commemorated – M Stansfield, page 300, and the **7 DWR Drill Hall WM panel 7, column 1.**
Mentioned in the Huddersfield Examiner (wounded in action) 08 6 1917.

MESSHAM, David – 307720 Private.
Born in New Ferry, Cheshire. Resided in Birkenhead. Enlisted at Halifax.
1/7th Battalion DWR; killed in action 13 4 1918 (German Spring Offensive).
Buried – Le Grand Beaumart British Cemetery, Steenwerck, France, 3, D, 16.
Commemorated – the **7 DWR Drill Hall WM panel 3, column 2.**
WM shows name as MASHAM.

METCALF, R G - see METCALFE, Reginald Joseph.
Commemorated – the **7 DWR Drill Hall WM panel 2, column 2.**
CWGC & SDGW show name as METCALFE.

METCALFE, Harry – 204303 Private.
Enlisted at Bradford.
1/7th Battalion DWR; 08 10 1917 (3rd Battle of Ypres, Passchendaele).
Buried – Poelcapelle British Cemetery, Belgium, 29, F, 17.
Commemorated – the **7 DWR Drill Hall WM panel 6, column 2.**
CWGC shows forename as Henry.

METCALFE, Henry – 2213 Private.
Son of A E and F E Metcalfe of 490, Huddersfield Road, Hey Heads, Stalybridge. Resided in Stalybridge. Enlisted at Milnsbridge.

1/7th Battalion DWR, D Company; died of wounds 24 9 1916, aged 26 (Battle of the Somme).
Buried – Contay British Cemetery, Contay, France. 2, D, 18.
Commemorated – Stalybridge WM; Micklehurst Liberal Club WM; Calico Printers Association WM; St James' School WM; R Vaughan, pages 24 & 61, the **7 DWR Drill Hall WM panel 5, column 1.**

METCALFE, Reginald Joseph – 305254 Lance Sergeant; Territorial Force War Medal.
Born at Hemsworth, Yorkshire, the son of Fred and Charlotte A Metcalfe, of 30, Church Street, Morley, Leeds. Resided in Leeds. Enlisted at Slaithwaite.
2/7th Battalion DWR; reported missing 03 5 1917, killed in action 14 5 1917, aged 19.
Commemorated – Arras Memorial, France and the **7 DWR Drill Hall WM panel 2, column 2.**
Mentioned in the Huddersfield Examiner (reported missing) 03 7 1917. TFWM awarded posthumously 20 4 1922.
WM shows name as R G METCALF.

METHURST, P see SMETHURST, Percy.
Commemorated – the **7 DWR Drill Hall WM panel 3, column 1.**
CWGC shows name as SMETHURST.

MIDGELEY, Joseph Edward – 269227 Private.
Born Lees, the son of Sugden and Jane Midgley, of 11 Birch Grove, Ingrow, Keighley. Enlisted at Keighley.
1/7th Battalion DWR; died of wounds 28 10 1917, aged 23.
Buried – Mont Huon Military Cemetery, Le Treport, France 6, B, 13B.
Commemorated - the **7 DWR Drill Hall WM panel 6, column 2.**
CWGC show name spelt MIDGLEY.
"LOVING THOUGHTS SHALL EVER LINGER ROUND THE GRAVE WHERE HE IS LAID"

MILLER, Percy – 5575 Private.
Born and resided in Carleton-in-Craven, Skipton, the son of George and Lehana Miller, of 2, Church Street, Carleton. Enlisted at Keighley.
1/7th Battalion DWR; killed in action 18 9 1916 (Battle of the Somme).
Buried – Lonsdale Cemetery, Authuile, France, 6, T, 6.
Commemorated – CPGW, page 173 & website, with photograph, and the **7 DWR Drill Hall WM panel 5, column 3.**
"EVER REMEMBERED"

MILLIARD, Fred – 2095 Private.
Born in Old Town, Lincs. Resided in Royton. Enlisted at Stallingborough, Lincs.
1/7th Battalion DWR; died of wounds 27 11 1915 (Ypres Sector).
Buried – Bard Cottage Cemetery, Belgium, 1, B, 19.
Commemorated – Saddleworth WM, and the **7 DWR Drill Hall WM panel 4, column 2.**
Mentioned in the Unit War Diary (killed in action) 27 11 1915.

MILLS, William – 305775 Private.
Son of Allen and Amelia Mills, of 1 Church Street, Lees, Oldham. Resided in Lees. Enlisted in Uppermill.
2/7th Battalion DWR; killed in action 21 11 1917, aged 27 (Battle of Cambrai).
Commemorated – Cambrai Memorial, Louverval, France, and the **7 DWR Drill Hall WM panel 7, column 3.**

MILNES, John – 5576 Private.
Born at Gilead Road, Longwood, Huddersfield. Resided at 15 Hill Top, Lindley. Enlisted at Huddersfield on 16 2 1916. Embarked for France & Flanders in August 1916.
1/7th Battalion DWR; killed in action 03 9 1916, aged 21 (Battle of the Somme, Thiepval).
Commemorated – Thiepval Memorial, France; Salendine Nook Baptist Church RoH; Crow Lane Board School, Milnsbridge; M Stansfield, page 304, and the **7 DWR Drill Hall WM panel 5, column 3.**

MINN, Charles c 33901 Private.
Born in Bradford, the son of Harry and Clara Minn, of 2 Spring Hill, Wilsden, Bradford. Resided in Wilsden. Enlisted at Keighley.
1/7th Battalion DWR; died of wounds 27 10 1918, aged 19 (Advance to Victory).
Buried – St Sever Cemetery Extension, Rouen, France S, 3, C, 2.
Commemorated – the **7 DWR Drill Hall WM panel 3, column 2.**

MOHAN, Joseph – 17202 Private.
Born at Ballybay, Ireland. Resided in Belfast. Enlisted at Cavan.
2/7th Battalion DWR; killed in action 27 11 1917 (Battle of Cambrai).
Commemorated – Cambrai Memorial, Louverval, France, and the **7 DWR Drill Hall WM panel 2, column 1.**

MOORE, Carl – 18865 Private.
Born in Middlestow, Yorks, the son of Henry P and Elizabeth Moore, of 8 Lister Avenue, Bradford. Resided and Enlisted at Bradford.
2/7th Battalion DWR; killed in action 17 4 1918, aged 24 (German Spring Offensive).
Buried – Bienvillers Military Cemetery, France, 13, B, 13.
Commemorated – the **7 DWR Drill Hall WM panel 2, column 1.**

MOORE, John Colin Dawson – 2nd Lieutenant.
Son of Emanuel and Emma E, of Keighley.
7th Battalion DWR; died of wounds (air raid) 20 7 1918, aged 22.
Buried – St Imoges Churchyard, France, C, 10.
Commemorated – 5 DWR Drill Hall WM panel 8, column 2; 62nd Division History, page 201, and the **7 DWR Drill Hall WM panel 3, column 3.**
Formerly 2579 LCpl, 5 DWR.
Mentioned in 5th DWR Unit War Diary (died of wounds) 31 7 1918. HDH Album 7 DWR Volume 2, (wounded, air raid, 12 1917) page 27.
"BECAUSE I LIVE, YE SHALL LIVE ALSO"

MOORE, Robert – 306709 Private.
Nephew of Mrs Sarah Withers, of 48 Pleasant Street, West Bromwich, Staffs. Enlisted at West Bromwich.
2/7th Battalion DWR; died at home 25 7 1917.
Buried – Manchester (Philips Park) Cemetery D, C.E, 689.
Commemorated – the **7 DWR Drill Hall WM panel 3, column 2.**

MORAN, John Patrick – 268418 Private.
Son of John and Ellen, of 15 Saxton Lane, Leeds. Enlisted at Leeds.
1/7th Battalion DWR; killed in action 11 10 1918, aged 21 (Advance to Victory, Battle of Iwuy).
Buried – Wellington Cemetery, Rieux-En-Cambresis, 3, C, 7.
Commemorated – the **7 DWR Drill Hall WM panel 6, column 3.**
"GOD TAKES OUR LOVED ONES FROM OUR HOMES, BUT NEVER FROM OUR HEARTS"

MORGAN, Albert – 306298 Private.
Born in 1890 in Mossley, the son of Ephraim. Husband of the late Annie Morgan, of Egmont Street, Mossley. Resided in Mossley. Enlisted at Milnsbridge.
2/7th Battalion DWR; died of wounds 19 5 1917, aged 29.
Buried – Mossley Cemetery, C.E. 1259.
Commemorated – St George's Church WM; Micklehurst Conservative Club WM; R Vaughan, page 80, and the **7 DWR Drill Hall WM panel 3, column 2.**
Mentioned in the Mossley and Saddleworth (wounded in bayonet charge) 19 5 1917.

MORGAN, Fred – 306520 Private.
Son of Daniel and Mary Morgan, of 163, Exeter Street, Bradford. Enlisted at Bradford.
2/7th Battalion DWR; killed in action 03 5 1917, aged 24 (Battle of Bullecourt).
Commemorated – Arras Memorial, France, and the **7 DWR Drill Hall WM panel 1, column 1.**

MORRISEY, Edward – 2507 Corporal.
Resided at Watersheddings, Lancs. Enlisted at Milnsbridge.
1/7th Battalion DWR; killed in action 18 9 1916 (Battle of the Somme).
Commemorated – Thiepval Memorial, France, and the **7 DWR Drill Hall WM panel 5, column 2.**
WM shows name as MORRISSEY.

MORTIMER, Ernest – 306635 Private.
Son of Albert and Harriet M Mortimer, of 13 Hopwood Street, Valley Road, Manningham, Bradford. Enlisted at Bradford.
2/7th Battalion DWR; killed in action 14 5 1917, aged 23.
Commemorated – Arras Memorial, France, and the **7 DWR Drill Hall WM panel 1, column 2.**

MORTIMER, John Cyril – 307645 Private.
Born at Holywell Green, Halifax., the son of Eli and Annie Mortimer, of 11 Spring View Gardens, Luddendenfoot. Enlisted at Halifax.
2/7th Battalion DWR, C Company; killed in action 30 12 1917, aged 19.
Buried – Belgian Battery Corner Cemetery, Belgium, 2, E, 3.
Commemorated – Luddendenfoot WM; Providence Congregational Church, Stainland; Luddendenfoot Congregational Church; CWD, page 559, and the **7 DWR Drill Hall WM panel 2, column 3.**
Mentioned in the Hebden Bridge Times 18 & 25 1 1918, with photograph.
"GONE BUT NOT FORGOTTEN"

MORTON, Herbert – 1196 (later 305192) Lance Sergeant.
Born on 05 1 1895 in Brighouse, the son of Samuel and Edith Morton, of 107 Market Street, Milnsbridge. Resided in Milnsbridge and at 4 Wood Top, Marsden, Huddersfield. Enlisted at Marsden, as local Territorial, on 06 2 1912, mobilised in August, 1914. Wounded twice and gassed twice.
1/7th Battalion DWR; killed in action 11 10 1918, aged 23 (Advance to Victory, Battle of Iwuy).
Buried – Wellington Cemetery, Rieux-En-Cambresis, 3, B, 6.
Commemorated – Marsden WM; M Stansfield, page 311, and the **7 DWR Drill Hall WM panel 6, column 2.**
"UPRIGHT AND JUST IN ALL HIS WAYS"

MUDD, Edgar – 5581 Private.
Born in Otley, the son of George and Dorothy Mudd, of 47 Boroughgate, Otley. Resided and enlisted at Otley.
1/7th Battalion DWR; killed in action 03 7 1916, aged 21 (Battle of the Somme).
Commemorated – Thiepval Memorial, France, and the **7 DWR Drill Hall WM panel 4, column 3.**

MULLAHY, John Francis – 34825 Private.
Born in Leicester, the son of Mr J F Mullahy, of 30 Navigation Street, Leicester. Enlisted at Leicester.
1/7th Battalion DWR; killed in action 11 10 1918 (Advance to Victory, Battle of Iwuy).
Buried – Naves Communal Cemetery Extension, France, 5, A, 22.
Commemorated - the **7 DWR Drill Hall WM panel 2, column 2.**
Formerly 27814 Trooper, Dragoons.

MULLARKY, James – 2296 Private.
Born on 16 11 1895 at 18 Castlegate, Huddersfield, the son of John and Mary Mullarky. Resided at 17 Pine Street, Huddersfield. Enlisted at Milnsbridge on 04 9 1914. Embarked for France & Flanders in April, 1915.
1/7th Battalion DWR, D Company; killed in action 21 11 1915, aged 20 (Ypres Salient).
Buried – Bard Cottage Cemetery, Belgium, 1, H, 16.
Commemorated – M Stansfield, page 313, and the **7 DWR Drill Hall WM panel 4, column 2.**
Mentioned in the Huddersfield Examiner (killed in action) 25 11 1915, (in memoriam) 20 11 1916.

MYERS, Frank – 5584 Private.
Born and resided in Bradford. Enlisted at Shipley.
1/7th Battalion DWR; killed in action 03 9 1916 (Battle of the Somme, Thiepval).
Commemorated – Thiepval Memorial, France, and the **7 DWR Drill Hall WM panel 5, column 1.**
WM shows number as 5583.

MYERS, John (William) – 7051 Private.
Born in York, the son of John and Jane Myers, of 120 Walmgate, York. Enlisted at York.
1/7th Battalion DWR; killed in action 16 11 1916, aged 24 (Battle of the Somme).
Buried – Foncquevillers Military Cemetery, France, 1, H, 6.
Commemorated – the **7 DWR Drill Hall WM panel 6, column 3.**
"REQUIESCAT IN PACE"

NAIGLE, Denis – 2458 (later 303002) Private.
Resided in Stalybridge, the son of Mrs Nora Naigle, of 6 Vaudrey Street, Stalybridge. Enlisted at Milnsbridge.
2/7th Battalion DWR; killed in action 30 8 1917, France, aged 21.
Buried – Favreuil British Cemetery, France, 1, D, 24.
Commemorated – Stalybridge WM and the **7 DWR Drill Hall WM panel 7, column 1.**
"SWEET JESUS HAVE MERCY ON HIS SOUL, R.I.P. FROM HIS LOVING MOTHER"

NAYLOR, Gilbert – 306652 Private.
Resided in Heckmondwike. Enlisted at Dewsbury.
2/7th Battalion DWR; killed in action 03 5 1917 (Battle of Bullecourt).
Commemorated – Arras Memorial, France, and the **7 DWR Drill Hall WM panel 1, column 3.**
Mentioned in the Goodall Collection (casualty return).

NAYLOR, John – 235538 Private.
Born and resided in Kirkstall, Leeds, the son of George William and Elizabeth Ann Naylor, of 4 Wyther Mount, Kirkstall, Leeds. Enlisted at Leeds.
1/7th Battalion DWR; killed in action 11 10 1916, aged 18 (Battle of the Somme).
Buried – St Aubert British Cemetery, France, 5, E, 30.
Commemorated – the **7 DWR Drill Hall WM panel 6, column 1.**
CWGC shows rank as Lance Corporal.
"GREATLY MISSED"

NAYLOR, Squire Norman – 306767 Private.
Brother-in-law of Mrs A G Naylor, of 1 The Wharrels, Lowtown, Pudsey, Leeds. Enlisted at Bradford.
2/7th Battalion DWR; killed in action 03 12 1917, aged 25 (Battle of Cambrai).
WM Commemorated – Cambrai Memorial, Louverval, France, and the **Drill Hall panel 1, column 3.**

NEALE, Charles – 306752 Private.
Son of Mrs Betsy Shinkins, of 139 Bolton Road, Bradford. Enlisted at Bradford.
2/7th Battalion DWR; killed in action 03 5 1917, aged 31 (Battle of Bullecourt).
Commemorated – Arras Memorial and the **7 DWR Drill Hall WM panel 3, column 2.**

NEESHAM, J M - see MEEHAN, James Matthew.
Commemorated – the **7 DWR Drill Hall WM panel 4, column 3.**
CWGC shows name as MEEHAM.

NEWBY, Arthur William – 1309 Private (Drummer).
Born in Saddleworth, the son of William and Eliza Newby, of Wool Road, Dobcross, Oldham. Resided in Dobcross. Enlisted at Uppermill.
1/7th Battalion DWR; killed in action 23 8 1915, aged 18 (Ypres Salient).
Buried – Bard Cottage Cemetery, Belgium 1, F, 28.
Commemorated – Saddleworth WM, and the **7 DWR Drill Hall WM panel 4, column 2.**
"GREATER LOVE HATH NO MAN R.I.P."

NEWELL, William – 25121 Private.
Born at Cape Town, South Africa, the son of John and Florence Newell, of Bradford. Resided in Heaton, Bradford. Enlisted at Bradford.
2/7th Battalion DWR; died of wounds 11 4 1918, aged 20 (German Spring Offensive).
Buried – Etaples Military Cemetery, France, 33, G, 13.
Commemorated – CPGW, website, and the **7 DWR Drill Hall WM panel 2, column 1.**
"MAY HIS REWARD BE AS GREAT AS HIS SACRIFICE"

NEWMAN, Cyril Brown – 2nd Lieutenant.
Born at Marsden, the son of John E and A E Newman, of 'West Leigh', Marsden, Huddersfield.
Commissioned from Leeds University OTC 23 7 1915. Embarked for France & Flanders, 14 6 1916.
7th Battalion DWR, C Company; killed in action 03 9 1916. aged 20 (Battle of the Somme, Thiepval).
Buried – Lonsdale Cemetery, Authuile, France, 8, E, 3.
Commemorated – Marsden WM; Leeds University RoH; Marsden Conservative Club RoH; CVA; J Fisher, page 107; M Stansfield, page 318, and the **7 DWR Drill Hall WM panel 4, column 1.**
Mentioned in the Unit War Diary (joined Battalion) 26 6 1916, (killed in action) 04 9 1916; the Huddersfield Examiner (killed in action) 07 9 1916 & 14 9 1916; the HDH Album 7 DWR Volume 2, (led draft from 3/7th DWR) page 13, (killed in action) page 15.
"IN LOVING MEMORY OF A DEAR SON"

NEWSHOLME, W H – see NEWSOME, William Lindley.
Commemorated – the **7 DWR Drill Hall WM panel 2, column 2.**
CWGC & SDGW show name as NEWSOME H L.

NEWSOME, William Lindley – 30342 Private.
Son of William and Katherine Newsome, of Bradford. Enlisted at Bradford.
1/7th Battalion DWR; died of wounds 30 4 1918, aged 24.
Buried – Boulogne Eastern Cemetery, 9, B, 5.
Commemorated – the **7 DWR Drill Hall WM panel 2, column 2.**
WM shows name as NEWSHOLME W H.

NICHOLL, Arnold – 2nd Lieutenant.
Son of Bright and Frances Nicholl, of Bayswater Terrace, Skircoat Green, Halifax. Enlisted as Trooper in East Riding Yeomanry in October, 1914. Commissioned into DWR July, 1915.
7th Battalion DWR; killed in action (shellfire) 18 7 1916, aged 25 (Battle of the Somme).
Buried – Authuile Military Cemetery, France, I, 12.
Commemorated – All Saint's Church, Salterhebble, Halifax; Heath Congregational Church, Halifax; Halifax Secondary School, Halifax; Halifax Civic Book of Remembrance; J Fisher, page 104; CWD, page 209, and the **7 DWR Drill Hall WM panel 4, column 1.**
Mentioned in the Unit War Diary (joined Battalion from 3/7th DWR) 10 5 1916, (killed in action) 18 7 1916; the Halifax Weekly Guardian, 29 7 1916, with photograph; HDH Album 7 DWR Volume 2, page 15.

NIELD, Charles Hilton – 1387 Corporal.
Born in Leesfield, Lancs, the son of Charles Hilton Nield and Letitia L Nield, of 48 High Street, Lees, Oldham. Enlisted at Lees.
1/7th Battalion DWR; killed in action 22 10 1915, aged 19 (Ypres Salient).
Buried – Talana Farm Cemetery, Belgium, 4, C, 17.
Commemorated – Saddleworth WM, and the **7 DWR Drill Hall WM panel 4, column 1.**
"STILL OURS IN MEMORY, THOUGHT AND LOVE"

NIELD, John Thomas (Tom) – 2953 Private.
Son of John and Hannah Nield, of Boarshurst, Greenfield, Oldham. Resided in Hollingworth. Enlisted at Greenfield.
1/7th Battalion DWR; killed in action 03 7 1916, aged 19 (Battle of the Somme).
Commemorated – Thiepval Memorial, France; Saddleworth WM and the **7 DWR Drill Hall WM panel 5, column 2.**

NIMMO, Frederick George – 307593 Private.
Born in Bradford. Resided with his wife, Ethel Nimmo, at 12 Holmes Street, Westgate, Bradford. Enlisted at Bradford.
2/7th Battalion DWR; killed in action 03 5 1917, aged 22 (Battle of Bullecourt).
Commemorated – Arras Memorial, France, and the **7 DWR Drill Hall WM panel 7, column 3.**

NIXON, Fred – 306868 – Private.
Born in Oakworth, the son of Oscar and Selina Nixon, of Oakworth, Keighley. Enlisted at Keighley.
2/7th Battalion DWR; died of wounds 20 12 1917, aged 21.
Buried – Etaples Military Cemetery, France, 31, D, 7.
Commemorated – the **7 DWR Drill Hall WM panel 3, column 2.**
"REST IN PEACE"
WM shows initial P.

NOBLE, William – 12011 (later 308090) Private.
Enlisted at Leicester.
2/7th Battalion DWR; killed in action 03 5 1917 (Battle of Bullecourt).
Commemorated – Arras Memorial, France, and the **7 DWR Drill Hall WM panel 3, column 2.**
Formerly 12011 Private, South Staffordshire Regiment.

NORTON, Charles – 25491 Private.
Resided and enlisted at Selby, Yorkshire.
1/7th Battalion DWR; died of wounds 10 5 1918 (German Spring Offensive).
Buried – Boulogne Eastern Cemetery, France, 9, B, 67.
Commemorated – the **7 DWR Drill Hall WM panel 2, column 1.**

Formerly 21319 Private, Labour Corps.

NOSSITER, Charles Elvin – 33907 Private.
Born in Leeds. Resided in New Wortley, Leeds. Enlisted at Leeds.
1/7th Battalion DWR; died 02 10 1918.
Buried – Abbeville Communal Cemetery Extension, France, 4, G, 4.
Commemorated – the **7 DWR Drill Hall WM panel 2, column 3.**

NUGENT, Edward William – 1655 Private.
Born in Forfar, Scotland. Resided at 'Three Nuns', Cross Grove Street, Huddersfield. Enlisted at Huddersfield.
1/7th Battalion DWR; killed in action (shellfire) 25 7 1915, aged 36 (Ypres Salient).
Buried – Bard Cottage Cemetery, Belgium 1, E, 16.
Commemorated – M Stansfield, page 322, and the **7 DWR Drill Hall WM panel 4, column 3.**

NUTTALL, Albert Armitage (Bert) – 2nd Lieutenant.
Born in Milnrow, Lancashire, the son of Robert H and Sarah H Nuttall, of Hollins House, Marsden. Manchester University OTC, October, 1914. Commissioned (LG) 23 8 1915. Embarked for France & Flanders in July, 1916.
1/7th Battalion DWR; died of wounds at Field Dressing Station on 15 8 1916, aged 20 (Battle of the Somme).
Buried – Forceville Communal Cemetery and Extension, France, 2, D, 1.
Commemorated – Marsden WM, Marsden Liberal Club RoH, J Fisher, page 107; R Vaughan, page 25; M Stansfield, page 322, and the **7 DWR Drill Hall WM panel 4, column 1.**
Mentioned in the Unit War Diary (joined the Battalion) 31 7 1916, (wounded in action & died of wounds) 14 8 1916; the Huddersfield Examiner (died of wounds) 18 8 1916, (killed in action) 07 9 1916, (commissioned 23 8 1915) 10 9 1915; HDH Album 7 DWR Volume 2 (joined Battalion & died of wounds) page 15.
"FELL AT THIEPVAL AGED 20 YEARS, FAITHFUL UNTO DEATH."

OAKES, John – 10676 (later 308135) Private.
Born in West Bromwich. Enlisted at Smethwick.
2/7th Battalion DWR; killed in action 03 5 1917 (Battle of Bullecourt).
Commemorated – Arras Memorial, France, and the **7 DWR Drill Hall WM panel 3, column 2.**

OAKLEY, John (Isaac) – 307039 Private.
Son of Frederick and Mary Oakley, of 65, Baxandall Street, West Bowling, Bradford. Enlisted at Bradford.
2/7th Battalion DWR, A Company; killed in action 26 1 1918.
Buried – Roclincourt Military Cemetery, France, 3, F, 19.
Commemorated – the **7 DWR Drill Hall WM panel 3, column 1.**

OATES, Ernest – 306647 Private.
Born in Littletown, the son of Henry and Hannah Oates, of Listing Lane, Gomersal. Resided at Gomersal. Enlisted at Liversedge.
2/7th Battalion DWR; died of wounds 18 4 1917, aged 25 (Hindenburg Line).
Buried – Boulogne Eastern Cemetery, France, 4, C, 7.
Commemorated – Cleckheaton WM, and the **7 DWR Drill Hall WM panel 1, column 1.**

O'BRIEN, John – 1335 Private.
Born and resided in Oldham. Enlisted at Greenfield.
1/7th Battalion DWR; died of wounds 25 12 1915 (Ypres Salient).

Buried – Boulogne Eastern Cemetery, France, 8, C, 74.
Commemorated – J Fisher, page 110, and the **7 DWR Drill Hall WM panel 4, column 2**.

ODDY, Albert – 268358 Private.
Born in Bradford, the son of Mr J l and Mrs M A Oddy, of 33 St Andrews Villas, Listerhills, Bradford. Resided in Bradford.
1/7th Battalion DWR, C Company; died of wounds 14 10 1918, aged 27 (Advance to Victory).
Buried – Bucquoy Road Cemetery, Ficheux, France, 3, G, 23.
Commemorated – J Fisher, page 110, and the **7 DWR Drill Hall WM panel 6, column 3**.
"TOO DEARLY LOVED TO BE FORGOTTEN"

ODDY, Amos – 306427 Private.
Born, resided and enlisted at Bradford.
10th Battalion DWR; reported missing (killed in action) 20 9 1917 (Veldhoek).
Buried – Tyne Cot Cemetery, Belgium, 45, E, 6.
Commemorated – the **7 DWR Drill Hall WM panel 7, column 3**.
Body recovered from unmarked grave, identified and reinterred, 1929.
Formerly 7th Battalion, also served in the 10th Battalion, see - **tunstillsmen.blogspot.com** (last accessed August, 2020).

O'HARA, Joseph Sykes – 306345 Private.
Son of Mr and Mrs Roger O'Hara, of 'Delves', Linguards, Slaithwaite. Resided at Slaithwaite.
Enlisted at Milnsbridge on 16 11 1915. Embarked for France & Flanders on 10 1 1917.
2/7th Battalion DWR; killed in action 27 11 1917, aged 23 (Battle of Cambrai).
Commemorated – Cambrai Memorial, Louverval, France; Slaithwaite WM; St James's Church, Slaithwaite; CVA; M Stansfield, page 323, and the **7 DWR Drill Hall WM panel 1, column 2**.
Mentioned in the Huddersfield and District Family History Society Journal Volume 32, No 1, page 30.

OLIVER, Thomas – 986 Private.
Born and resided in Oldham. Enlisted at Lees.
1/7th Battalion DWR; killed in action 09 8 1915 (Ypres Salient).
Buried – Bard Cottage Cemetery, Belgium 1, E, 18.
Commemorated – the **7 DWR Drill Hall WM panel 4, column 2**.

ORR, Herbert – 305971 Lance Sergeant.
Son of Robert and Alice Orr, of 12 Warrington Street, Lees. Resided in Lees, Oldham, Enlisted at Milnsbridge.
2/7th Battalion DWR, killed in action 03 5 1917, aged 23 (Battle of Bullecourt).
Commemorated – Arras Memorial, France, and the **7 DWR Drill Hall WM panel 3, column 2**.

OTLEY, James – 265543 Private.
Resided in Keighley. Enlisted at Skipton.
1/7th Battalion DWR; killed in action 11 10 1918, (Advance to Victory, Battle of Iwuy).
Buried – Wellington Cemetery, Rieux-En-Cambresis, 3, C, 8.
Commemorated - the **7 DWR Drill Hall WM panel 1, column 1**.
CWGC & SDGW show name as OTTLEY.

PALMER, Joseph – 305637 Private.
Born in 1894 in Bury, Lancs. Resided in Mossley. Enlisted at Milnsbridge.
1/7th Battalion DWR; died of wounds 15 8 1917 (Nieuport Sector).
Buried – Adinkerke Military Cemetery, Belgium, C, 21.

Commemorated - Mossley Town Hall WM; Saddleworth WM; St George's Church WM; R Vaughan, pages 24, 92, 157 & 159, and the **7 DWR Drill Hall WM panel 6, column 1.**

PARKINSON, Ernest – 5997 (later 307613) Lance Corporal.
Born at Leeds, the son of Charles and Mary Ann Parkinson. Husband of Lily Parkinson, of 15 Strathmore Avenue, Harehills, Lane, Leeds. Enlisted at Leeds.
2/7th Battalion DWR; killed in action 03 5 1917, aged 25 (Battle of Bullecourt).
Commemorated – Arras Memorial, France, and **7 DWR Drill Hall WM panel 6, column 2.**

PARKINSON, James Herring – Lieutenant.
Son of Walter Henshaw Parkinson and Ada Wellesley Parkinson, of Manscombe House, Manscombe Lake, Bridport, Dorset.
8th Battalion Lincolnshire Regiment; died 02 7 1916, aged 31 (Battle of the Somme).
Commemorated – Tyne Cot Memorial, Belgium and the **7 DWR Drill Hall WM panel 3, column 3.**
Not DWR.

PARSONS, John Arthur – 22445 Private.
Born at Hardwick, Nottinghamshire, the son of Reuben and Mary Parsons, of 11 Maxwell Street, Long Eaton. Resided in Long Eaton, Derbyshire. Enlisted at Ilkeston.
2/7th Battalion DWR; killed in action 27 3 1918, aged 19 (German Spring Offensive).
Buried – Pommier Communal Cemetery, France, 4.
Commemorated – the **7 DWR Drill Hall WM panel 2, column 2.**
"SAFE IN JESU'S ARMS"

PARSONS, Walter Douglas – Lieutenant.
Son of Hannah McIntosh Parsons, of 65 Shirland Gardens, Maida Vale, London.
7th Battalion DWR; died 13 4 1918, aged 24 (German Spring Offensive).
Commemorated – Tyne Cot Memorial, Belgium, and the **7 DWR Drill Hall WM panel 3, column 3.**
Formerly 5508 & 50225 Private, Cheshire Regiment.
Mentioned in the Unit War Diary (wounded in action) 21 11 1917; the HDH Album 7 DWR Volume 2, (joined 7 DWR November 1917) page 29 & (killed in action) page 33.

PARTRIDGE, Charles – 305334 Private.
Born in Attercliffe, Sheffield. Resided in Leek. Enlisted at Matlock.
2/7th Battalion DWR; died of wounds 11 8 1917.
Buried – Grevillers British Cemetery, France, 6, C, 19.
Commemorated – the **7 DWR Drill Hall WM panel 1, column 3.**
Formerly 1638 Private, Nottinghamshire and Derbyshire Regiment.

PAYNE, Sydney Tuft – 269163 Private.
Born in Farsley, Leeds, the son of Andrew John and Emily Payne, of Station House, Upper Broughton, Melton Mowbray. Resided in Melton Mowbray. Enlisted at Normanton, Yorks.
2/7th Battalion DWR; died of wounds 12 3 1918, aged 25 (German Spring Offensive).
Buried – Wimereux Communal Cemetery, France, 8, D, 3A.
Commemorated – the **7 DWR Drill Hall WM panel 7, column 1.**
"IN THE MIDST OF LIFE WE ARE IN DEATH"

PEACE, Arthur (Robert) – 307824 Private.
Son of Harrison Kilner and Elizabeth Peace, of 113 Woodhead Road, Hinchcliffe Mills, Huddersfield. Enlisted at Holmfirth in July, 1916. Embarked for France & Flanders in December, 1916.
1/7th Battalion DWR; died (nephritis) at Field Ambulance on 12 3 1917, aged 31.
Buried – La Gorgue Communal Cemetery, 3, C, 5.

Commemorated – Memorial Hospital (Holme and Holmbridge plaque) WM; M Stansfield, page 330, and the **7 DWR Drill Hall WM panel 6, column 2.**
Mentioned in the Huddersfield Examiner (died, nephritis at Base Hospital) 27 3 1917.

PEAKMAN, Wilfred – 22447 Private.
Born at Oldbury, Worcestershire, the son of Thomas and Pheobe Peakman, of 128 Bromford Lane, West Bromwich. Resided and enlisted at West Bromwich.
2/7th Battalion DWR; killed in action 25 3 1918, aged 19 (German Spring Offensive).
Commemorated – Arras Memorial, France, and the **7 DWR Drill Hall WM panel 2, column 2.**

PEARSON, Joseph Sykes – Captain, Croix de Guerre (France).
Son of Henry Edward and Clara Pearson, of Cliffe Ash, Golcar, Huddersfield. Husband of Elsie Marion Pearson, of 19 Trinity Street, Huddersfield. Former pre-war Colne Valley Territorial Major & Adjutant. Course with Army Service Corps for Mechanical Transport.
1/7th Battalion; died (pneumonia, following influenza) 07 11 1918, aged 26.
Buried – Les Baraques Military Cemetery, Sangatte, France, 6, D, 4.
Commemorated – Memorial in Golcar Church Yard; St John's Church, Golcar; J Fisher, pages 111 & 134, with photograph; M Stansfield, page 333, and the **7 DWR Drill Hall WM panel 3, column 3.**
Mentioned in the Units War Diary (CO 2/7th DWR 22 9 o 14 10 1915) 23 9 1915, (relinquished appointment of Adjutant) 02 12 1916, (attended Transport Officers' Course) 18 12 1916; the Huddersfield Examiner (granted leave for wedding) 14 4 1915, (died, influenza) 11 11 1918; HDH Album 7 DWR Volume 2, page 3.
CWGC show Unit as Army Service Corps.
"THE DEARLY LOVED HUSBAND OF ELSIE MARION PEARSON, 'NEVER FORGOTTEN'"

PEDLEY, Walter – 29009 Private.
Born, resided and enlisted at Shipley.
2/7th Battalion DWR; killed in action 28 11 1917 (Battle of Cambrai).
Commemorated – Cambrai Memorial, Louverval, France, and the **Drill Hall W M panel 2, column 3.**
Also served in the 10th Battalion, see - **tunstillsmen.blogspot.com** (last accessed August, 2020).

PEEL, Oliver – 30621 Private.
Born in Bradford, the son of John James and Esther Ann Peel, of 83 Brompton Road, East Bowling, Bradford. Husband of Evelyn Peel, of 13 Sheridan Street, East Bowling. Enlisted at Bradford.
1/7th Battalion DWR; killed in action 08 10 1917, aged 25 (3rd Battle of Ypres, Passchendaele).
Commemorated – Tyne Cot Memorial, Belgium, and the **7 DWR Drill Hall WM panel 2, column 1.**
Also served in the 10th Battalion, see - **tunstillsmen.blogspot.com** (last accessed August, 2020).

PEMBERTON, Edward – 1108 (later 305161) Corporal.
Born in 1893 in Mossley. Resided in Mossley. Enlisted at Micklehurst, Lancs.
1/7th Battalion DWR; killed in action 29 4 1918 (German Spring Offensive).
Commemorated – Tyne Cot Memorial, Belgium; St George's Church WM; R Vaughan, pages 125 & 159, and the **7 DWR Drill Hall WM panel 6, column 1.**
WM shows initial as A.

PERRY, Charles – 305599 Private.
Son of John and Harriet Perry, of 7 Hibbert's Place, Derker Street, Oldham. Resided in Oldham with his wife, Betty Ellen Dyson (formerly Perry), of 5 Hibbert's Place, Derker Street, Oldham. Enlisted at Uppermill.
2/7th Battalion DWR; killed in action 27 11 1917, aged 33 (Battle of Cambrai).
Commemorated – Cambrai Memorial, Louverval, France, and the **7 DWR Drill Hall WM panel 7, column 1.**

PETTY, Heymond – 5493 Private.
Born in Morley, Leeds, the brother of Mrs Martha Kay, of 3 Thomas Street, Denholme, Bradford. Resided in Bradford. Enlisted at Morley.
1/7th Battalion DWR; died of wounds 03 7 1916 (Battle of the Somme).
Commemorated – Thiepval Memorial, France, and the **7 DWR Drill Hall WM panel 5, column 1.**

PHILIBIN, Joseph – 884 Sergeant.
Born and resided in Oldham. Enlisted at Lees.
1/7th Battalion DWR; killed in action 04 7 1916 (Battle of the Somme).
Buried – Mill Road Cemetery, Thiepval, France, 11. A, 10.
Commemorated – the **7 DWR Drill Hall WM panel 4, column 3.**
CWGC shows name as PHILBIN, SDGW shows name as PHILLIBIN.

PICKBOURNE, Wallace Horace – 307113 Private.
Born in Nottingham, the son of George and Sophia Pickbourne, of 29 Baden Powell Road, Sneinton, Nottingham. Enlisted at Nottingham.
1/7th Battalion DWR; killed in action 24 6 1917, aged 20.
Buried – Sailly-Labourse Communal Cemetery Extension, France, B, 2.
Commemorated – the **7 DWR Drill Hall WM panel 6, column 2.**
WM shows initial as H, CWGC & SDGW show forename as Walter.
"TILL WE MEET AGAIN"

PICKLES, Angus – 307825 Private.
Born in Bradford, the son of Naylor and Violet Pickles, of Shelf. Husband of Eunice Ethel Pickles, of Waitati, New Zealand. Resided at 11 Albert Street, Queensbury. Enlisted at Bradford.
1/7th Battalion DWR; killed in action 11 10 1918, aged 28 (Advance to Victory, Battle of Iwuy).
Buried – Wellington Cemetery, Rieux-En-Cambresis, 1, E, 4.
Commemorated – Shelf Bethel United Methodist Church; Holy Trinity Church, Queensbury RoH; Queensbury WM; CWD page 428 and the **7 DWR Drill Hall WM panel 1, column 2.** Mentioned in the Bradford Weekly Telegraph 08 11 & 20 12 1918 with photograph.
CWGC shows rank as Lance Corporal; SDGW shows rank as Acting Lance Corporal.
"LOVED IN LIFE, HONOURED IN DEATH, TREASURED IN MEMORY, ONE OF THE BEST"

PICKLES, Hartley - 3742 (later 242894) Private.
Born in Halifax, the son of Albert and Emma Pickles, of 81 Well i'th' Lane, Rochdale, Lancs. Resided in Rochdale. Enlisted at Bradford.
1/7th Battalion DWR; killed in action, aged 27 (Battle of the Somme, Leipzig Salient).
Commemorated – Thiepval Memorial, Somme, France and the **7 DWR Drill Hall WM panel 5, column 1.**

PICKLES, John – 240756 Private.
Resided in Dewsbury, the husband of Mrs Smithson (formerly Pickles), of 30 Carlisle Street, Batley Carr, Dewsbury. Enlisted at Mirfield.
1/7th Battalion DWR; killed in action 12 10 1918 (Advance to Victory, Battle of Iwuy).
Buried – Naves Communal Cemetery Extension, France, 2, A, 8.
Commemorated – the **7 DWR Drill Hall WM panel 6, column 1.**
No SDGW entry.

PICKUP, William – 1596 Private.
Born and resided in Oldham, the son of James Pickup, of 79 Stockfield Road, Chadderton, Oldham. Enlisted at Springhead.
1/7th Battalion DWR; killed in action 18 8 1915, aged 20 (Ypres Salient)

Commemorated – Ypres (Menin Gate) Memorial, Belgium, and the **7 DWR Drill Hall WM panel 4, column 2.**
Mentioned in the Unit War Diary (killed in action) 18 8 1915.

PLEASANT, Stanley – 306592 Private.
Son of James and Annie Pleasant, of 18 Ackworth Street, West Bowling, Bradford. Enlisted at Bradford.
2/7th Battalion DWR; killed in action 03 5 1917, aged 21 (Battle of Bullecourt).
Commemorated – Arras Memorial, France, and the **7 DWR Drill Hall WM panel 1, column 3.**
CWGC shows name as PLEASANTS.

PLEWS, Thomas George – 306972 Private.
Brother of Jessie Plews, of 103 Upperthorpe Road, Sheffield. Enlisted at Sheffield.
2/7th Battalion DWR; killed in action 03 5 1917, aged 42 (Battle of Bullecourt).
Commemorated – Arras Memorial, France, and the **7 DWR Drill Hall WM panel 3, column 2.**
CWGC shows forename as Thornas.

POGSON, Harry – 2191 Private.
Born in Rosemary Lane, Huddersfield, the son of James Pogson, of 57 Thomas Street, Northgate. Resided in Huddersfield. Enlisted at Milnsbridge in September, 1914.
1/7th Battalion DWR; died of wounds 19 12 1915, aged 19 (Ypres Salient).
Buried – Bard Cottage Cemetery, Belgium, 1, D, 18.
Commemorated – J Fisher, page 110; M Stansfield, page 339, and the **7 DWR Drill Hall WM panel 4, column 2.**
Mentioned in the Huddersfield Examiner (RSM's batman, died of wounds) 10 1 1916.
WM shows name as DYSON H.

POGSON, John Wadsworth – 2774 Corporal.
Born on 01 8 1893, at Dingle Road, Marsh, Huddersfield, the son of Arthur and Ellen Pogson, of 29, Cliffe End Road, Longwood. Resided in Longwood, Huddersfield. Enlisted at Milnsbridge on 08 11 1914.
1/7th Battalion DWR, A Company; died of wounds (Shrapnel to thigh) No.6 British Red Cross Hospital (The Liverpool Merchant's Hospital) on 13 7 1916, aged 22 (Battle of the Somme).
Buried – Etaples Military Cemetery, France, 14, A, 12A.
Commemorated – St Mark's Parish Church, Longwood; St Stephen's Church, Lindley; Salendine Nook Baptist Church; Salendine Nook Baptist Chapelyard, F, 20; M Stansfield, page 340, and the **7 DWR Drill Hall WM panel 4, column 1.**
"FATHER IN THY GRACIOUS KEEPING LEAVE WE NOW OUR LOVED ONE SLEEPING"

POPE, Francis – 47350 Private.
Born in Longridge, Lancs, the son of Peter and Ellen Pope, of Longridge. The husband of Elizabeth Pope, of 278 Railway Street, Nelson, Lancs. Enlisted at Nelson.
1/7th Battalion DWR; died of wounds 12 10 1918, aged 31 (Advance to Victory).
Buried – Queant Communal Cemetery British Extension, France, D, 41.
Commemorated – the **7 DWR Drill Hall WM panel 2, column 1.**
Formerly 210789 Private, Army Service Corps.
"R.I.P."

PORTER, William Scotney – 22492 Private.
Born in Sheffield, the son of William and Mary Ellen Porter, of Althorpe, Doncaster. Resided in Althorpe. Enlisted at Grimsby.
2/7th Battalion DWR, D Company; died of wounds 12 10 1918, aged 19 (Advance to Victory).

Buried – Doullens Communal Cemetery Extension No 1, France, 5, C, 17.
Commemorated – the **7 DWR Drill Hall WM panel 2, column 2.**
"NOT DEAD BUT GONE BEFORE"

POUCHER, Wilfred – 307312 Private.
Resided in Norton, Yorks. Enlisted at Doncaster.
1/7th Battalion DWR; killed in action 19 4 1918 (German Spring Offensive).
Buried – Meteren Military Cemetery, France, 4, K, 868.
Commemorated – the **7 DWR Drill Hall WM panel 7, column 2.**

POWNALL, George – 362 Private.
Son of Alfred Pownall, of 127 Edgefield Terrace, Milnsbridge. Enlisted at Milnsbridge.
1/7th Battalion DWR; died of wounds 12 7 1916, aged 25 (Battle of the Somme).
Buried – Aveluy Wood Cemetery (Lancashire Dump), Mesnil-Martinsart, France, Special Memorial A, 3.
Commemorated – Milnsbridge WM; J Fisher, page 113; M Stansfield, page 342, and the **7 DWR Drill Hall WM panel 5, column 2.**
"THEIR GLORY SHALL NOT BE BLOTTED OUT"

PRATT, Arthur – 204297 Private.
Resided in Bradford, the husband of Ada Pratt, of 23 Thornbury Road, Bradford. Enlisted at Bradford.
1/7th Battalion DWR; died of wounds 28 7 1917, aged 24 (Nieuport Sector).
Buried – Coxyde Military Cemetery, Belgium, 3, L, 14.
Commemorated – the **7 DWR Drill Hall WM panel 6, column 3.**

PRESTON, Wilfrid – 2nd Lieutenant.
Born on 29 11 1890 at Jesmond, Newcastle-on-Tyne, the son of William and Sarah Preston of 'Hill Crest', 153 Halifax Old Road, Birkby, Huddersfield. Commissioned in August, 1914.
7th Battalion DWR; died of wounds 04 7 1916, aged 25 (Battle of the Somme).
Buried – Bouzincourt Communal Cemetery Extension, France, 2, B, 8.
Commemorated – Fartown and Birkby WM; Huddersfield Parish Church, Woodhouse Hill; J Fisher, page 107; M Stansfield, page 342, and the **7 DWR Drill Hall WM panel 4, column 1.**
Mentioned in the Unit War Diary (joined Battalion from 3/7th DWR) 29 5 1916, (wounded in action) 03 7 1916, the Huddersfield Examiner (died of wounds) 06 12 1916 & 12 7 1916, (in memoriam) 03 7 1918 & 02 7 1920; HDH Album 7 DWR Vol 2, page 11.

PRICE, Hugh – 2nd Lieutenant.
Son of Daniel and Kate Price, of 2 Delaval Road, Whitley Bay, Northumberland.
1/7th Battalion DWR, died 11 10 1918, aged 27 (Advance to Victory).
Buried – St Aubert British Cemetery, France, 5, E, 28.
Commemorated – the **7 DWR Drill Hall WM panel 3, column 3.**
Mentioned in the Unit War Diary (killed in action) 13 10 1918; HDH Album 7 DWR Volume 2, (killed in action) page 39.
Formerly 3rd West Yorkshire Regiment, attached to 1/7th DWR.
"HE SLEEPS WITH THE UNRETURNING BRAVE"

PRICE, Sydney – 5472 (later 7212 & 308057) Private.
Born in Bradford. Enlisted at Bradford.
1/7th Battalion DWR; died of wounds 24 3 1917.
Buried – Merville Communal Cemetery Extension, France, 3, A, 2.
Commemorated – the **7 DWR Drill Hall WM panel 6, column 3.**

PRIESTLEY, Eli Garnett – 29643 Private.
Born in Halifax. Resided at 17, Cotton Street, Halifax. Enlisted at Halifax.
2/7th Battalion DWR; died of wounds 24 4 1918 (German Spring Offensive).
Buried – St Sever Cemetery Extension, Rouen, France, P, 9, N, 7B.
Commemorated – Halifax Civic Book of Remembrance; CWD, page 224, and the **7 DWR Drill Hall WM panel 2, column 2.**
Mentioned in the Halifax Courier 01 5 1918.

PROCTOR, Percy Oswald – 306649 Private.
Son of William and Sarah Maria Procter, of 26 Greaves Street, Little Horton, Bradford. Enlisted at Bradford.
2/7th Battalion DWR; killed in action 28 11 1917, aged 30 (Battle of Cambrai).
Commemorated – Cambrai Memorial, Louverval, France, and the **7 DWR Drill Hall WM panel 1, column 3.**
CWGC shows name spelt PROCTER.

PURSGLOVE, Tom – 306247 Lance Sergeant.
Born in Rawmarsh, the son of Tom and Nellie Ann Pursglove, of Dinnington. Resided in Laughton Common, Dinnington, Rotherham. Enlisted at Redford, Sussex.
2/7th Battalion DWR; died of wounds 18 9 1917, aged 24 (Battle of the Somme).
Buried – Grevillers British Cemetery, France, 7, A, 12.
Commemorated – the **7 DWR Drill Hall WM panel 1, column 3.**
WM shows name as PURSLOVE and rank as Corporal.
"THY WILL, BE DONE"

QUARMBY, Frederick – 2nd Lieutenant.
Son of Mr and Mrs J W Quarmby, of Spark Green, Meltham. Husband of Esther Ann Quarmby, of Clarke Lane, Meltham, Huddersfield. Leeds University OTC, commissioned in July, 1915. Embarked to France & Flanders in May, 1916.
7th Battalion DWR; reported missing, presumed killed in action, 18 9 1916, aged 24 (Battle of the Somme, Leipzig Salient).
Buried – Longueau British Cemetery, France, 4, B, 14.
Commemorated – St Bartholomew's Church, Meltham; Almondbury Grammar School RoH; Leeds University RoH; M Stansfield, page 345, and the **7 DWR Drill Hall WM panel 4, column 1.**
Mentioned in the Unit War Diary (joined Battalion from 3/7th DWR); the Huddersfield Examiner (reported missing) 18 10 1916; HDH Album 7 DWR Volume 2, (reported missing 17 9 1916) page 17; G Howcroft, page 74.
"THY WILL, BE DONE"

QUARMBY, James Schofield – 2nd Lieutenant.
Son of John Sykes and Laura Helena Quarmby, of Green Lea, Meltham, Huddersfield.
7th Battalion DWR; killed in action 02 12 1917, aged 20 (Battle of Cambria).
Buried – Hermies Hill British Cemetery, France, 1, B, 11.
Commemorated – St Bartholomew's Church, Meltham; CVA; M Stansfield, page 345, and the **7 DWR Drill Hall WM panel 4, column 1.**
Formerly Earl of Chester's Imperial Yeomanry, 40413 Pte, Manchester Regiment, commissioned into DWR, March, 1917.
Mentioned in the Unit War Diary (patrol action) 04 7 1917, 29 8 1917 & 01 9 1917, (killed in action) 11 1917; the 62nd Divisional History, page 194.
"MAY YOU AND YOUR COMRADES REST IN PEACE"

RADCLIFFE, J – Lieutenant.
Son of John and Elizabeth Radcliffe, of Farlane, Greenfield, Saddleworth, Yorks.
1/7th Battalion DWR, OC C Company; killed in action (shellfire) 24 2 1918, aged 26.
Buried – Belgian Battery Corner Cemetery, Belgium, 1, H1, 1.
Commemorated – Saddleworth WM; J Fisher, page 133, and the **7 DWR Drill Hall WM panel 3, column 3.**
Mentioned in the Unit War Diary (joined Battalion) 22 12 1915, (killed in action) 23 2 1918; HDH Album 7 DWR Volume 2, pages 15, 21, (appointed Divisional Burial Officer 04 4 1917) 23, 25 & 31; Howcroft G (killed in action) page 107.
"BLESSED ARE THE PURE IN HEART"

RAFTER, George Shale - 3839 Private.
Born in Bradford, the son of John and Margaret Rafter, of 1 Newby Street, West Bowling, Bradford. Enlisted at Bradford.
1/7th Battalion DWR; died of wounds 15 10 1916, aged 26 (Battle of the Somme).
Buried – Boulogne Eastern Cemetery, France, 8, D, 142.
Commemorated – the **7 DWR Drill Hall WM panel 5, column 3.**
"SWEET BE THY REST"

RAISBECK, Maurice – 306618 Private.
Son of Lewis and Sarah Raisbeck, of Greenroyd, Coach Road, Baildon, Shipley. Enlisted at Shipley.
2/7th Battalion DWR; killed in action 03 5 1917, aged 23 (Battle of Bullecourt).
Commemorated – Arras Memorial, France, and the **7 DWR Drill Hall WM panel 1, column 3.**
SDGW shows forename as Morris.

RAMSDEN, Arthur – 204481 Private; Territorial Force War Medal.
Born in Holmfirth, the son of John Thomas and Frances Ramsden, of Bank Top, Holmbridge, Huddersfield. Enlisted at Holmfirth, mobilised with local Territorials. Embarked for France & Flanders in June, 1917.
1/7th Battalion DWR; killed in action 29 7 1917, aged 18 (Nieuport Sector).
Commemorated – Nieuport Memorial, Belgium; Memorial Hospital (Holme and Holmbridge plaque) WM; 5 DWR Drill Hall WM, panel 9 column 2; M Stansfield, page 347, and the **7 DWR Drill Hall WM panel 6, column 1.**
Mentioned in the Huddersfield Examiner (reported missing) 26 9 1917.
Awarded the TFWM, posthumously, on 22 4 1920.
5 DWR WM, CWGC & M Stansfield shows number as 204881.

RAMSDEN, Tom – 203023 Private.
Born in Ovenden, Halifax, the son of Harry and Emma Ramsden, of 40 Keighley Road, Ovenden. Resided in Ovenden. Enlisted at Halifax.
1/6th Battalion DWR; killed in action, whilst acting as Battalion Scout, 15 4 1918, aged 23 (German Spring Offensive).
Commemorated – Tyne Cot Memorial, Belgium, CWD, page 226, and the **7 DWR Drill Hall WM panel 7, column 3.** Mentioned in S Barber, page 179.

RAPP, Reginald – 2nd Lieutenant.
Son of Thomas William and Lilian Rapp, of 9 Lune Street, Saltburn-by-the-Sea, Yorks.
7th Battalion DWR, A Company; died 18 6 1915, aged 19 (Ypres Sector).
Buried – Rue-David Military Cemetery, Fleurbaix, France, 1, A, 21.
Commemorated – Saltburn WM; J Fisher, page 132, and the **7 DWR Drill Hall WM panel 4, column 1.**

Mentioned in the Unit War Diary (shot by sniper) 18 6 1915; G Howcroft, page 17; HDH Album 7 DWR Volume 2, page 5; personal album held in Brotherton Library, Leeds University.
"GRANT HIM ETERNAL REST O LORD AND MAY THY LIGHT SHINE UPON HIM"

RATCLIFFE, Lewis – 307594 Private.
Born and enlisted at Bradford.
2/7th Battalion DWR; killed in action 27 11 1917 (Battle of Cambrai).
Commemorated – Cambrai Memorial, Louverval, France, and the **7 DWR Drill Hall WM panel 7, column 2.**
NA Nominal Roll shows Louis.

RAWLEY, F W – see ROWLEY, Frederick William.
Commemorated – the **7 DWR Drill Hall WM panel 2, column 1.**
WM & SDGW shows RAWLEY, CWGC & NA Roll shows ROWLEY.

RAWLINSON, T – see ROLLINSON, Thomas.
Commemorated – the **7 DWR Drill Hall WM panel 2, column 1.**
CWGC & SDGW show name spelt as ROLLINSON.

READ, Colin John – 306710 Private.
Son of Frederick and Mary Ann Read, of Jubilee Cottage, Orchard Road, Willenhall, Staffs. Resided in Willenhall. Enlisted at Lichfield.
2/7th Battalion DWR; killed in action 27 11 1917, aged 34 (Battle of Cambrai).
Commemorated – Cambrai Memorial, Louverval, France, and the **7 DWR Drill Hall WM panel 7, column 3.**

READING, Walter – 12008 (later 3080870) Private.
Enlisted at Walsall.
2/7th Battalion DWR; killed in action 03 5 1917 (Battle of Bullecourt).
Commemorated – Cambrai Memorial, Louverval, France, and the **7 DWR Drill Hall WM panel 7, column 1.**

REDMAN, Ethelbert – 307831 Private.
Husband of Mary Redman, of 4 Wainsgate Lane, Wadsworth, Hebden Bridge. Enlisted at Hebden Bridge.
1/7th Battalion DWR; died of wounds at No 3 Canadian CCS on 10 3 1918, aged 37 (German Spring Offensive).
Buried – Lijssenthoek Military Cemetery, Belgium, 27, EE, 5.
Commemorated – Wadsworth WM; Wainsgate Baptist Church, Wadsworth; CWD, page 568, and the **7 DWR Drill Hall WM panel 7, column 1.**
Mentioned in Hebden Bridge Times 22 3 1918, with photograph.

REDMAN, Lewis – 307609 Private.
Born at Thornton, Lancs. Enlisted at Barrow-in-Furness.
2/7th Battalion DWR; killed in action 03 5 1917 (Battle of Bullecourt).
Commemorated – Arras Memorial, France, and the **7 DWR Drill Hall WM panel 3, column 1.**

REDMAN, P - see REDMOND, Peter.
Commemorated – the **7 DWR Drill Hall WM panel 2, column 1.**
CWGC & SDGW show surname as REDMOND.

REDMOND, Peter – 24834 Private: Brighouse Tribute Medal.
Resided in Dublin, Ireland. Enlisted at Huddersfield.
2/7th Battalion DWR; killed in action 26 11 1917 (Battle of Cambrai).
Commemorated – Cambrai Memorial, Louverval, France, and the **7 DWR Drill Hall WM panel 2, column 1.**
WM shows name as REDMAN.

REVELL, Albert – 22301 Private.
Resided in Hull, the son of M and A Revell, of Hull. Enlisted at Hull.
2/7th Battalion DWR; died of wounds 09 3 1918, aged 19.
Buried – Maroeuil British Cemetery, France, 4, G, 14.
Commemorated – the **7 DWR Drill Hall WM panel 2, column 2.**
WM shows surname as REVILL.

RICHARDSON, Hedley – 3835 Private.
Born in Addingham. Resided in Leeds. Enlisted at Bradford.
1/7th Battalion DWR; killed in action 04 7 1916 (Battle of the Somme).
Commemorated – Thiepval Memorial, France, and the **7 DWR Drill Hall WM panel 5, column 2.**
WM shows number as 3853.

RICHARDSON, Robert – 308026 Corporal.
Son of William John and Ann Richardson, of Alnmouth. Husband of Jane Richardson, of Poplar Cottage, Alnmouth. Enlisted at Alnwick.
1/7th Battalion DWR; killed in action 11 3 1918, aged 35.
Buried – Oxford Road Cemetery, Belgium, 3, D, 10.
Commemorated – the **7 DWR Drill Hall WM panel 2, column 2.**
"THY WILL, BE DONE"

RICHARDSON, William Henry – 1781 Private.
Born at Golcar, Huddersfield, the son of Mrs Richardson, of 102 Handle Street, Golcar, formerly of Lowergate, Longwood. Resided in Huddersfield. Enlisted at Milnsbridge in August, 1914.
1/7th Battalion DWR; killed in action (shell fragment to head) 29 10 1915 (Ypres Salient).
Buried – Talana Farm Cemetery, Belgium, 3, D, 5.
Commemorated – St John's Church, Golcar; M Stansfield, page 354, and the **7 DWR Drill Hall WM panel 4, column 3.**

RIGBY, Richard – 307155 Private.
Resided in Bury, the son of Fred and Elizabeth Rigby, of Bury. Husband of Agnes Rigby, of Manchester. Enlisted at Bury.
1/7th Battalion DWR; died of wounds 30 4 1918,, aged 25 (German Spring Offensive).
Buried – Etaples Military Cemetery, France, 66, A, 31.
Commemorated – the **7 DWR Drill Hall WM panel 6, column 1.**
WM shows surname as WRIGLEY.
"TO THE SACRED MEMORY OF MY BELOVED HUSBAND, MAY HE REST IN PEACE, AMEN"

RILEY, Thomas Henry – 306431 Private.
Born and resided in Skipton, the son of Mrs Sarah Elizabeth Riley, of 33 Russell Street, Skipton. Enlisted at Skipton.
1/7th Battalion DWR; killed in action 28 2 1918, aged 25.
Buried – Duhallow ADS Cemetery, Belgium, 8, F, 12.
Commemorated – the **7 DWR Drill Hall WM panel 7, column 1.**
"GONE BUT NOT FORGOTTEN"

RIPLEY, Hadfield – 306483 Private.
Born in Heckmondwike, the son of John Ripley, of 20 Lower Smithies, Heckmondwike. Resided in Dewsbury. Enlisted at Heckmondwike.
1/7th Battalion DWR; died of wounds 12 4 1918, aged 26 (German Spring Offensive).
Buried – Meteren Military Cemetery, France, 4, L, 895.
Commemorated – Cleckheaton WM and the **7 DWR Drill Hall WM panel 7, column 1.**

ROBB, David Arthur – 8427 Regimental Sergeant Major.
Son of Alexander and Jessie Robb. Husband of Clara Robb, of 'The Drill Hall', Alva, Clackmannanshire. From Argyll and Sutherland Highlanders, pre war, as Staff Instructor. Embarked for France and Flanders as CSM, promoted RSM by December, 1915.
1/7th Battalion DWR; died 17 11 1916, aged 32 (Battle of the Somme).
Buried – Foncquevillers Military Cemetery, France, 1, H, 9.
Commemorated – the **7 DWR Drill Hall WM panel 3, column 3.**
Formerly Argyll and Sutherland Highlanders, attached 7 DWR.
Mentioned in the Unit War Diary (killed in action, shellfire) 17 11 1916; G Howcroft, pages 79 & 126; HDH Album 7 DWR Volume 2, pages 7, 9, 17, 18 & 19, with photograph.
WM shows initials as R H.
"UNTIL THE DAY BREAK"

ROBERTS, William Henry – 24028 Private.
Born at Bilson, Staffs. Resided in Small Heath. Enlisted at Newcastle-on-Tyne.
1/7th Battalion DWR; killed in action 29 4 1918 (German Spring Offensive).
Commemorated – Tyne Cot Memorial, Belgium, and the **7 DWR Drill Hall WM panel 2, column 2.**
Formerly 55045 Private, Devonshire Regiment & 101774 Private, Labour Corps.

ROBINSON, Alexander – 5600 Private.
Born in Bradford, the son of Jabez and Elizabeth Robinson, of 157 Dudley Hill Road, Undercliffe, Bradford. Enlisted at Bradford.
1/7th Battalion DWR; killed in action 03 7 1916, aged 20 (Battle of the Somme).
Commemorated – Thiepval Memorial, France, and the **7 DWR Drill Hall WM panel 5, column 1.**

ROBINSON, Edward – 305262 Private.
Son of James and Alice Robinson, of 9 Platt Street, Springhead, Lees. Enlisted at Lees.
1/7th Battalion DWR; died of wounds 02 11 1918, aged 26 (Advance to Victory).
Buried – Thiant Communal Cemetery, France, C, 7.
Commemorated – Saddleworth WM; and the **7 DWR Drill Hall WM panel 1, column 2.**
"THE LORD BE WITH YOU TILL WE MEET AGAIN"

ROBINSON, Edward – 306878 Private.
Resided in Ingleton, the son of Thomas and Elizabeth Ann Robinson, of 2 Storrs Cottages, Ingleton. Enlisted at Settle.
2/7th Battalion DWR; killed in action 03 5 1917, aged 20 (Battle of Bullecourt).
Commemorated – Arras Memorial, France; Ingleton WM; CPGW, page 243 and website, with photograph, and the **7 DWR Drill Hall WM panel 2, column 3.**

ROBINSON, Samuel – 3455 (later 307785) Private.
Born in Doncaster, the son of Samuel and Mary Ann Robinson, of 15 Birkland Street, Bulwell, Nottingham. Resided in Bulwell. Enlisted at Nottingham.
1/7th Battalion DWR; killed in action 30 4 1918, aged 34 (German Spring Offensive).
Buried – La Clytte Military Cemetery, Belgium, 5, E, 21.
Commemorated – the **7 DWR Drill Hall WM panel 6, column 2.**

"PEACE PERFECT PEACE, WITH OUR LOVED ONE FAR AWAR"

ROBINSON, Walter – 852 Lance Corporal.
Born at Swinton, Lancs, the son of Joseph and Esther Ann Robinson. Husband of Clara Robinson, of 8 Salop Street, Oldham. Enlisted at Lees.
1/7th Battalion DWR; died of wounds 15 12 1915, aged 24 (Ypres Sector).
Buried – Boulogne Eastern Cemetery, France 8, C, 67.
Commemorated – the **7 DWR Drill Hall WM panel 4, column 1.**
"YEARS PASS BY, MY HEART STILL SORE, AS TIME GOES ON I MISS YOU MORE (WIFE)"

ROEBUCK, Arthur – 202216 Private.
Born in Bradford, husband of Edith Roebuck, of 2 Lower Back William Street, Little Horton Lane, Bradford. Enlisted at Bradford.
1/7th Battalion DWR; died at home 28 10 1918, aged 33.
Buried – Bradford (Bowling) Cemetery, 10, 634.
Commemorated – the **7 DWR Drill Hall WM panel 3, column 1.**
"NOT FORGOT"

ROGERS, John Wixdale – 308098 Private.
Son of Henry Arthur and Martha Rogers, of 5 Thompson Street, Bilston, Staffs. Enlisted at Bilston.
2/7th Battalion DWR; killed in action 03 5 1917, aged 22 (Battle of Bullecourt).
Commemorated – Arras Memorial, France, and the **7 DWR Drill Hall WM panel 1, column 2.**
CWGC shows second name as WISEDALE, SDGC shows name as WIXDALE.

ROGERS, Walter – 5500 Private.
Born and enlisted at Sheffield.
1/7th Battalion DWR; killed in action 15 11 1916 (Battle of the Somme).
Buried – Foncquevillers Military Cemetery, France, 1, H, 5.
Commemorated - the **7 DWR Drill Hall WM panel 5, column 2.**
CWGC shows name as RODGERS and state date of death as 16 11 1916.

ROGERSON, David Pickett – 7175 (later 308028) Private.
Resided in Bamburgh, Northumberland. Enlisted at Alnwick.
1/7th Battalion DWR; killed in action 29 4 1918 (German Spring Offensive).
Buried – La Clytte Military Cemetery, Belgium, 5, E, 20.
Commemorated – the **7 DWR Drill Hall WM panel 6, column 2.**
Formerly 3044 Private, Northumberland Fusiliers.

ROLLINSON, George Reynard – 307031 Private.
Son of Alfred and C R Rollison, of 129 Round Street, West Bowling, Bradford. Enlisted at Bradford.
2/7th Battalion, A Company; killed in action 14 5 1917 (Hindenburg Line).
Commemorated – Arras Memorial, France, and the **7 DWR Drill Hall WM panel 1, column 1.**

ROLLINSON, Thomas – 307830 Private.
Born in Honley, Huddersfield, the son of Mr C and Mrs S E Rollinson, of Honley. Husband of Mary Rollinson, of 11 Oldfield Buildings, Honley. Resided in Honley. Enlisted at Huddersfield in August, 1916.
1/7th Battalion DWR; died of wounds 24 2 1918, aged 30.
Buried – Menin Road South Military Cemetery, Belgium, 3, H, 30.
Commemorated – Honley WM; M Stansfield, page 363, and the **7 DWR Drill Hall WM panel 7, column 2.**
WD show name as RAWLINSON.

"HE DIED FOR HIS COUNTRY, EVER REMEMBERED, HONLEY, HUDDS."

ROLLOND, A – 7074 Private - see **BOLLAND,** Arthur.
Commemorated –the **7 DWR Drill Hall WM panel 5, column 1.**
CWGC & SDG shows name as BOLLAND.

ROSS, James – 306768 Private.
Son of Mrs M Ross, of 72 Clayton Street, Sunbridge Road, Bradford. Enlisted at Bradford.
2/7th Battalion DWR; killed in action 29 3 1918 (German Spring Offensive).
Buried – Bienvillers Military Cemetery, France, 12, A, 10.
Commemorated – the **7 DWR Drill Hall WM Panel 3, column 2.**

ROSS, Robert – 7174 (later 308027) Corporal.
Born at Stobswood, Northumberland, the son of Alexander and Mary Ann Graham Ross, of 6 Hedgehope Terrace, Chevington Drift, Morpeth, Northumberland. Resided in Acklington. Enlisted at Alnwick.
1/7th Battalion DWR; killed in action 13 4 1918, aged 22 (German Spring Offensive).
Commemorated – Tyne Cot Memorial, France, and the **7 DWR Drill Hall WM panel 7, column 1.**
Formerly 2961 Private, Northumberland Fusiliers.
CWGC shows rank as Sergeant; SDGW shows rank as Acting Sergeant.

ROWLEY, Frederick William – 34826 Private.
Son of Frederick William and Mary Ann Rowley, of 38 Frank Street, London Road, Stoke-on-Trent.
Enlisted at Newcastle upon Tyne.
1/7th Battalion DWR; died 12 10 1918, aged 19 (Advance to Victory).
Buried – Bucquoy Road Cemetery, Ficheux, France, 4, F, 28.
Commemorated - the **7 DWR Drill Hall WM panel 2, column 1.**
Formerly D/27832 Dragoons.
CWGC & SDGW show second name as William, WM shows number as 34825.
"HE DIED THAT WE MIGHT LIVE"

RUFF, Samuel – Lieutenant.
Son of Thomas and Lavinia Ruff, of 'Belsize', 48 Scarcroft Hill, York.
1/7th Battalion DWR; died 17 11 1916, aged 24 (Battle of the Somme).
Buried – Foncquevillers Military Cemetery, France, 1, H, 10.
Commemorated - J Fisher, page 133, and the **7 DWR Drill Hall WM panel 4, column 1.**
Mentioned in the Unit War Diary (transferred to 1/7th Battalion) 31 7 1915, (killed in action) 17 11 1916; G Howcroft, pages 12 & 79; HDH Album 7 DWR Volume 2, pages 8, 15, 17 & 19.
CWGC show rank as 2nd Lieutenant.
"CROWNED WITH THE SUNSHINE OF ETERNAL YOUTH"

RUKIN, Clement – 307002 Private.
Resided in Brighouse, the son of Joseph and Ann Rukin, of Clifton, Brighouse. Enlisted at Halifax in March, 1916.
2/7th Battalion DWR; died of wounds, as POW in Germany, 24 7 1917, aged 39.
Buried – Niederzwehren Cemetery, Kassel, Germany 2, J, 1.
Commemorated – Clifton WM; Clifton Methodist Church WM; St John the Evangelist Church, Clifton, Brighouse; CWD, page 436; M Sharp, pages 63, 66 & 77, and the **7 DWR Drill Hall WM panel 7, column 3.**
Mentioned in the Brighouse Echo 31 8 1917.
"FAITHFUL UNTO DEATH"

RUSHWORTH, Herbert – 3836 Private.
Born and enlisted at Bradford.
1/7th Battalion DWR; killed in action 03 9 1916 (Battle of the Somme, Thiepval).
Buried – Lonsdale Cemetery, Authuile, France, 10, H, 3.
Commemorated – the **7 DWR Drill Hall WM panel 5, column 2.**
WM shows number as 2380.

RUSHWORTH, Jonas William – 307388 Private.
Born in Bradford. Resided in Queensbury, Bradford. Enlisted at Bradford.
1/7th Battalion DWR; killed in action 03 9 1916 (Battle of the Somme, Thiepval).
Commemorated – Thiepval Memorial, France; Queensbury WM; Holy Trinity Church, Queensbury, RoH and the **7 DWR Drill Hall WM panel 6, column 2.**

RUSLING William – 205105 Private.
Born in Goole. Resided in Selby, the husband of Rosetta Rusling, of Chapel Haddlesey, Selby. Enlisted at Goole.
1/7th Battalion DWR; died of wounds 14 4 1918, aged 32 (German Spring Offensive).
Buried – Etaples Military Cemetery, France, 29, B, 18.
Commemorated – the **7 DWR Drill Hall WM panel 7, column 1.**
"NEARER MY GOD TO THEE"

RYDHALGH, Thomas – 305834 Private.
Born at Halifax. Resided at 13 Mount Street, Halifax. Enlisted at Halifax in 1916.
1/7th Battalion DWR; killed in action (shellfire) 25 7 1917, aged 28 (Ypres Salient).
Buried – Ramscappelle Road Military Cemetery, Belgium, 1, B, 10.
Commemorated – St Mary's Church, Rhodes Street, Halifax; St Hilda's Church, Gibraltar Road, West End, Halifax; Halifax Civic Book of Remembrance; Halifax Butcher's Association RoH; Halifax Bowling Club RoH; CWD, page 231, and the **7 DWR Drill Hall WM panel 6, column 1.**
Mentioned in the Halifax Weekly Guardian 11 8 1917
WM & SDGW show name as RIDEHALGH and number as 307834.

SADDINGTON, William Henry – 306959 Private.
Son of Mr W H Saddington, of 41 Fowler Street, Pitsmoor, Sheffield. Enlisted at Sheffield.
2/7th Battalion DWR; killed in action 03 5 1917, aged 20 (Battle of Bullecourt).
Commemorated – Arras Memorial, France, and the **7 DWR Drill Hall WM panel 6, column 2.**
WM shows name LADDINGTON.

SANDERSON, Walter – 12820 (later 267237) Lance Corporal.
Born and resided in Sedbergh, Yorkshire. Enlisted at Sedburgh.
2/7th Battalion DWR; died of wounds 26 3 1918 (German Spring Offensive).
Buried – Pommier Communal Cemetery, France, 7.
Commemorated – CPGW website, and the **7 DWR Drill Hall WM panel 3, column 1.**

SANDS, Arthur – 306147 Private.
Son of Joshua and Hannah Sands. Resided in Oldham. Enlisted at Greenfield.
2/7th Battalion DWR; died of wounds 21 5 1918, aged 47 (German Spring Offensive).
Buried – Doullens Communal Cemetery Extension No 2, France 2, C, 2.
Commemorated – the **7 DWR Drill Hall WM panel 6, column 3.**
"HE GAVE HIS BEST, HIS LIFE, FROM SISTER SARAH"

SAVAGE, Harry – 2628 Private.
Resided in Newport, Shropshire. Husband of Martha Savage, of 127 New Cottage, Donnington Wood, Wellington, Shropshire. Enlisted at Milnsbridge.
1/7th Battalion DWR; killed in action 18 9 1916, aged 29 (Battle of the Somme).
Commemorated – Thiepval Memorial; Donnington Wood, Salop, WM and the **7 DWR Drill Hall WM panel 5, column 2.**
WM shows 2828.

SCARGILL, Willie – 307390 Private.
Born in Halifax. Resided at 3, Ward's End, Halifax, the son of Ernest and Emma Scargill, of 62 New Road, Halifax. Enlisted at Halifax.
1/7th Battalion DWR; killed in action 24 11 1917, aged 23 (3rd Battle of Ypres, Passchendaele).
Buried – Perth Cemetery (China Wall), Belgium, 5, H, 1.
Commemorated – Halifax Civic Book of Remembrance; CWD, page 239, and the **7 DWR Drill Hall WM panel 7, column 1.**
Mentioned in the Halifax Courier 03 12 1917 & Halifax Weekly Guardian 08 12 1917, with photograph.
"THE BELOVED SON OF ERNEST AND EMMA SCARGILL, GONE BUT NOT FORGOTTEN"

SCHOFIELD, Harold – 2506 Private.
Born and resided in Greenfield, the son of W Henry Schofield, of Haybottoms, Greenfield. Enlisted at Milnsbridge.
1/7th Battalion DWR; killed in action 26 7 1916 (Battle of the Somme).
Buried – Bard Cottage Cemetery, Belgium 1, E, 17.
Commemorated – Saddleworth WM and the **7 DWR Drill Hall WM panel 4, column 2.**

SCHOFIELD, James Albert – 6720 (later 307837) Private.
Born on 26 2 1887 in Huddersfield, the son of Walter and Mary Ann Schofield, of Laurel Lea, 344 Leeds Road, Huddersfield. Husband of Helena Schofield, of 14 Second Avenue, Long Lane, Dalton. Enlisted on 04 8 1916.
1/7th Battalion DWR; killed in action 19 4 1918, age 31 German Spring Offensive.
Buried – Meteren Military Cemetery, France, 4, N, 970.
Commemorated – St Andrew's Church, Leeds Road, Huddersfield; St John's Church, Kirkheaton; M Stansfield, page 372, and the **7 DWR Drill Hall WM panel 4, column 2.**

SCHOFIELD, Lewis Thorpe – 241541 Private.
Born in Marsden, the son of Sam Thorpe Schofield and Mary Schofield, of 6 Wood Top, Marsden, Huddersfield. Enlisted at Marsden, a local Territorial in August, 1914.
1/7th Battalion DWR; died of wounds (gas) 29 4 1918, aged 25 (German Spring Offensive).
Buried – Boulogne Eastern Cemetery, France, 9, B, 19.
Commemorated – Marsden WM; Marsden Conservative Club RoH; M Stansfield, page 373, and the **7 DWR Drill Hall WM panel 7, column 2.**

SCHOFIELD, Oliver – 2317 Private.
Born in Delph. Resided in Blackmoorfoot, Linthwaite. Enlisted at Milnsbridge in October, 1914. Embarked for France & Flanders in April, 1915.
1/7th Battalion DWR; killed in action (whilst in dugout) 23 9 1915, aged 33 (Ypres Sector).
Buried – Bard Cottage Cemetery, Belgium 1, H, 20.
Commemorated – Helme Parish Church, Linthwaite, WM; St Bartholomew's Church, Meltham; M Stansfield, page 373, and the **7 DWR Drill Hall WM panel 4, column 2.**
Mentioned in the Unit War Diary (killed in action) 23 9 1915; the Huddersfield Examiner (listed on Helme WM) 31 3 1920; the HDH Album 7 DWR Volume 2 (original grave photo) page 4; the Iron Duke Journal 092-1954, page 71.

SCHOFIELD, Tom – 305780 Private.
Resided at Lees. Enlisted at Uppermill.
1/7th Battalion DWR; killed in action 03 9 1916 (Battle of the Somme, Thiepval).
Commemorated – Thiepval Memorial, France, and the **7 DWR Drill Hall WM panel 6, column 2.**

SCOTT, John Edward - 24086 Private.
Born in Yeadon, Leeds. Enlisted at Shipley.
2/7th Battalion DWR; killed in action 25 3 1918 (German Spring Offensive).
Commemorated – Arras Memorial, France, and the **7 DWR Drill Hall WM panel 2, column 1.**
Also served in the 10th Battalion, see - **tunstillsmen.blogspot.com** (last accessed August, 2020).

SCOTT, Sam – 3806 Private.
Born in Guiseley, Leeds, the son of Cornelius and George Scott, of Tramuse Cottage, Back Lane, Guiseley. Resided and enlisted at Guiseley.
1/7th Battalion DWR, attached to 1/5th Battalion King's Own Yorkshire Light Infantry; killed in action 28 8 1916, aged 24 (Battle of the Somme).
Buried – Lonsdale Cemetery, Authuile, France, 10, A, 2.
Commemorated – the **7 DWR Drill Hall WM panel 5, column 1.**
"MAY HIS REWARD BE AS GREAT AS HIS SACRIFICE"

SEWARD, Fred – 5522 Private.
Born in Hull. Husband of Annie Elizabeth Seward, of 46 Madeley Street, Hessle Road, Hull. Enlisted at Hull.
1/7th Battalion DWR; killed in action 17 9 1916, aged 37 (Battle of the Somme, Leipzig Salient).
Commemorated – Thiepval Memorial, France, and the **7 DWR Drill Hall WM panel 5, column 3.**

SHACKLETON, Tom Humfress – 307196 Private.
Born at Dams Rrol, Norway. Husband of Lillie Shackleton, of 27 East Street, Shipley. Enlisted at Shipley.
1/7th Battalion DWR; killed in action 26 4 1918, aged 30 (German Spring Offfensive).
Buried – Brandhoek New Military Cemetery No 3, Belgium, 1, O, 22.
Commemorated – the **7 DWR Drill Hall WM panel 7, column 2.**
SDGW shows middle name as Humphrey.

SHARD, Charles – 3776 Private.
Born and enlisted at Bradford.
1/7th Battalion DWR; killed in action 28 8 1918 (Advance to Victory).
Buried – Lonsdale Cemetery, Authuile, France, 8, C, 5.
Commemorated – the **7 DWR Drill Hall WM panel 5, column 2.**
WM shows name as SHEARD.

SHARP, Fred – 306622 Private.
Resided in Holme Street, Liversedge. Enlisted at Heckmondwike.
2/7th Battalion DWR; died (appendicitis) 16 4 1917.
Buried – Achiet-Le-Grand Communal Cemetery Extension, France 1, C, 4.
Commemorated – Cleckheaton WM and the **7 DWR Drill Hall WM panel 1, column 1.**

SHARP, Willie – 307672 Private.
Born in Cleckheaton, the son of Mr and Mrs James Sharp, of 'Springfield House', Scholes, Cleckheaton. Husband of Ethel Sharp, of 70 Prospect Place, Scholes. Resided in Liversedge. Enlisted at Heckmondwike.
1/7th Battalion DWR; killed in action 16 4 1917, aged 34 (German Spring Offensive).

Commemorated – Tyne Cot Memorial, France; Cleckheaton WM and the **7 DWR Drill Hall WM panel 6, column 3.**

SHARPE, G - see THORPE, George.
Commemorated – 7 DWR Drill Hall WM panel 2, column 3.
CWGC & SDGW show name as THORPE.

SHARROCKS, John Charles – 3551 (later 603198) Private.
Born in Hayfield, Derbyshire. Resided in Spring Terrace, Binn Road, Marsden, Huddersfield. Enlisted at Milnsbridge. Formerly Sherwood Forrester's Territorials for three years. Embarked for France & Flanders in March, 1916.
1/7th Battalion DWR; killed in action 18 9 1916, aged 26 (Battle of the Somme).
Commemorated – Thiepval Memorial, France; Marsden WM; CVA; J Fisher, page 114; M Stansfield, page 389, and the **7 DWR Drill Hall WM panel 5, column 3.**
Formerly Nottinghamshire & Derbyshire Regiment.
Mentioned in the Huddersfield Examiner (wounded in action) 25 7 1916, (died of wounds) 05 10 1916, (killed in action) 25 10 1917.
WM & Huddersfield Examiner show name as SHORROCKS & initial as J.

SHAW, Albert – 305673 Sergeant.
Born in 1893 in Mossley. Resided in Mossley. Enlisted at Milnsbridge.
1/7th Battalion DWR; killed in action 18 9 1916 (Battle of the Somme).
Buried – Bray Vale British Cemetery, Bray-Sur-Somme, France, 4, A, 10.
Commemorated – Mossley Town Hall WM; Saddleworth WM; St George's Church WM; St John the Baptist Church WM; R Vaughan, pages 24 & 60, and the **7 DWR Drill Hall WM panel 6, Column 3.**

SHAW, C – 5776 Private.
Commemorated – the **7 DWR Drill Hall WM panel 5, Column 2.**
No trace of this man either by name or number, CWGC or SDGW.

SHAW, Dan – 305612 Corporal.
Resided in 32 Golcar Hill, Golcar. Enlisted at Milnsbridge in October, 1914. Embarked for France & Flanders in January, 1917.
2/4th Battalion DWR; died of wounds at No 3 CCS on 20 9 1917, aged 20.
Buried – Grevillers British Cemetery, France, 7, A, 14.
Commemorated – St John's Church, Golcar; CVA; M Stansfield, page 380, and the **7 DWR Drill Hall WM panel 7, column 3.**
Mentioned in the Huddersfield Examiner (died of wounds) 23 10 1917.

SHAW, George Albert – 307789 Private.
Son of Mr L Shaw, of 22 Birk's Hall Terrace, Pellon, Halifax. Enlisted at Halifax in June, 1915.
1/7th Battalion DWR; died of wounds at 62 CCS on 14 4 1918, aged 39 (German Spring Offensive).
Buried – Haringhe (Bandaghem) Military Cemetery, Belgium, 2, C, 20.
Commemorated – Halifax Civic Book of Remembrance; CWD, page 245, and the **7 DWR Drill Hall WM panel 7, column 1.**
Mentioned in the Halifax Weekly Courier 27 4 1918.

SHAW, Gilbert – 2026 Lance Corporal.
Born in 1883 in Mossley. Resided in Mossley. Enlisted on 05 9 1914 at Milnsbridge. Embarked for France & Flanders on 15 4 1915.
1/7th Battalion DWR; killed in action, shellfire, 09 9 1915 (Ypres Salient).
Buried – Colne Valley Cemetery, Belgium, D, 4 (collective).

Commemorated – Mossley Town Hall WM; St George's Church WM; St John the Baptist Church WM; United Methodist Church WM; R Vaughan, pages 16, 24 & 36, and the **7 DWR Drill Hall WM panel 4, column 1.**
CWGC & SDGW show number as 2024.

SHAW, Harold – 480 Lance Sergeant.
Resided in Springhead, Oldham, the son of Napoleon and Sarah Maria Shaw, of Whams House, Den Lane, Oldham. Enlisted at Lees.
1/7th Battalion DWR; killed in action 26 11 1915, aged 28 (Ypres Salient).
Buried – Bard Cottage Cemetery, Belgium 1, B, 20.
Commemorated – Saddleworth WM and the **7 DWR Drill Hall WM panel 4, column 1.**
"FAITHFUL UNTO DEATH"

SHAW, John William – 2331 Lance Sergeant.
Resided in Marsden, the son of William Shaw, of 13 Warehouse Hill, Marsden. Enlisted at Milnsbridge.
1/7th Battalion DWR; died of wounds in Bradford War Hospital on 31 7 1916, aged 25 (Battle of the Somme).
Buried – St Bartholomew's Churchyard, Marsden, Yorkshire, SW, 23, 4.
Commemorated – CVA; M Stansfield, page 384, and the **7 DWR Drill Hall WM panel 5, column 3.**
Mentioned in the Huddersfield Examiner (wounded in action) 25 7 1916, (died of wounds) 04 8 1916, (reported wia, dow) 19 9 1918.

SHAW, Norman – 307089 Private.
Born in Leeds, the son of Mr and Mrs J B Shaw, of Horsforth, Leeds. Resided in Horsforth. Enlisted at Leeds.
1/7th Battalion DWR; killed in action 14 8 1917 aged 22 (Nieuport Sector).
Buried – Coxyde Military Cemetery, Belgium, 2, H, 19.
Commemorated – the **7 DWR Drill Hall WM panel 6, column 3.**

SHAW, Seth – 2118 Private.
Resided in Lees, the son of Thomas and Mary Ann Shaw, of Waterhead, Oldham. Husband of Edith Langstaff (formerly Shaw), of 127 High Street, Lees. Enlisted at Uppermill.
1/7th Battalion DWR, D Company; died 22 7 1916 (Battle of the Somme).
Buried – Connaught Cemetery, Thiepval, France, 13, C, 5.
Commemorated – the **7 DWR Drill Hall WM panel 5, Column 3.**
"HE DID HIS DUTY"

SHAW, Thomas – 1033 Lance Corporal.
Born at Waterhead, Oldham. Resided in Oldham, the husband of Emma Shaw, of 31 Stoneleigh Street, Oldham. Enlisted at Lees.
1/7th Battalion DWR; killed in action (shellfire) 06 8 1915, aged 21 (Ypres Salient).
Buried – Ferme-Olivier Cemetery, Belgium, 1, H, 6.
Commemorated – the **7 DWR Drill Hall WM panel 4, column 1.**
Mentioned in the Unit War Diary (killed in action) 06 8 1915.
"NO ONE KNOWS, NO ONE CAN TELL, BUT THOSE WHO HAVE TO SAY FAREWELL"

SHAW, William – 269176 Private.
Born, resided and enlisted at Huddersfield.
1/7th Battalion DWR; reported missing, presumed killed in action, on 09 10 1917.
Commemorated – Tyne Cot Memorial, Belgium; All Saint's Church, Paddock, RoH (now in Huddersfield Drill Hall); M Stansfield, page 385, and the **7 DWR Drill Hall WM panel 6, column 1.**

SHAW, Willie – 12764 Private.
Born in Halifax. Resided at 4 Swift Street, Salterhebble, Halifax. Enlisted at Halifax.
1/7th Battalion DWR; died of wounds 08 5 1918 (German Spring Offensive).
Buried – Boulogne Eastern Cemetery, France, 9, B, 62.
Commemorated – Sacred Heart & St Bernard's Church, Halifax; Halifax Civic Book of Remembrance; CWD, page 246, and the **7 DWR Drill Hall WM panel 3, column 2.**
Mentioned in the Halifax Weekly Guardian 10 5 1919.
CWGC shows rank as Lance Corporal.

SHEARD, C - see SHARD, Charles.
Commemorated – the **7 DWR Drill Hall WM panel 5, column 2.**
CWGC & SDGW show surname as SHARD.

SHERWOOD, Alfred Sydney – 26152 Private.
Born in Maidstone, Kent. Resided in Wandsworth, London. Enlisted at Camberwell.
1/7th Battalion DWR; killed in action 14 4 1918 (German Spring Offensive).
Buried – Le Grand Beaumart British Cemetery, Steenwerck, France, 3, I, 19.
Commemorated – the **7 DWR Drill Hall WM panel 2, column 3.**
Formerly 5/1195 Private, Queen's Regiment & 81436 Private, Labour Corps.

SHORROCKS, J - see SHARROCKS, John Charles.
Commemorated – the **7 DWR Drill Hall WM panel 5, column 3.**
CWGC & SDGW show surname as SHARROCKS.

SHUTTLEWORTH, Walter – 882 Drummer.
Born and resided in Oldham, the son of Henry and Harriet Shuttleworth. Enlisted at Lees.
1/7th Battalion DWR; died at home 16 1 1916, aged 24.
Buried – Oldham (Greenacres) Cemetery, GIA, CE, 146
Commemorated – the **7 DWR Drill Hall WM panel 4, column 3.**

SIME, Charles Sinclair – 26693 Private.
Born in Govan, Scotland. Enlisted at Glasgow.
1/7th Battalion DWR; died of wounds 26 4 1918 (German Spring Offensive).
Buried – Haringhe (Bandaghem) Military Cemetery, Belgium, 5, A, 16.
Commemorated – the Scottish National War Memorial (Edinburgh Castle) and the **7 DWR Drill Hall WM panel 2, column 1.**
Formerly 15325 Private, Royal Highlanders & 22410 Royal Scots Fusiliers.
WM shows name as SIMS.

SIMPSON, Archibald – 308116 Private.
Born and resided at Hawksclough, Hebden Bridge, the son of James and Grace Simpson, of Mytholmroyd. Husband of Eliza Ann Simpson, of 7 Aspinall Street, Banksfield, Mytholmroyd. Enlisted at Halifax in October, 1916. Embarked for France & Flanders in January, 1917.
2/7th Battalion DWR; died of wounds (to head), at 23 CCS on 29 11 1917, aged 39 (Battle of Cambrai).
Buried – Grevillers British Cemetery, France, 8, C, 1.
Commemorated – St Michael's Parish Church, Mytholmroyd; Wesleyan Methodist Church, Mytholmroyd; CWD, page 575, and the **7 DWR Drill Hall WM panel 7, column 1.**
Mentioned in the Hebden Bridge Times 07 12 1917, with photograph.
"LOVE ONE ANOTHER, LEST WE FORGET"

SIMS, C S - see SIME, Charles Sinclair.
Commemorated – 7 DWR Drill Hall WM panel 2, column 1.
CWGC & SDGW show name as SIME.

SINGLETON, Albert – 306249 Private.
Resided in Oldham. Enlisted at Greenfield.
1/7th Battalion DWR; killed in action 28 5 1917.
Buried – St Vaast Post Military Cemetery, 4, H, 3.
Commemorated - the 7 DWR Drill Hall WM panel 2, column 2.

SINGLETON, Clarence – 306140 Private.
Resided in Linthwaite, the son of Mr and Mrs Joe Singleton, of 55 Royd House, Linthwaite, Huddersfield. Enlisted at Milnsbridge.
2/7th Battalion DWR; reported missing, presumed killed in action, on 03 5 1917, aged 19 (Battle of Bullecourt).
Commemorated – Arras Memorial, France; Linthwaite WM; CVA, M Stansfield, page 390, and the **7 DWR Drill Hall WM panel 1, column 3.**
Mentioned in the Huddersfield Examiner (wounded in action) 01 6 1917.

SKELDON, Thomas – 306050 Private.
Born on 15 9 1899 in Mossley. Resided in Mossley. Enlisted at Thoresby Camp, Nottingham.
2/7th Battalion DWR; killed in action 03 5 1917 (Battle of Bullecourt).
Commemorated – Arras Memorial, France; Abney Congregational Church RoH and window; R Vaughan, pages 20, 75 & 154, and the **7 DWR Drill Hall WM panel 1, column 3.**
Mentioned in the Mossley and Saddleworth Reporter, in memoriam, 26 4 1919.

SLATER, Herbert – 1614 Lance Corporal.
Born in 1886 in Stalybridge. Had been a pre war Territorial, enlisted at Mossley. Embarked for France & Flanders on 15 4 1915.
1/7th Battalion DWR, H Company; killed in action 18 9 1916 (Battle of the Somme).
Commemorated – Thiepval Memorial, France; Mossley Town Hall WM; St George's Church WM; J Fisher, page 114; R Vaughan, pages 24, 25 & 61 and **7 DWR Drill Hall WM panel 5, column 3.**
Mentioned in the Huddersfield Examiner (killed in action) 12 10 1916.

SLATER, William – 535 (later 305058) Corporal.
Born at Oldham. Resided in Oldham. Enlisted at Lees.
1/7th Battalion DWR; died of wounds 20 4 1918 (German Spring Offensive).
Buried – Haringhe (Bandaghem) Military Cemetery, Belgium, 5, C, 12.
Commemorated - the 7 DWR Drill Hall WM panel 6, column 2.

SMETHURST, Percy – 1967 Corporal.
Son of Oscar and Elizabeth Smethurst, of 1 Bonny Brow, Rhodes, Manchester.
1/7th Battalion DWR; killed in action 03 9 1916, aged 23 (Battle of the Somme, Thiepval).
Buried – Le Grand Beaumart British Cemetery, Steenwerck, France, 3, F, 5.
Commemorated – the 7 DWR Drill Hall WM panel 3, column 1.
WM shows name as METHURST.

SMITH, Alvin – 5615 Private.
Born and resided in Lothersdale, Yorkshire, the son of Edmund and Sarah Jane Smith, of Dale End Farm, Lothersdale. Enlisted at Skipton.
1/7th Battalion DWR; killed in action 17 9 1916 aged 20 (Battle of the Somme, Leipzig Salient).

Commemorated – Thiepval Memorial, France; CPGW, page 174, with photograph, and the **7 DWR Drill Hall WM panel 5, column 1.**

SMITH, Arthur Lewis – 2464 Private.
Resided in Golcar, Huddersfield the brother of Mr F K Smith, of 5 Wellhouse Fields, Golcar. Enlisted at Milnsbridge.
1/7th Battalion DWR; killed in action 08 12 1915, aged 20 (Ypres Salient).
Buried – Bard Cottage Cemetery, Belgium 1, D, 20.
Commemorated – St John's Church, Golcar; CVA, J Fisher, page 110; M Stansfield, page 394, and the **7 DWR Drill Hall WM panel 4, column 3.**
CVA shows number as 2646.

SMITH, David – 13207 Private.
Born in Keighley, the son of William and Elizabeth Smith, of 2 Hive Street, Fell Lane, Keighley. Enlisted at Keighley.
1/7th Battalion DWR; died of wounds 14 4 1918, aged 30 (German Spring Offensive).
Buried – Mendinghem Military Cemetery, Belgium, 6, B, 46.
Commemorated – the **7 DWR Drill Hall WM panel 2, column 3.**
"LET YE WHO FOLLOW ON BE WORTHY OF MY SACRIFICE"

SMITH, Ernest – 306302 Private.
Resided in Heckmondwike, the son of John and Agnes Smith, of 79, Brighton Street, Heckmondwike. Enlisted at Cleckheaton.
1/7th Battalion DWR; killed in action 29 4 1918, aged 20 (German Spring Offensive).
Commemorated – Tyne Cot Memorial, Belgium, and **7 DWR Drill Hall WM panel 6, column 3.**

SMITH, George Marshall – 29445 Private.
Born in Yeadon, Leeds, the son of Grimshaw and Mary Hannah Smith, of 4, Swaine Hill Terrace, Yeadon. Resided in Yeadon. Enlisted at Keighley. Embarked for France & Flanders on 15 4 1915.
2/7th Battalion DWR; killed in action 27 11 1917, aged 20 (Battle of Cambrai).
Commemorated – Cambrai Memorial, Louverval, France; the 5 DWR Drill Hall WM, panel 10, column 3. and the **7 DWR Drill Hall WM panel 2, column 3.**
7 DWR WM shows initials as H M. 5 DWR WM shows initials as G N.

SMITH, George Thomas – 305420 Corporal.
Resided in Cardiff, the son of Thomas and Fanny Smith. Enlisted at Mossley.
1/7th Battalion DWR; killed in action 03 9 1916, aged 20 (Battle of the Somme, Thiepval).
Commemorated – Thiepval Memorial, Somme, France; All Saints Church WM St George's Church WM; R Vaughan, pages 24, 25 & 58. and the **7 DWR Drill Hall WM panel 6, column 3.**

SMITH, Herbert – 306453 Private.
Born in Skipton, the son of William Smith, of 47 Leonard Street, Barnoldswick. Resided in Barnoldswick. Enlisted at Skipton.
1/7th Battalion DWR; killed in action 13 4 1918 (German Spring Offensive).
Commemorated – Tyne Cot Memorial, Belgium; CPGW, page 341, with photograph, and the **7 DWR Drill Hall WM panel 6, column 1.**

SMITH Herbert John – 306796 Private.
Resided in Greystones Farm, Eastwood, Todmorden, the son of Frederick and Mary Ann Smith, of 4 Cornfield Street, Todmorden. Enlisted at Halifax.
2/7th Battalion DWR; killed in action 27 11 1917, aged 25 (Battle of Cambrai).

Commemorated – Cambrai Memorial, Louverval, France; St James's Church, Hebden Bridge; Blackshaw Head Wesleyan Methodist Church; CWD, page 576, and the **7 DWR Drill Hall WM panel 1, column 2.**
Mentioned in Hebden Bridge tines 28 12 1917; the Halifax Weekly Guardian 29 12 1917 & the Todmorden Advertiser 04 1 1918.

SMITH, H M - see SMITH, George Marshall.
Commemorated – 7 DWR Drill Hall WM panel 2, column 3.
CWGC & SDGW show name as George Marshall Smith.

SMITH, John – 268472 Lance Corporal.
Resided in Oldham, the son of Thomas R and Elizabeth Smith, of 57 Mayfield Road, Oldham. Husband of Annie Short (formerly Smith), of 11 Evelyn Street, Oldham. Enlisted at Lees.
$1/7^{th}$ Battalion DWR; killed in action 18 3 1918, aged 32 (Geman Spring Offensive).
Buried – Oxford Road Cemetery, Belgium, 3, D, 7.
Commemorated – the **7 DWR Drill Hall WM panel 7, column 3.**

SMITH, Joseph – 268432 Private.
Enlisted at Leeds.
$2/7^{th}$ Battalion DWR; killed in action 03 5 1917 (Battle of Bullecourt).
Commemorated – Arras Memorial, France, and the **7 DWR Drill Hall WM panel 3, column 2.**

SMITH, Percy – 3700 Private.
Born and enlisted at Bradford.
$1/7^{th}$ Battalion DWR; killed in action 17 8 1916, aged 25 (Battle of the Somme).
Commemorated – Thiepval Memorial, France, and the **7 DWR Drill Hall WM panel 5, column 3.**

SMITH, Percy Edgar – 307540 Private.
Born and resided in Skipton, the husband of Lily Smith, of 20 Sheep Street, Skipton. Enlisted at Keighley.
$1/7^{th}$ Battalion DWR; killed in action 16 3 1918, aged 28.
Buried – Duhallow ADS Cemetery, Belgium, 5, A, 15.
Commemorated – the **7 DWR Drill Hall WM panel 7, column 3.**
Mentioned in S Barber, page 51.
WM shows initials as T E, CPGW shows middle name as Edward.

SMITH, Samuel – 306550 Private.
Son of William H and Hannah Smith. Enlisted at Bradford.
$2/7^{th}$ Battalion DWR; killed in action 03 5 1917 (Battle of Bullecourt).
Commemorated – Arras Memorial, France, and the **7 DWR Drill Hall WM panel 3, column 1.**

SMITH, Thomas – 7180 Lance Corporal.
Born in Berwick-on-Tweed, the son of Mrs Charlotte Wilson Smith, of 13 Quay Walls, Berwick-on-Tweed. Enlisted at Berwick-on-Tweed.
$1/7^{th}$ Battalion DWR; killed in action 18 9 1916, aged 19 (Battle of the Somme).
Buried – Bray Vale British Cemetery, Bray-Sur-Somme, France, 4, B, 24.
Commemorated – the **7 DWR Drill Hall WM panel 5, Column 3.**
Formerly 1568 Private, Northumberland Fusiliers
"WITH CHRIST WHICH IS FAR BETTER"

SMITH, T E - see SMITH, Percy Edgar.
Commemorated – the **7 DWR Drill Hall WM panel 7, column 3.**

CWGC, SDGW & S Barber show forenames as Percy Edgar.

SMITH, Walter – 306915 Private.
Enlisted at Keighley.
2/7th Battalion DWR; killed in action 12 8 1917.
Buried – Noreuil Australian Cemetery, France, G, 15.
Commemorated – the **7 DWR Drill Hall WM panel 1, column 1.**

SMITH, William – 242019 Private.
Born on 25 12 1894 in Lindley, the son of Herbert and Hannah Smith, of 23 Lockwood Scar, Huddersfield. Enlisted at Huddersfield.
2/7th Battalion DWR; killed in action 25 3 1918, aged 23 (German Spring Offensive).
Commemorated – Arras Memorial, France; Emmanuel Church, Lockwood; M Stansfield, page 398, and the **7 DWR Drill Hall WM panel 3, column 2.**
Mentioned in the Huddersfield Examiner (wounded in action) 05 6 1917.

SNELL, Henry – 1650 Private.
Born 1898 in Bristol, the son of Henry and Alice Elizabeth Snell, of 6 Ashton Place, Fame Street, Stalybridge. Resided in Stalybridge. Enlisted at Mossley.
1/7th Battalion DWR, originally F Company; killed in action 03 9 1916, aged 19 (Battle of the Somme, Thiepval).
Commemorated – Thiepval Memorial, France, R Vaughan, page 25, and the **7 DWR Drill Hall WM panel 5, column 1.**

SPACKMAN, Edwin Alfred – 15384 Corporal.
Born in Marylebone, London, the son of John and Elizabeth Spackman, of 109 Hall Place, Paddington. Resided in Lambeth. Enlisted at St Paul's Churchyard, London.
1/7th Battalion DWR; killed in action 13 4 1918, aged 23 (German Spring Offensive).
Commemorated – Tyne Cot Memorial, France, and the **7 DWR Drill Hall WM panel 2, column 2.**
WM shows name as SPACHMAN.

SPEAK, Herbert – 306856 Corporal.
Resided in Mytholmroyd, the son of William and Martha Speak, of 17 Albert Street, Mytholmroyd. Enlisted at Halifax in March, 1916.
2/7th Battalion DWR; killed in action (by sniper) 20 11 1917, aged 28 (Battle of Cambrai).
Commemorated – Cambrai Memorial, France; Mytholmroyd Churchyard; Mount Zion Primitive Methodist Church, Mytholmroyd; CWD, page 577, and the **7 DWR Drill Hall WM panel 7, column 3.**
Mentioned in Hebden Bridge Times 07 12 1917, with photograph, & 22 11 1918.

SPENCER, John – 1302 Lance Corporal.
Born in Loveclough, Lancs, the son of Thomas Rothwell and Annie Amy Sedgwick Spencer, of 'Ulleswater', 54 Dalmorton Road, New Brighton, Cheshire. Resided in Waterfoot. Enlisted into Loyal North Lancashire Regiment at Bolton in May 1910. Transferred to 7th Battalion in 1912.
1/7th Battalion DWR; killed in action 21 6 1915, aged 23.
Buried – Rue-David Military Cemetery, Fleurbaix, France, 1, B, 26.
Commemorated – Saddleworth WM and the **7 DWR Drill Hall WM panel 4, column 1.**

SPENCER, John – 202247 Private.
Born in Queensbury, Yorkshire, the son of George and Mary Ada Spencer, of 29 Mount Tabor, Halifax. Enlisted at Halifax.
1/7th Battalion DWR; died of wounds 25 4 1918, aged 27 (German Spring Offensive).

Commemorated – Tyne Cot Memorial, Belgium; Mount Tabor Wesleyan Methodist Church, Halifax; Halifax Civic Book of Remembrance; CWD, page 257, and the **7 DWR Drill Hall WM panel 7, column 3.**
Mentioned in the Halifax Courier 25 4 1919.

SPENDLOVE, Alfred – 306926 Private.
Born and resided in Hazlewood, Derbyshire, the son of Mrs F Spendlove, of The Post Office, Hazlewood. Enlisted at Derby.
2/7th Battalion DWR; died 06 5 1918 (German Spring Offensive).
Buried – Couin New British Cemetery, France, D, 36.
Commemorated – the **7 DWR Drill Hall WM panel 3, column 1.**

SPICER, Albert – 307486 Private.
Resided in Tividale, Staffs. Enlisted at Oldbury, Birmingham.
1/7th Battalion DWR; killed in action 03 5 1917 (Battle of Bullecourt).
Buried – St Vaast Post Military Cemetery, France, 4, G, 5.
Commemorated – the **7 DWR Drill Hall WM panel 6, column 1.**
Formerly 5424 Gunner, Royal Field Artillery.

SQUIRE, William Henry – 22305 Private.
Resided in Willenhall, Staffs. Enlisted at Bilston.
2/7th Battalion DWR; died of wounds 03 4 1918 (German Spring Offensive).
Buried – Etaples Military Cemetery, France, 33, C, 7A.
Commemorated – the **7 DWR Drill Hall WM panel 2, column 3.**

STANIFORTH, Percy – 307325 Private.
Born in Sheffield. Resided in Eckington. Enlisted at Sheffield.
1/7th Battalion DWR; killed in action 13 4 1918 (German Spring Offensive).
Commemorated – Tyne Cot Memorial, Belgium, and the **7 DWR Drill Hall WM panel 3, column 1.**

STANSFIELD, Harry – 242218 Private.
Born at Bradford. Resided in Southowram, Halifax. Enlisted at Bradford.
1/7th Battalion DWR; killed in action 13 4 1918.
Commemorated – Tyne Cot Memorial, Belgium; CWD page 490 and the **7 DWR Drill Hall WM panel 3, column 1.**
Formerly 27077 Private, King's Own Yorkshire Light Infantry.

STANTON, W - see STENSON, Walter.
Commemorated – **7 DWR Drill Hall WM panel 6, column 1.**
CWGC & SDGW show surname as STENSON.

STEAD, Harry – 307612 Private.
Born in Bradford. Husband of A Stead, of 22 Tumbling Hill Street, Thornton Road, Bradford. Enlisted at Bradford.
2/7th Battalion DWR; killed in action 21 5 1918 (German Spring Offensive).
Buried – Bienvillers Military Cemetery, France, 20, A, 8.
Commemorated – the **7 DWR Drill Hall WM Panel 3, column 2.**

STEELE, Sydney – 26633 Private.
Born in Ashington. Resided 45 Fairbank Road, Bradford. Enlisted at Morpeth.
1/7th Battalion DWR; killed in action, 17 3 1918.
Buried – Duhallow ADS Cemetery, Belgium, 8, F, 20.

Commemorated – the **7 DWR Drill Hall WM panel 2, column 1.**
Originally 1/5th Battalion DWR.
WM shows number as 20635.

STEER, Samuel – 5515 Private.
Son of Samuel and Florence Steer, of 15 Rutland Road, Neepsend, Sheffield. Enlisted at Sheffield.
1/7th Battalion DWR; killed in action 03 7 1916, aged 25 (Battle of the Somme).
Commemorated – Thiepval Memorial, France, and the **7 DWR Drill Hall WM panel 5, column 2.**

STEGGLES, Albert – 307915 Private.
Resided and enlisted at Bradford.
1/7th Battalion DWR; killed in action 08 10 1917 (3rd Battle of Ypres, Passchendaele).
Commemorated – Tyne Cot Memorial, Belgium, and the **7 DWR Drill Hall WM panel 6, column 1.**

STENSON, Walter – 308058 Private.
Born, resided and enlisted at Skipton.
1/7th Battalion DWR; killed in action 08 10 1918 (Advance to Victory).
Commemorated – Tyne Cot Memorial, Belgium, and the **Drill Hall WM panel 6, column 1.**
WM shows name as Stanson.

STENTON, Joseph – 201889 Private.
Resided in Liversedge, the son of George and Emma Stenton, of 18, West View, Hightown Heights, Liversedge. Enlisted at Cleckheaton.
2/7th Battalion DWR; killed in action 13 6 1918, aged 31.
Buried – Bienvillers Military Cemetery, France, 20, D, 5.
Commemorated – Cleckheaton WM and the **7 DWR Drill Hall WM Panel 3, column 1.**
"DEARLY LOVED HUSBAND OF EMMA STENTON, LIVERSEDGE"

STEPHENSON, Alfred – 307791 Lance Corporal.
Resided at 15 Darley Street, Halifax. Husband of Ann Stephenson, of 11 Grant Street, Commercial Road, Halifax. Enlisted at Halifax in August, 1914.
1/7th Battalion DWR; died of wounds 07 5 1918, aged 35 (German Spring Offensive).
Buried – Arneke British Cemetery, France, 2, C, 17.
Commemorated – Halifax Civic Book of Remembrance; CWD, page 259, and the **7 DWR Drill Hall WM Panel 1, column 1.**
Mentioned in the Halifax Weekly Guardian 18 5 1918.
CWGC shows rank as Corporal, CWD shows number as 207791.
"DUTY NOBLY DONE"

STEPHENSON, William – 23518 Private.
Born in Bingley, the son of Robert and Jane Stephenson, of Bingley. Husband of Esther Stephenson, of 905 Talbot Avenue, Elmswood, Winnipeg, Canada. Enlisted at Bingley.
1/7th Battalion DWR; killed in action 28 2 1918, aged 29.
Buried – Oxford Road Cemetery, Belgium, 3, D, 8.
Commemorated – the **7 DWR Drill Hall WM panel 2, column 2.**

STEVENSON, Fred – 5624 Private.
Born in Bradford, the son of John William and Rosetta Stevenson, of 106 Cotewall Road, West Bowling, Bradford. Enlisted at Bradford.
1/7th Battalion DWR; died of wounds 27 7 1916 (Battle of the Somme).
Buried – Etaples Military Cemetery, France, 14, E, 1.
Commemorated – the **7 DWR Drill Hall WM panel 5, column 2.**

"GONE BUT NOT FORGOTTEN"

STEWART, Gordon – 1575 Private.
Born in 1897 in Rawtenstall, Lancashire, the son of George and Janet Stewart, of The Square, Tarland, Aberdeenshire. Enlisted at Mossley. Embarked for France & Flanders on 15 4 1915.
1/7th Battalion DWR; killed in action 28 9 1915, aged 18 (Ypres Salient).
Buried – Bard Cottage Cemetery, Belgium 1, I, 26.
Commemorated – Mossley Town Hall WM; St George's Church WM; Abney Congregational Church RoH and window; R Vaughan, pages 16, 24, 39, 40, 154, 171, and the **7 DWR Drill Hall WM panel 4, column 2.**
Mentioned in the Unit War Diary (killed in action) 28 9 1915.
"MY PRESENCE SHALL GO WITH THEE AND I WILL GIVE THEE REST"

STONEY, Herbert – 3783 Private.
Born and resided in Pateley Bridge, Yorkshire, the son of Mrs Margaret Stoney, of Bewerley, Pateley Bridge. Enlisted at Bradford.
1/7th Battalion DWR, attached 1/5th Battalion KOYLI; killed in action 23 7 1916, aged 28 (Battle of the Somme).
Buried – Authuile Military Cemetery, France, I, 7.
Commemorated – the **7 DWR Drill Hall WM panel 5, column 3.**
"WITH LOVING REMEMBRANCE, FROM MOTHER AND SISTER AND ALL"

STOTT, John William – 307844 Private.
Resided at Moor Hey Farm, Stainland, Halifax. Enlisted at Halifax in August, 1916.
1/7th Battalion DWR; killed in action 25 7 1917, aged 21.
Buried – Ramscappelle Road Military Cemetery, Belgium, 1, B, 11.
Commemorated – St Andrew's Church, Stainland; Providence Congregational Church, Stainland; CWD, page 446, and the **7 DWR Drill Hall WM panel 6, column 3.**
Mentioned in the Huddersfield Examiner (killed in action) 28 8 1917; the Brighouse Echo 17 10 1917.

SUGDEN, George – 307195 Private.
Born, resided and enlisted at Bradford.
1/7th Battalion DWR; killed in action 08 10 1917 (3rd Battle of Ypres, Passchendaele).
Commemorated – Tyne Cot Memorial, France, and the **7 DWR Drill Hall WM panel 6, column 3.**
SDGW shows number as 307185.

SUGDEN, Norman – 306461 Private.
Born and enlisted at Bradford.
1/7th Battalion DWR; killed in action 26 7 1917.
Buried – Ramscappelle Road Military Cemetery, Belgium, 1, B, 13.
Commemorated – the **7 DWR Drill Hall WM panel 6, column 1.**

SULLIVAN, James – 1420 Private.
Born in 1897 in Ashton-under-Lyne. Pre war Territorial, enlisted on 22 5 1913 at Mossley.
1/7th Battalion DWR; killed in action (shellfire) 08 12 1915 (Ypres Salient).
Buried – Bard Cottage Cemetery, Belgium 1, D, 19.
Commemorated – R Vaughan, pages 24 & 43, and the **7 DWR Drill Hall WM panel 4, column 3.**

SUMMERS, Fred – 33430 Private.
Born in Stretford, Manchester, the son of Charles and Fanny Summers, of 8 Meadow Street, Moss Side, Manchester. Enlisted at Manchester.
1/7th Battalion DWR; died of wounds 28 4 1918 (German Spring Offensive).

Buried – Boulogne Eastern Cemetery, France, 9, A, 48.
Commemorated – the **7 DWR Drill Hall WM panel 2, column 3.**
"DUTY CALLED HIM, HE WAS THERE"

SUNDERLAND, Edgar – 306917 Private, Brighouse Tribute Medal.
Resided in Brighouse. Enlisted at Halifax.
2/7th Battalion DWR; killed in action 03 5 1917 (Battle of Bullecourt).
Commemorated – Arras Memorial, France; Brighouse WM; CWD, page 447, and the **7 DWR Drill Hall WM panel 2, column 2.**
Mentioned in the Brighouse Echo 29 6 1917.

SURTEES, Herbert – 3527 Private.
Resided in Meltham, Huddersfield, formerly of Coldwell Street, Hoyle House, Meltham. Enlisted at Milnsbridge.
1/7th Battalion DWR; killed in action 03 7 1916, aged 30 (Battle of the Somme).
Commemorated – Thiepval Memorial, France; St Bartholomew's Church, Meltham; M Stansfield, page 410, and the **7 DWR Drill Hall WM panel 4, column 3.**

SUTCLIFFE, George (Grant) – 4492 (later 306913) Private.
Resided in Shaw Terrace, Ripponden. Enlisted at Halifax.
2/7th Battalion DWR; died of wounds at Rouen General Hospital on 15 5 1917.
Buried – St Sever Cemetery Extension, Rouen, France, P, 2, O, 10A.
Commemorated – Ripponden WM; St Bartholomew's Church, Ripponden; Soyland UDC Memorial; J Fisher, page 115; CWD, page 583, and the **7 DWR Drill Hall WM panel 1, column 3.**
Mentioned in the Huddersfield Examiner (killed in action) 27 8 1918; the Hebden Bridge Times 25 5 1917 & the Halifax Courier 12 6 1917.

SUTCLIFFE, Harold – 306956 Private.
Enlisted at Sheffield.
2/7th Battalion DWR; killed in action 27 11 1917 (Battle of Cambrai).
Commemorated – Cambrai Memorial, Louverval, France, and the **7 DWR Drill Hall WM panel 1, column 3.**

SUTCLIFFE, Thomas Henry – 308190 Private.
Resided in Luddendenfoot, Yorkshire, the nephew of John Thomas, of Springfield, Midgley, Luddendenfoot. Enlisted at Halifax in March, 1916. Embarked for France & Flanders in January, 1917.
2/7th Battalion DWR; died of wounds (shrapnel to lungs) 17 9 1917, aged 36 (Battle of the Somme).
Buried – Favreuil British Cemetery, France, 1, F, 21.
Commemorated – Providence United Methodist Church, Midgley; Luddenden & Midgley WM; CWD, page 584, and the **7 DWR Drill Hall WM panel 7, column 2.**
Mentioned in the Hebden Bridge Times 05 10 1917 & Halifax Weekly Guardian 06 10 1917.
"HE DIED FOR FREEDOM"

SWAINE, Samuel – 306753 Private.
Enlisted at Bradford.
2/7th Battalion DWR; killed in action 25 6 1917.
Buried – Adanac Military Cemetery, Miraumont, France, 4, H, 21.
Commemorated – R Vaughan, page 25, and the **7 DWR Drill Hall WM panel 7, column 1.**

SWAN, Robert – 302184 Private.
Resided and enlisted at Halifax.
8th Battalion DWR; killed in action 11 8 1917 (3rd Battle of Ypres, Passchendaele).

Commemorated – Ypres (Menin Gate) Memorial, Belgium, Northowram WM, CWD, page 265, and the **7 DWR Drill Hall WM panel 6, column 1.**
WM shows name as SWANN R and number as 307185.

SWIFT, Sydney – 3668 Private.
Born and enlisted at Bradford.
1/7th Battalion DWR; killed in action 04 7 1916 (Battle of the Somme).
Commemorated – Thiepval Memorial, France and the **7 DWR Drill Hall WM panel 5, column 1.**

SWIFT, W – 2nd Lieutenant.
West Yorkshire Regiment, attached to 1/7th Battalion DWR; killed in action 11 01 1918.
Buried – Wellington Cemetery, Rieux-en-Cambresis, 1, E, 10.
Commemorated – the **7 DWR Drill Hall WM panel 3, column 3.**
Mentioned in the Unit War Diary (joined the Bn) 30 4 1918, (killed in action) 13 10 1918; HDH Album 7 DWR (joined Bn) page 35 & (killed in action) page 39.

SWITHENBANK, Harry – 203785 Private.
Born at Bradford, the son of Mr C and Mrs S Swithenbank of Springfield Farm, Hodgson Lane, Birkenshaw, Bradford. Enlisted at Bradford.
1/7th Battalion DWR; killed in action 11 10 1918, aged 34 (Advance to Victory, Battle of Iwuy).
Buried – Wellington Cemetery, Rieux-En-Cambresis, 2, A, 9.
Commemorated - the **7 DWR Drill Hall WM panel 1, column 1.**
"THY WILL, BE DONE"

SYKES, David – 2316 Private.
Resided in Elms Hill, Slaithwaite, Huddersfield, and 273, Brierley Wood, Huddersfield. Enlisted at Milnsbridge.
1/7th Battalion DWR; died of wounds (head and leg) at No 13 General Hospital on 29 9 1915, aged 29 (Ypres Salient).
Buried – Boulogne Eastern Cemetery, France, 8, B, 87.
Commemorated – Slaithwaite WM; St James's Church, Slaithwaite; M Stansfield ,page 414, and the **7 DWR Drill Hall WM panel 4, column 2.**
Mentioned in the Huddersfield Examiner (died of wounds) 15 10 1915.

SYKES, David – 235098 Private.
Born at Lepton, Huddersfield, the son of John and Mary Sykes, of Green Balk Lane, Lepton, Huddersfield. Enlisted at Huddersfield.
2/7th Battalion DWR; killed in action 26 3 1918, aged 37 (German Spring Offensive).
Buried – Hannescamps New Military Cemetery, France, C, 17.
Commemorated – Lepton Parish Church; M Stansfield, page 414, and the **7 DWR Drill Hall WM panel 3, column 2.**
"THERE'S SOMEONE WHO THINKS OF YOU ALWAYS AND TRIED HARD TO BE CONTENT"

SYKES, Edgar – 2746 Private.
Born and resided in Slaithwaite, Huddersfield, the son of Allen Sykes, of Holme, Slaithwaite. Resided in Hollins Glen, Slaithwaite. Previously a local Territorial. Embarked for France & Flanders in April, 1915.
1/7th Battalion DWR; died (gassed and drowned) 19 12 1915, aged 21 (Ypres Salient).
Buried – Bard Cottage Cemetery, Belgium 1, A, 28.
Commemorated – Slaithwaite WM; St James's Church, Slaithwaite; J Fisher, page 110; M Stansfield, page 415, and the **7 DWR Drill Hall WM panel 4, column 3.**
"DEARLY LOVED"

SYKES, France – 305462 Corporal.
Resided in Marsden, Huddersfield, the son of Mrs Mary Ellen Dyson, of 13 North View Cottages, Marsden. Enlisted at Milnsbridge on 12 8 1914. Embarked for France & Flanders in January, 1917.
2/7th Battalion DWR; killed in action 03 5 1917, aged 19 (Battle of Bullecourt).
Commemorated – Arras Memorial, France; Memorial in Marsden Churchyard; CVA; M Stansfield, page 416, and the **7 DWR Drill Hall WM panel 1, column 1.**
Mentioned in the Huddersfield Examiner (killed in action) 01 6 1917.

SYKES, Harry – 306582 Private.
Son of Mrs M Sykes, of 13 Portland Street, Low Moor, Bradford. Enlisted at Bradford.
2/7th Battalion DWR; died of wounds 20 4 1918 (German Spring Offensive).
Buried – Bienvillers Military Cemetery, France, 13, B, 1.
Commemorated - the **7 DWR Drill Hall WM panel 7, column 3.**

SYKES, Herbert – 3971 Private.
Born in Linthwaite, the son of Bradley and Mrs Sykes of Coldwell Street, Linthwaite. Resided in Linthwaite, Huddersfield. Enlisted at Milnsbridge in March, 1916.
1/7th Battalion DWR; killed in action 14 7 1916, aged 19 (Battle of the Somme).
Commemorated – Thiepval Memorial, France; Linthwaite WM; M Stansfield, page 419, and the **7 DWR Drill Hall WM panel 5, column 2.**

SYKES, John William – 306629 Lance Corporal.
Enlisted at Bradford.
2/7th Battalion DWR; killed in action 03 5 1917 (Battle of Bullecourt).
Commemorated – Arras Memorial, France, and the **7 DWR Drill Hall WM panel 1, column 3.**

SYKES, Norman – 1044 Sergeant.
Born in Marsden, Huddersfield, the son of Hiram and Mary Sykes, of Church Avenue, Linthwaite. Enlisted at Slaithwaite in the local 2nd Volunteer Battalion in 1903, transferred to 7th Battalion (TF) in 1906, discharged in 1909. Re enlisted in April, 1916, with rank of Corporal and promoted to Sergeant in September, 1915. Embarked for France & Flanders in April, 1915.
1/7th Battalion DWR; died of wounds at Forward Dressing Station on 17 10 1915, aged 28 (Ypres Salient).
Buried – Ferme-Olivier Cemetery, Belgium, 2, K, 1.
Commemorated – Linthwaite WM; M Stansfield, page 422, and the **7 DWR Drill Hall WM panel 4, column 1.**
Mentioned in the Unit War Diary (died of wounds) 15 10 1915.
"SON OF HIRAM AND MARY SYKES: THY WILL, BE DONE"

TATTERSALL, James Ormerod – 307477 Private.
Born at Stackstead, Lancs, the son of James and Mary Ann Tattersall, of Barnoldswick. Enlisted at Barnoldswick.
1/7th Battalion DWR; killed in action 14 2 1917, aged 23.
Commemorated – Tyne Cot Memorial, Belgium; CPGW, page 328, with photograph, and the **7 DWR Drill Hall WM panel 7, column 1.**
Mentioned in P Thompson, page 175.

TAYLOR, Anthony – 16799 Private.
Born and resided in Berwick-on-Tweed. Enlisted at Newcastle-on-Tyne.
2/7th Battalion DWR; killed in action 28 11 1917 (Battle of Cambrai).
Commemorated – Cambrai Memorial, Louverval, France, and the **7 DWR Drill Hall WM panel 2, column 1.**

TAYLOR, Frank – 26641 Private.
Born at Wheldrake, York, the son of John Henry and Jessie Taylor. Resided in Wheldrake. Enlisted at York.
1/7th Battalion DWR; died of wounds 06 5 1918 (German Spring Offensive).
Buried – Boulogne Eastern Cemetery, France, B, 51.
Commemorated – the **7 DWR Drill Hall WM panel 2, column 3.**

TAYLOR, James – 30573 Private.
Resided in Oldham, the husband of Alice Ann Taylor, of 52 Quail Street, Oldham. Enlisted at Milnsbridge.
1/7th Battalion DWR; killed in action 13 4 1918 (German Spring Offensive).
Commemorated – Tyne Cot Memorial, Belgium; Saddleworth WM and the **7 DWR Drill Hall WM panel 6, column 1.**

TAYLOR, Jabez William – 29986 Private.
Born in Meltham. Enlisted at Huddersfield.
2/7th Battalion DWR; died 26 3 1918 (German Spring Offensive).
Buried – Pommier Communal Cemetery, France, 1.
Commemorated – St Bartholomew's Church, Meltham; M Stansfield, page 429, and the **7 DWR Drill Hall WM panel 2, column 3.**
WM shows initials as J E; SDGW & M Stansfield show names as Jabez William.

TAYLOR, John Thomas – 790 Private.
Son of Walter Taylor of Handel Street, Golcar. Enlisted at Milnsbridge, a local pre-war Territorial for 4 years.
1/7th Battalion DWR; killed in action 22 10 1915, aged 22 (Ypres Salient).
Buried – Talana Farm Cemetery, Belgium, 4, C, 18.
Commemorated – Longwood WM; St John's Church Golcar; M Stansfield, page 430, and the **7 DWR Drill Hall WM panel 4, column 2.**

TAYLOR, John William – 4667 (later 307045) Private.
Son of Owen Harrison and Mary Taylor, of 149 Maperton Road, Bradford. Enlisted at Bradford.
2/7th Battalion DWR; died of wounds 15 4 1917, aged 20 (Hindenburg Line).
Buried – Mory Abbey Military Cemetery, Mory, France, 1, B, 3.
Commemorated – the **7 DWR Drill Hall WM panel 1, column 2.**
See Shell Hole Boy poem, page 168.

TAYLOR, Joseph – 1907 (later 305503) Lance Corporal.
Born in 1881 in Mossley, the son of James and Ellen Taylor. Husband of Elizabeth Ellen Taylor, of 12 Hopkins Buildings, Roaches, Mossley, Manchester. Enlisted on 01 9 1914 at Mossley.
1/7th Battalion DWR; killed in action 18 9 1916, aged 35 (Battle of the Somme).
Commemorated – Thiepval Memorial, Somme, France; Mossley Town Hall WM; St John the Baptist Church WM; St Augustine's Church RoH; Methodist Sunday School RoH; R Vaughan, page 61, and the **7 DWR Drill Hall WM panel 6, column 2.**

TAYLOR, William – 307333 Private.
Born in Filey, the son of George and Ellen Taylor, of 7 Cromwell Avenue, Filey.
1/7th Battalion DWR; killed in action 13 4 1918, aged 25 (German Spring Offensive).
Commemorated – Tyne Cot Memorial, Belgium, and the **7 DWR Drill Hall WM panel 7, column 3.**
Formerly 26912 Private, King's Own Yorkshire Light Infantry.

TERRY, William Edward – 241496 Private.
Born in Eccleshill. Enlisted at Bradford.
1/7th Battalion DWR; died 13 4 1918.
Commemorated – Tyne Cot Memorial, Belgium, and the **7 DWR Drill Hall WM panel 3, column 1.**
WM shows name as TURRET W H, number as 242496.

TETLOW, Luke Mallinson – Lieutenant.
Son of John and Florence Tetlow, of Prospect Mills, Cleckheaton, Yorkshire. Enlisted at Cleckheaton, commissioned May 1915.
1/7th Battalion DWR, B Company; killed in action (gunshot wound to head) 30 5 1915, aged 21.
Buried – Rue-David Military Cemetery, Fleurbaix, France, 1, A, 20.
Commemorated – Cleckheaton WM; Whitechapel Church, Cleckheaton; J Fisher, page 133, and the **7 DWR Drill Hall WM panel 4, column 1.**
Mentioned in the Unit War Diary (killed in action) 30 5 1915; the Huddersfield Examiner (in memoriam) 30 5 1916 & 29 5 1918; HDH Album 7 DWR Volume 2, pages 4 & 5, G Tetlow, page 5.
"WHO DIES IF ENGLAND LIVES"

THEOBALD, George Herbert – 33806 Private.
Born at Warley, Brentwood, the son of Alfred and Alice Theobald, of Thruxted Farm, Chatham, Canterbury. Enlisted at Scarborough.
1/7th Battalion DWR; died of wounds 12 10 1918, aged 19 (Advance to Victory).
Buried – Bucquoy Road Cemetery, Ficheux, France, 3, F, 10.
Commemorated – the **7 DWR Drill Hall WM panel 2, column 2.**
Formerly 67543 Private, Royal West Surrey Regiment.

THOMAS, Walton – 13603 Private.
Born in Burley-in-Wharfedale, the son of John Mason and Alice Thomas, of Elm Tree, Burley-in-Wharfedale. Enlisted at Ilkley.
1/7th Battalion DWR, C Company; killed in action 12 4 1918, aged 22 (German Spring Offensive).
Commemorated – Tyne Cot Memorial, Belgium, and the **7 DWR Drill Hall WM panel 2, column 3.**
Also served in the 10th Battalion, see - **tunstillsmen.blogspot.com** (last accessed August, 2020).

THOMPSON, Frank – 306602 Private.
Husband of Hettie Thompson, of 14 Beacon Street, Old Road, Great Horton, Bradford. Enlisted at Bradford.
2/7th Battalion DWR; killed in action 03 5 1917, aged 23 (Battle of Bullecourt).
Commemorated – Arras Memorial, France, and the **7 DWR Drill Hall WM panel 2, column 2.**

THOMPSON, James Tennant – 5281 (later 7200 & 308047) Corporal.
Born in Skipton, the son of Thomas Benjamin and Jane Thompson. Enlisted at Keighley.
1/7th Battalion DWR; killed in action 29 4 1918, aged 24 (German Spring Offensive).
Commemorated – Tyne Cot Memorial, Belgium; CPGW, page 379, and the **7 DWR Drill Hall WM panel 6, column 2.**

THORNBORROW, John – 26406 Private.
Born in Shropshire, the son of Thomas Steele and Jane Thornborrow, of 19 Woodhouse Lane, Horsehay, Shropshire. Enlisted at Ironbridge.
2/7th Battalion DWR; died of wounds 07 7 1918.
Buried – Les Baraques Military Cemetery, Sangatte, France, 4, C, 12.
Commemorated – Dawley, Horsay & Dosley WMs, Salop, and the **7 DWR Drill Hall WM panel 3, column 2.**
"DEEPLY MOURNED AND SADLY MISSED BY HIS MOTHER AND SISTER NELL"

THORP, John Eric – 2nd Lieutenant, Territorial Force War Medal.
Son of John William and Clara E Thorp, of 49 Grasmere Road, Huddersfield. Pre war Territorial.
2/7th Battalion DWR, attached to 186th Light Trench Mortar Battery; died 03 5 1917, aged 26 (Hindenburg Line).
Buried – Queant Road Cemetery, Buissy, France, 2, F, 26.
Commemorated – the **7 DWR Drill Hall WM panel 3, column 3.**
Mentioned in the Unit War Diary (gazetted to 2/7th DWR) 28 8 1915.
Formerly 1128 Company Quartermaster Sergeant, 5 DWR.
Territorial Force War Medal awarded posthumously, 07 2 1923.
WM shows name as THORPE.
"UNTIL THE MORNING DAWNS AND SHADOWS FLEE AWAY"

THORPE, George – 26430 Private.
Born in Woburn Green, Buckinghamshire. Resided in Caversham, Oxfordshire. Enlisted at Caversham.
2/7th Battalion DWR; killed in action 28 11 1917 (Battle of Cambrai).
Commemorated – Cambrai Memorial, Louverval, France, and the **7 DWR Drill Hall WM panel 2, column 3.**
Formerly 25354 Private, Royal Berkshire Regiment & 95777 Private, Labour Corps.
WM shows name as SHARPE.

TIDSWELL, Harry – 22799 Private.
Resided in Halifax, the son of Samuel and Emma Tidswell, of 56 Ellison Street, Lee Mount, Halifax. Enlisted at Halifax.
2/7th Battalion DWR; killed in action 03 5 1917, aged 22 (Battle of Bullecourt).
Commemorated – Arras Memorial, France, and the **7 DWR Drill Hall WM panel 2, column 3.**
WM shows initial as G and number as 23799.

TIDSWELL, Harry – 306895 Private.
Enlisted at Halifax.
2/7th Battalion DWR; killed in action 03 5 1917 (Battle of Bullecourt).
Commemorated – Arras Memorial; Halifax Civic Book of Remembrance; CWD, page 273, and the **7 DWR Drill Hall WM panel 2, column 3.**

TOMLINSON, Francis Edgar – 1257 Lance Corporal.
Born and resided in Linthwaite, Huddersfield, the son of Mr Ed and Clara Jane Tomlinson, of Flathouse, 583 Jovil, Linthwaite. Enlisted at Slaithwaite in May, 1912. Pre war local Territorial, mobilised on 05 8 1914. Embarked for France & Flanders in April, 1915.
1/7th Battalion DWR, Machine Gun Section; killed in action 16 5 1916.
Buried – Rue-David Military Cemetery, Fleurbaix, 1, B, 25.
Commemorated –Linthwaite WM; M Stansfield, page 443, and the **7 DWR Drill Hall WM panel 4, column 3.**
Mentioned in the 1/5th DWR Unit War Diary (killed in action) 15 5 1915; the Huddersfield Examiner (killed in action) 21 5 1915.

TOWLER, Albert Edward – 307569 Private.
Born at Brindle, Lancs. Husband of Martha Ann Towler, of 83 Park Road, Thackley, Idle, Bradford. Enlisted at Bradford.
1/7th Battalion DWR, C Company; killed in action 11 10 1917, aged 26 (3rd Battle of Ypres, Passchendaele).
Commemorated – Tyne Cot Memorial and the **7 DWR Drill Hall WM panel 6, column 3.**
WD shows number as 307567.

TOWNLEY, William – 306201 Private.
Resided in Oldham. Enlisted at Greenfield.
1/7th Battalion DWR; killed in action 17 3 1918.
Buried – Duhallow ADS Cemetery, Belgium, 9, C, 10.
Commemorated – the **7 DWR Drill Hall WM panel 7, column 1.**

TOWNSEND, Edward – 307024 Private.
Brother of William Townsend, of 84 Lonsdale Street, Bradford. Enlisted at Bradford. Embarked for France & Flanders in Jan 1917.
2/7th Battalion DWR; killed in action 27 11 1917, aged 37 (Battle of Cambrai).
Commemorated – Cambrai Memorial, Louverval, France, and the **7 DWR Drill Hall WM panel 2, column 1.**

TOWNSEND, William – 305294 Private.
Born in 1897 in Mossley, the son of Mr M A Townsend, of 2 Lees Road, Mossley. Enlisted at Mossley. Embarked for France & Flanders in Jan 1917.
2/7th Battalion DWR; died of wounds 08 5 1917 (Hindenburg Line).
Buried – Achiet-Le-Grand Communal Cemetery Extension, France 1, F, 10.
Commemorated – St George's Church WM; St John the Baptist Church WM; United Methodist Church WM; R Vaughan, pages 77, 160 & 161, and the **7 DWR Drill Hall WM panel 1, column 3.**
"AT THE GOING DOWN OF THE SUN AND IN THE MORNING WE WILL REMEMBER THEM"

TUCKER, Robert Bruce – 242927 Private.
Resided in Holmbridge, the son of Mrs Tucker of Damhouse, Holmfirth, Huddersfield. Enlisted at Halifax on 05 7 1916. Embarked for France & Flanders in October, 1916.
1/7th Battalion DWR; killed in action 29 4 1918 (German Spring Offensive).
Buried – Klein-Vierstraat British Cemetery, Belgium, 5, C, 11.
Commemorated – Memorial Hospital (Holme and Holmbridge plaque) WM; M Stansfield, page 447, and the **7 DWR Drill Hall WM panel 6, column 3.**

TUNNACLIFFE, James – 305660 Private.
Resided in Stalybridge. Enlisted at Milnsbridge.
10th Battalion DWR (from 2/7th DWR); killed in action 20 9 1917 (Veldhoek).
Commemorated – Tyne Cot Memorial, Belgium; Stalybridge WM and the **7 DWR Drill Hall WM panel 7, column 2.**
Also served in the 10th Battalion, see - **tunstillsmen.blogspot.com** (last accessed August, 2020).
WM shows name as TUNNACLIFE.

TURNER, John – 267821 Private.
Resided in Denshaw. Enlisted at Shaw, Oldham.
2/7th Battalion DWR; killed in action 03 5 1917 (Battle of Bullecourt).
Commemorated – Arras Memorial, France; Saddleworth WM and the **7 DWR Drill Hall WM panel 3, column 1.**
Mentioned in the Huddersfield Examiner (reported missing) 17 6 1917.

TURNER, Lewis – 306836 Private.
Son of Miles and Mary Turner, of 36 Moorfield Street, Halifax. Resided at 44, King Cross Street, Halifax. Husband of Emma Jane Turner, of 10 Osborne Grove, Lightcliffe, Halifax. Enlisted at Halifax in March, 1916.
2/7th Battalion DWR; killed in action 29 5 1918, aged 30 (German Spring Offensive).
Buried – Bienvillers Military Cemetery, France, 21, A, 5.

Commemorated – St Paul's Church, King Cross, Halifax; Halifax Civic Book of Remembrance; CWD, page 276, and the **7 DWR Drill Hall WM Panel 3, column 2.**
Mentioned in the Halifax Weekly Guardian, with photograph, 15 6 1918.
"UNTIL THE DAY BREAKS AND THE SHADOWS FLEE AWAY"

TURNER, Samuel – 308096 Private.
Son of George and Jane Turner, of 5E Ivy House Lane, Coseley, Bilston, Staffs. Enlisted at Wolverhampton.
2/7th Battalion DWR, D Company; killed in action 27 11 1917 (Battle of Cambrai).
Commemorated – Cambrai Memorial, Louverval, France, and the **7 DWR Drill Hall WM panel 1, column 2.**

TURRET, W H – see **TERRY, William Edward.**
Commemorated – the **7 DWR Drill Hall WM panel 3, column 1.**
CWGC shows name as TERRY William Edward.

UTTLEY, Sidney – 1853 Corporal.
Born in Marsden, Huddersfield, the son of William and Emily Uttley, of Bankfield, Manchester Road, Marsden. Enlisted at Milnsbridge in August, 1914. Served four years as Territorial.
1/7th Battalion DWR; died of wounds at No 10 CCS on 24 7 1915, aged 30 (Ypres Salient).
Buried – Lijssenthoek Military Cemetery, Belgium, 4, A, 18.
Commemorated – Marsden WM; M Stansfield, page 450, and the **7 DWR Drill Hall WM panel 4, column 1.**

VARLEY, Joe – 1174 Lance Sergeant.
Born in Marsden, Huddersfield, the son of Luke and Agnes Varley, of 28 Plains, Marsden. Enlisted at Slaithwaite in August, 1914. Embarked for France & Flanders in April, 1915.
1/7th Battalion DWR; killed in action 20 9 1915, aged 20 (Ypres Slaient).
Buried – Bard Cottage Cemetery, Belgium, 1, H, 22.
Commemorated – Marsden WM; M Stansfield, page 451, and the **7 DWR Drill Hall WM panel 4, column 1.**
Mentioned in the Unit War Diary (killed in action) 20 9 1915; the Huddersfield Examiner (killed in action) 28 9 1915.
"GOD MOVES IN A MYSTERIOUS WAY"

WADSWORTH, J – 2774 Corporal.
See POGSON, John Wadsworth – 2774 Corporal, listed on panel 4, column 1.
Commemorated – the **7 DWR Drill Hall WM panel 5, column 2.**

WAGSTAFF, John William – 1147 Corporal.
Born on 05 11 1893 at Newsome, the son of Joseph and Emma Wagstaff, of 33 Cliffe End Road, Longwood, Huddersfield. Enlisted at Milnsbridge on 10 7 1911. Pre war local Territorial, mobilised on 05 8 1914. Embarked for France & Flanders in April, 1915.
1/7th Battalion DWR; killed in action 01 10 1915, aged 21 (Ypres Salient).
Buried – Bard Cottage Cemetery, Belgium, 1, I, 28.
Commemorated – St Mark's Parish Church, Longwood; Salendine Nook Baptist Church; M Stansfield, page 456, and the **7 DWR Drill Hall WM panel 4, column 1.**
Mentioned in the Unit War Diary (killed in action) 01 10 1915; the Huddersfield Examiner (killed in action) 06 10 1915.
"JESUS IN THY PRECIOUS KEEPING, WE NOW LEAVE OUR LOVED ONES SLEEPING"

WAITE, Harry – 5636 Private.
Son of M M and Sarah Ann Waite, of 2 Binns Street, Bingley. Enlisted at Bingley.
1/7th Battalion DWR; died of wounds 28 8 1916, aged 23 (Battle of the Somme).
Buried – Bingley Cemetery, Yorkshire, F4, 48.
Commemorated – the **7 DWR Drill Hall WM panel 4, column 3.**

WAKEFIELD, Herbert William Harold – 306935 Private.
Son of George and Kate Margaret Wakefield, of 25 Osborne Street, Radford, Nottingham. Enlisted at Nottingham.
2/7th Battalion DWR; killed in action 14 5 1917 aged 27 (Hindenburg Line).
Commemorated – Arras Memorial, France, and the **7 DWR Drill Hall WM panel 6, column 2.**
WM shows initials as A W H.

WALFORD, Richard – 5539 Private.
Born in Heckmondwike, the son of William Henry and Anastasia Walford, of 63A Common Road, Staincliffe, Batley. Enlisted at Batley.
1/7th Battalion DWR; killed in action 03 9 1916, aged 23 (Battle of the Somme, Thiepval).
Commemorated – Thiepval Memorial, France, and the **7 DWR Drill Hall WM panel 5, column 1.**

WALKER, Ernest – 205414 Private.
Born in Huddersfield. Resided in Golcar, Huddersfield, the son of Joe and Mary Elizabeth Walker, of Linthwaite. Husband of Annie Walker, of 14 Lowestwood, Golcar. Enlisted at Huddersfield.
1/7th Battalion DWR; died of wounds 03 5 1918, aged 29 (German Spring Offensive).
Buried – Esquelbecq Military Cemetery, France, 2, B, 30.
Commemorated – St John's Church, Golcar; M Stanfield, page 457, and the **7 DWR Drill Hall WM panel 7, column 3.**
"THY WILL, BE DONE"

WALKER, Frederick – 16524 Private, Military Medal.
Born at Ryhope, County Durham, the son of James and Margaret Walker, of St Paul's Terrace, Ryhope. Resided at Ryhope. Enlisted at Sunderland.
1/7th Battalion DWR; killed in action 29 4 1918 (German Spring Offensive).
Buried – La Clytte Military Cemetery, Belgium, 5, C, 12.
Commemorated – the **7 DWR Drill Hall WM panel 2, column 1.**
Formerly 17709 Trooper, Hussars.
Mentioned in the London Gazette (MM award) 07 10 1918, page 11838; L Magnus (MM award) page 257.
"TILL THE DAY BREAKS AND THE SHADOWS FLEE AWAY"

WALKER, George William Quarmby – Lieutenant.
Son of Benjamin Henry Sykes Walker and Hannah Walker, of 'Croft House', Slaithwaite, Huddersfield. Commissioned 10 1914.
1/7th Battalion DWR; killed in action (shellfire) 07 7 1916, aged 20 (Battle of the Somme).
Buried – Authuile Military Cemetery, France, H, 12.
Commemorated – Slaithwaite War MM; St James's Church, Slaithwaite; J Fisher, pages 107, 119 & 133; M Stansfield, page 457, and the **7 DWR Drill Hall WM panel 4, column 1.**
Mentioned in the Unit War Diary (promoted Lieutenant) 28 2 1916, (killed in action) 07 7 1916; the Huddersfield Examiner (killed in action) 13 7 1916, (in memoriam) 08 7 1918; HDH Album 7 DWR Volume 2, (killed in action) page 13.
"FOR WHAT IS OUR HOPE OR JOY OR CROWN OF REJOICING"

WALKER, James – 1278 Lance Corporal.
Born and resided in Stalybridge, the son of Sam and Sarah Jane Walker. Enlisted at Mossley.
1/7th Battalion DWR; died of wounds 28 12 1915, aged 19 (Ypres Salient).
Buried – Etaples Military Cemetery, France, 6, B, 25.
Commemorated – Stalybridge WM; J Fisher, page 110, and the **7 DWR Drill Hall WM panel 4, column 1.**
"THERE IS A LINK DEATH CANNOT SEVER, LOVE AND REMEMBRANCE LAST FOR EVER"

WALKER, John – 2007 Private.
Son of John and Sarah Walker, of Amber Hill, Nr Boston, Lincs. Resided at Bridge Street, Slaithwaite. Enlisted at Slaithwaite in August, 1914.
1/7th Battalion DWR; died (heart failure) at No 2 West Riding Field Ambulance Dressing Station on 05 11 1915, aged 42.
Buried – Ferme-Olivier Cemetery, Belgium, 1, H, 2.
Commemorated – Slaithwaite WM; St James's Church, Slaithwaite; M Stansfield, page 458, and the **7 DWR Drill Hall WM panel 4, column 3.**

WALKER, Joseph – 306650 Private.
Enlisted at Bradford.
2/7th Battalion DWR; killed in action 25 3 1918 (German Spring Offensive).
Commemorated – Arras Memorial, France, and the **7 DWR Drill Hall WM panel 7, column 1.**

WALKER, Samuel – 2897 Private.
Resided in Stalybridge, the son of James and Annie Walker, of Ashton-under-Lyne. Husband of Amelia Walker, of 1 Hutchinson Buildings, Stalybridge. Enlisted at Milnsbridge.
1/7th Battalion DWR; killed in action 03 9 1916, aged 24 (Battle of the Somme, Thiepval).
Buried – Connaught Cemetery, Thiepval, France, 12, M, 7.
Commemorated – Stalybridge WM and the **7 DWR Drill Hall WM panel 5, Column 1.**

WALKER, Walter Mellnotte – 306501 Private.
Resided at 2 Cooper Lane, Shelf, Halifax. Enlisted at Bradford.
2/7th Battalion DWR; killed in action 03 5 1917 (Battle of Bullecourt).
Commemorated – Arras Memorial, France; St Michael's Church, Shelf; Shelf Primitive Methodist Church; CWD, page 457, and the **7 DWR Drill Hall WM panel 2, column 1.**
Mentioned in the Halifax Weekly Guardian 30 3 1918.

WALLER, Charles Edward – 203918 Private.
Born at Kearby, Yorkshire. Resided in Huddersfield, the son of Maria Louisa and William Brown (stepfather), of Roehead, Mirfield. Enlisted at Mirfield.
1/7th Battalion DWR; died of wounds (gas) 28 4 1918, aged 20 (German Spring Offensive).
Buried – Boulogne Eastern Cemetery, France, 9, A, 39.
Commemorated – the **7 DWR Drill Hall WM panel 7, column 1.**
"REST IN PEACE"

WALSH, John James – 306108 Private.
Born at Saddleworth, the son of John and Amy Walsh, of Lee Street, Uppermill, Oldham. Resided in Uppermill. Enlisted at Milnsbridge.
2/7th Battalion DWR; died of wounds 21 5 1917, aged 26 (Hindenburg Line).
Buried – Boulogne Eastern Cemetery, France, 4, B, 34.
Commemorated – Pots and Pans (Uppermill section) WM, St Chad's Church, Uppermill, Saddleworth Church Magazine, 1917; and the **7 DWR Drill Hall WM panel 1, column 1.**

WM shows name as J Walsh, SDGW shows name as James Walsh, CWGC shows name as John James Walsh (known as James).

WALSH, Joseph – 306300 Private.
Born in 1892 in Mossley. Resided in Mossley. Enlisted at Milnsbridge.
2/7th Battalion DWR; killed in action 28 11 1917, aged 25 (Battle of Cambrai).
Commemorated – Cambrai Memorial, Louverval, France; R Vaughan, pages 105 & 153, and the **7 DWR Drill Hall WM panel 7, column 3.**
Mentioned in a letter from Lieutenant B J Trowsdale to the family, 12 1917.

WALSH, Maurice – 26357 Private.
Born in Ballyporeen, County Tipperary, the son of Maurice and Mary O'Brien Walsh, of Carrigavistale, Ballyporeen. Enlisted at Clonmel, Ireland.
2/7th Battalion DWR; died of wounds 09 12 1917 (Battle of Cambrai).
Buried – St Sever Cemetery Extension, Rouen, France, P, 5, M, 6A.
Commemorated - the **7 DWR Drill Hall WM panel 2, column 2.**
Formerly 35800 Private, Army Service Corps.

WALSH, Thomas – 306532 Private.
Son of Michael and Mary Walsh, of 6 Royle Fold, Heckmondwike. Enlisted at Heckmondwike.
2/7th Battalion DWR; killed in action 03 5 1917, aged 32 (Battle of Bullecourt).
Buried – Ecoust Military Cemetery, Ecoust St Mein, France, 1, A, 12.
Commemorated – Cawley's Ltd (Spenborough Guardian 11 1919) and the **7 DWR Drill Hall WM panel 1, column 1.**

WARD, Edwin – 306668 Private.
Son of Sam and Louise Ward, of 3 North Wing, Bradford. Husband of Ada Ward, of 34 Bennerley Road, Wandsworth, London. Resided in Camberwell. Enlisted at Bradford.
2/7th Battalion DWR; killed in action 14 5 1917, aged 30 (Hindenburg Line).
Commemorated – Arras Memorial and the **7 DWR Drill Hall WM panel 7, column 3.**
WM shows number as 306688 [306688 is Lance Corporal Harry West – see below].

WAREING, Joseph – 2286 Private.
Resided in Oldham. Enlisted at Milnsbridge.
1/7th Battalion DWR; killed in action 28 9 1915 (Ypres Sector).
Buried – Bard Cottage Cemetery, Belgium 1, I, 27.
Commemorated – Saddleworth WM and the **7 DWR Drill Hall WM panel 4, column 2.**

WARING Sydney – 7000 Private.
Enlisted at Dewsbury.
1/7th Battalion DWR; killed in action 17 11 1916 (Battle of the Somme).
Buried – Foncquevillers Military Cemetery, France, 1, H, 8.
Commemorated – the **7 DWR Drill Hall WM panel 6, column 3.**

WARRINGTON, Albert – 24795 Corporal.
Born in Halifax, the son of William and Annie Warrington, of 13 Ainley Bottom, Elland. Enlisted at Elland.
1/7th Battalion DWR; died of wounds 15 4 1918, aged 25 (German Spring Offensive).
Buried – Boulogne Eastern Cemetery, France, 8, I, 197.
Commemorated – Elland WM; Elland Providence Congregational Church; CWD, page 459, and the **7 DWR Drill Hall WM panel 2, column 2.**
Mentioned in the Brighouse Echo 31 5 1918.

"THY WILL, BE DONE"

WARRINGTON, Benjamin – 306820 Private, Brighouse Tribute Medal.
Resided in Delf Hill, Rastrick, Brighouse. Enlisted at Halifax.
2/7th Battalion DWR; killed in action 03 5 1917, aged 25 (Battle of Bullecourt).
Commemorated – Arras Memorial, France; Brighouse WM; Rastrick WM; CWD, page 459, and the **7 DWR Drill Hall WM panel 1, column 1.**
Mentioned in the Brighouse Echo 25 5 & 01 6 1917, with photograph.

WARWICK, George – 417 Sergeant, Military Medal.
Born in Woolwich, London. Resided in Idle, Bradford, previously of Brougham Road, Marsden.
Enlisted at Marsden in 1909. Pre war local Territorial, mobilised on 05 8 1914.
1/7th Battalion DWR; killed by accidental bomb explosion 22 7 1916, aged 36.
Buried – Connaught Cemetery, Thiepval, France, 8, D, 5.
Commemorated – M Stansfield, page 464, and the **7 DWR Drill Hall WM panel 5, Column 3.**
Mentioned in the Huddersfield Examiner (accidentally killed) 22 8 1916, (MM award) 19 2 1917.

WATERHOUSE, George – 7226 Private.
Husband of A Waterhouse, of 93 College Road, Bradford. Enlisted at Bradford.
1/7th Battalion DWR; died of wounds 24 11 1916, aged 24 (Battle of the Somme).
Buried – Boulogne Eastern Cemetery, France, 8, D, 189.
Commemorated – the **7 DWR Drill Hall WM panel 6, column 2.**

WATERWORTH, John – 307580 Private.
Resided in Barnoldswick. Enlisted at Skipton.
1/7th Battalion DWR; killed in action 13 4 1918 (German Spring Offensive).
Commemorated – Tyne Cot Memorial, Belgium; CPGW, page 341, and the **7 DWR Drill Hall WM panel 6, column 2.**

WATSON, Thomas – 11689 Private.
Born, resided and enlisted at Bradford.
2/7th Battalion DWR; killed in action 28 11 1917 (Battle of Cambrai).
Commemorated – Cambrai Memorial, Louverval, France, and **7 DWR Drill Hall WM panel 2, column 3.**

WATSON, William Ralph – 5537 Private.
Born in Sheffield, the son of William and Annie Watson, of 10 Vale Road, Parkwood Springs, Sheffield. Enlisted at Sheffield.
1/7th Battalion DWR; died of wounds 03 7 1916, aged 24 (Battle of the Somme).
Buried – Bouzincourt Communal Cemetery Extension, France, 2, D, 18.
Commemorated – the **7 DWR Drill Hall WM panel 5, column 2.**

WEAVER, Ernest – 7223 Private.
Born and enlisted at West Bromwich.
1/7th Battalion DWR; killed in action 18 9 1916 (Battle of the Somme).
Commemorated – Thiepval Memorial, France and the **7 DWR Drill Hall WM panel 5, column 1.**

WEBB, James – 813 Sergeant.
Born in Warrington, Cheshire. Resided in Ashton-under-Lyne. Enlisted at Micklehurst.
1/7th Battalion DWR; died of wounds 04 10 1915 (Ypres Sector).
Buried – Stalybridge (St Paul's) New Yard.

Commemorated – Stalybridge WM; Stalybridge (St Paul's) Churchyard, Special Memorial 48-63; R Vaughan, page 25, and the **7 DWR Drill Hall WM panel 4, column 1.**

WEBSTER, John – 341 Sergeant.
Born in 1888 in Mossley. Resided in Mossley. Enlisted into the 2nd Volunteer Battalion in 1906, pre war Territorial, from 26 6 1908, Micklehurst. Embarked for France & Flanders on 15 4 1915.
1/7th Battalion DWR; died of wounds 03 9 1916 (Battle of the Somme, Thiepval).
Commemorated – Thiepval Memorial, France; Mossley Town Hall WM; All Saints Church WM; R Vaughan, pages 24, 58 & 169, and the **7 DWR Drill Hall WM panel 5, column 2.**

WEST, Harry – 306688 Lance Corporal.
Enlisted at West Bromwich.
2/7th Battalion DWR; killed in action 23 9 1917 (Hindenburg Line).
Buried – Favreuil British Cemetery, France, 1, E, 26.
Commemorated – the **7 DWR Drill Hall WM panel 7, column 1.**
Mentioned in the Unit War Diary (wounded in action) 22 9 1917.
"GOD MOVES IN MYSTERIOUS WAYS HIS WONDERS TO PERFORM"

WESTERN, W H - see WESTON, William Harold.
CWGC shows surname spelt WESTON.

WESTON, William Harold – 306931 Private.
Born and resided in Papplewick, Notts, the son of Henry and Annie Weston, of Seven Mile House, Papplewick. Enlisted at Hucknell.
2/7th Battalion DWR, B Company; killed in action 03 5 1917, aged 36 (Battle of Bullecourt).
Buried – Noreuil Australian Cemetery, France, G, 15.
Commemorated – the **7 DWR Drill Hall WM panel 6, column 2.**
WM shows surname spelt WESTERN.
"PEACE, PERFECT PEACE"

WHARAM, Frederick – 307890 Corporal.
Enlisted at Leeds.
1/7th Battalion DWR; died of wounds 11 10 1918 (Advance to Victory).
Buried – Ramillies British Cemetery, France, C, 20.
Commemorated – the **7 DWR Drill Hall WM panel 6, column 1.**
Formerly 1849 Private, West Yorkshire Regiment.
WM shows rank as Private.

WHARF, (Joe) William – 1939 Private.
Born on 08 7 1896 at 17 Prospect Place, Prospect Street, Huddersfield, the son of Percy and Ruth Wharf, of 10 Thornton Lodge Cottages, and The Fire Station, Princess Street, Huddersfield. Enlisted at Huddersfield on 31 8 1914.
1/7th Battalion DWR, A Company; killed in action (shellfire) 08 12 1915, aged 18 (Ypres Salient).
Buried – Bard Cottage Cemetery, Belgium 1, D, 21.
Commemorated – St Paul's Church, Southgate, Huddersfield; M Stansfield, page 467, and the **7 DWR Drill Hall WM panel 4, column 2.**
Mentioned in the Huddersfield Examiner (wounded in action) 21 6 1915.
"HIS NAME LIVETH FOR EVERMORE"

WHARTON, George Henry – 1400 (later 305279) Private.
Born in 1896 in Marsden. Resided in Huddersfield, the son of Henry Hind and Jane Wharton, of 29 Mark Street, Paddock, Huddersfield. Enlisted at Milnsbridge in April/May 1913. Pre war local Territorial, mobilised on 05 8 1914.
1/7th Battalion DWR; killed in action 17 9 1916, aged 20 (Battle of the Somme, Leipzig Salient).
Commemorated – Thiepval Memorial, France; All Saint's Church, Paddock, WM (held in Huddersfield Drill Hall); Shared Church, Paddock; M Stansfield, page 467, and the **7 DWR Drill Hall WM panel 1, column 1.**

WHEELER, Alfred Daniel – 29499 Sergeant.
Resided in Mold, Flintshire. Husband of Mrs J Wheeler, of 45 Wingford Road, Brixton Hill, London. Enlisted at Lambeth.
1/7th Battalion DWR; 13 4 1918, aged 35 (German Spring Offensive).
Commemorated – Tyne Cot Memorial, France, and the **7 DWR Drill Hall WM panel 2, column 2.**

WHILES, John William – 241680 Lance Corporal.
Born in Castle Bytham, Grantham. Enlisted at Bedford.
1/7th Battalion DWR; killed in action 29 4 1918 (German Spring Offensive).
Commemorated – Tyne Cot Memorial, Belgium, and the **7 DWR Drill Hall WM panel 6, column 1.**
WM shows rank as Private.

WHITAKER, James – 307737 Private.
Son of Mr and Mrs Wilson Whitaker, of 19 Chapel Lane, Oakworth, Keighley. Enlisted at Keighley.
1/7th Battalion DWR, C Company; killed in action 25 4 1918, aged 28 (German Spring Offensive).
Commemorated – Tyne Cot Memorial, Belgium and the **7 DWR Drill Hall WM panel 3, column 1.**
WM shows WHITTAKER W, no trace.

WHITE, Frank – 201682 Private.
Son of Fred and Sarah Ann White, of 4 Field View, Keighley Road, Illingworth, Halifax. Enlisted at Halifax in May, 1915.
2/7th Battalion DWR; killed in action 29 3 1918, aged 22 (German Spring Offensive).
Buried – St Amand British Cemetery, France, 1, C, 3.
Commemorated – St Mary's Church, Illingworth; Halifax Civic Book of Remembrance; CWD, page 290, and the **7 DWR Drill Hall WM panel 7, column 1.**
Mentioned in Halifax Weekly Guardian 20 4 1918.
"HIS MEMORY IS AS DEAR TO-DAY AS IN THE HOUR HE PASSED AWAY"

WHITEHEAD, Walter Kenyon – 4372 (later 306826) Private.
Son of William Maude Whitehead, widower, of 66 Upper Washer Lane, King Cross Halifax. Enlisted at Halifax in March 1916.
2/7th Battalion DWR; died 20 9 1917 (Veldhoek), aged 32.
Commemorated – Tyne Cot Memorial, Belgium; St Paul's Church, Halifax, RoH; J Fisher, page 115, and the **7 DWR Drill Hall WM panel 7, column 2.**
Also served in the 10th Battalion, see - **tunstillsmen.blogspot.com** (last accessed August, 2020).
WM shows number as 300826, Huddersfield Examiner shows number as 300826, 13 10 1917.

WHITELEY, Fred – 24225 Private.
Born in Meltham, the son of Joe Whiteley, of Hollingworth Green, Meltham, Huddersfield. Husband of Alice Lang (formerly Whiteley), of 3 Fence Nook, Littleborough. Enlisted at Meltham.
2/7th Battalion DWR; died of wounds 04 12 1917, aged 24.
Buried – Hermies Hill British Cemetery, France, 2, C, 6.

Commemorated – St Bartholomew's Church, Meltham; CVA, M Stansfield, page 470, and the **7 DWR Drill Hall WM panel 2, column 3.**
"GONE BUT NOT FORGOTTEN FROM HIS LOVING WIFE AND CHILDREN, LESLIE AND IRENE"

WHITEMAN, J J - see WIGHTMAN, John Joseph.
Commemorated – 7 DWR Drill Hall WM panel 7, column 2.
CWGC, SDGW & M Stansfield show surname spelt WIGHTMAN.

WHITHAM, T – see WHITTLAM, Thomas.
No trace under Whitham.
Commemorated – the 7 DWR Drill Hall WM panel 3, column 1.

WHITING, Henry John – 268389 Private.
Born and enlisted at Burton-on-Trent.
2/7th Battalion DWR; killed in action 15 4 1918 (German Spring Offensive).
Buried – Gommecourt British Cemetery No 2, Hebuterne, France, 5, J, 2.
Commemorated – the 7 DWR Drill Hall WM panel 7, column 1.

WHITTAKER, Reginald – 1341 Private.
Born in 1897 in Ashton-under-Lyne. Resided in Springhead. Enlisted on 15 1 193 at Uppermill. Embarked for France & Flanders on 15 4 1915.
1/7th Battalion DWR; killed in action (shellfire) 09 5 1915, aged 18 (Ypres Salient).
Buried – Rue David Military Cemetery, Fleurbaix, France, 1, H, 2.
Commemorated – Saddleworth (Pots and Pans, Springhead) WM; All Saints Church WM, St George's Church WM; St Anne's Church, Lydgate, RoH; R Vaughan, pages 24, 33 & 169, and the **7 DWR Drill Hall WM panel 4, column 3.**
Mentioned in Unit War Diary (killed in action) 09 5 1915.

WHITTAKER, W - see WHITAKER, James.
Probably WHITAKER, James.
Commemorated – the 7 DWR Drill Hall WM panel 3, column 1.

WHITTLAM, Thomas – 306343 Private.
Born in 1883 in Barnsley. Resided in Mossley, the husband of Marian Whittlam, of 5439, 18th Avenue, Rosemont, Montreal, Canada. Enlisted at Milnsbridge.
2/7th Battalion DWR; killed in action 25 3 1918 (German Spring Offensive).
Commemorated – Arras Memorial, France; Stalybridge WM; St George's Church WM; Micklehurst Conservative Club WM; R Vaughan, pages 112, 165, 169 & 175, and the **7 DWR Drill Hall WM panel 3, column 1.**
WM shows 306643 WHITHAM T.

WHITWAM, Harold Ernest – Captain.
Born in Golcar, Huddersfield, the son of Joe and Annie Whitwam, of 'Clifton House', Golcar, and 'Arcadia', Cecil Avenue, Richmond Park, Bournemouth. From Leeds University Officers' Training Corps, joined the Colne Valley Territorials in 1909. Embarked for France & Flanders in April, 1915, as Lieutenant. Invalided home in October, 1915, gas poisoning. Returned to France in September, 1917.
1/7th Battalion DWR; killed in action 09 10 1917, aged 27 (3rd Battle of Ypres, Passchendaele).
Commemorated – Tyne Cot Memorial, Belgium; York Minster Memorial; Leeds University RoH, page 207; St John's Church, Golcar; CVA, J Fisher, pages 107, 111 & 132; M Stansfield, page 473, and the **7 DWR Drill Hall WM panel 3, column 3.**

Mentioned in the Unit War Diary (joined Battalion) 17 9 1917, (killed in action, Vlamertinghe) 08 10 1917; the Huddersfield Examiner (B Coy, 1915) 04 8 1915, (killed in action) 15 10 1917, (in memoriam (08 10 1918); 7 DWR Albums Volumes 1 & 2 - multiple entries.

WHITWAM, Nelson – 1908 Sergeant.
Born in Golcar, Huddersfield, the son of Herbert and Ellen Whitwam, of Golcar. Husband of Annie Whitwam, of 92 Croft Terrace, Town End, Golcar. Enlisted at Milnsbridge.
1/7th Battalion DWR; died of wounds at No 10 CCS on 04 10 1915, aged 27 (Ypres Salient).
Buried – Lijssenthoek Military Cemetery, Belgium, 1, C, 36.
Commemorated – Golcar Churchyard Memorial; St John's Church, Golcar; M Stansfield, page 474, and the **7 DWR Drill Hall WM panel 4, column 1.**
"THY WILL, BE DONE"

WHITWORTH, Frank – 306034 Private.
Resided in Milnsbridge, the son of Edwin and Harriett Whitworth, of Ashworth Road, Dewsbury. Husband of Agnes Whitworth, of 17 Chapel Lane, Milnsbridge. Enlisted at Doncaster.
2/7th Battalion DWR; killed in action 03 5 1917, aged 37 (Battle of Bullecourt).
Commemorated – Arras Memorial, France; CVA; M Stansfield, page 475, and the **7 DWR Drill Hall WM panel 2, column 2.**
Mentioned in the Huddersfield Examiner (reported missing) 27 6 1917.

WIGGLESWORTH, Harry – 3683 Private.
Born and enlisted at Bradford.
1/7th Battalion DWR; killed in action 03 9 1916 (Battle of the Somme, Thiepval).
Commemorated – Thiepval Memorial, France, and the **7 DWR Drill Hall WM panel 5, column 2.**

WIGHTMAN, John Joseph – 305810 Private.
Born on 27 8 1893 at Marsden Road, Huddersfield. Resided in Huddersfield, the son of Thomas James and Livey Wightman, of 165 Marsden Road, Huddersfield. Enlisted at Milnsbridge on 11 10 1914.
2/7th Battalion DWR; died of wounds at No 5 General Hospital, Rouen, 05 12 1917, aged 24.
Buried – St Sever Cemetery Extension, France, Rouen, P, 5, I, 9A.
Commemorated – M Stansfield, page 475, and the **7 DWR Drill Hall WM panel 7, column 2.**
*WM shows name as Whiteman, CWGC, SDGW & M Stansfield show surname spelt **WIGHTMAN**.*
WM shows name as WHITEMAN, all other sources as WHIGHTMAN.
"HE, NOBLY STRIVING, NOBLY FELL"

WILD, Clifford – 267078 Private.
Born and Resided in Keighley, the son of Alfred and Mary Wild, of 77 Emily Street, Keighley. Enlisted at Bradford.
1/7th Battalion DWR; died of wounds 13 10 1918, aged 22 (Advance to Victory).
Buried – Bucquoy Road Cemetery, Ficheux, France, 3, F, 3.
Commemorated – the **7 DWR Drill Hall WM panel 6, column 3.**
"IT IS WELL WITH THE BOY"

WILKINSON, Charlie – 306667 Private.
Son of Mr and Mrs Charles James Wilkinson, of 45 Preston Street, Listerhills, Bradford. Enlisted at Bradford.
2/7th Battalion DWR, Machine Gun section; killed in action 03 5 1917, aged 26 (Battle of Bullecourt).
Commemorated – Arras Memorial, France, and the **7 DWR Drill Hall WM panel 2, column 2.**
Mentioned in the Huddersfield Examiner (reported missing) 09 8 1917.

WILKINSON, Rufus – 306526 Private.
Enlisted at Bradford.
2/7th Battalion DWR; killed in action 27 11 1917 (Battle of Cambrai).
Commemorated – Cambrai Memorial, Louverval, France, and the **7 DWR Drill Hall WM panel 7, column 2.**

WILLIAMS, Edward Robert – 1485 Private.
Born and resided in Oldham, the son of Arthur and Mary Williams, of Oldham. Enlisted at Lees.
1/7th Battalion DWR; died of wounds 20 9 1916, aged 21 (Battle of the Somme).
Buried – Puchevillers British Cemetery, France, 4, D, 13.
Commemorated – the **7 DWR Drill Hall WM panel 5, column 3.**
"HERO OF OURS BELOVED BY NOBLE PURPOSE LED, REST THOU IN PEACE"

WILLIAMS, Frank – 1434 Private.
Born in 1892 in Stalybridge. Resided in Mossley. Pre war Territorial, enlisted on 27 5 1913 at Mossley. Embarked for France & Flanders on 15 4 1915.
1/7th Battalion DWR; killed in action 17 9 1916 (Battle of the Somme, Leipzig Salient).
Commemorated – Thiepval Memorial, France; Saddleworth WM; All Saints Church WM; St George's Church WM; R Vaughan, pages 16, 24, 60 & 169, and the **7 DWR Drill Hall WM panel 5, column 2.**

WILLIAMS, George Henry – 16159 (later 308173) Private.
Enlisted at Nottingham.
2/7th Battalion DWR; killed in action 27 11 1917 (Battle of Cambrai).
Commemorated – Cambrai Memorial, Louverval, France, and the **7 DWR Drill Hall WM panel 2, column 3.**
WM shows name as H G Williams, CWGC & SDGW show names as George Henry.

WILLIAMS, William Henry – 7190 Lance Corporal, Military Medal.
Enlisted at West Bromwich.
1/7th Battalion DWR; killed in action 28 2 1917.
Buried – Le Fermont Military Cemetery, Riviere, France, 2, E, 7.
Commemorated – the **7 DWR Drill Hall WM panel 6, column 2.**
Mentioned in the London Gazette (MM award) 16 11 1916, page 11144.

WILLIAMSON, William John – 266267 Private.
Born in London. Resided at 42 Skipton Road, Earby, the son of James and Mary E Williamson, of 21 Albion Street, Earby, Colne, Lancs. Enlisted at Skipton.
10th Battalion DWR; died of wounds (gunshot to back, right leg and arm) 01 10 1917, aged 29.
Buried – New Irish Farm Cemetery, Belgium, 31, F, 23.
Commemorated – Earby WM; CPGW, page 310, with photograph, and the **7 DWR Drill Hall WM panel 6, column 2.**
Also served in the 10th Battalion, see - **tunstillsmen.blogspot.com** (last accessed August, 2020).

WIMPENNY, A - see WINPENNY, Arthur.
Commemorated – 7 DWR Drill Hall WM panel 2, column 3.
CWGC & SDGW show surname as WINPENNY.

WIMPENNY, Joe – 307856 Private.
Born at Golcar, the son of Mrs B Wimpenny, of Chain, Marsden. Resided in Gladstone Buildings, Marsden. Enlisted at Huddersfield in August, 1916. Embarked for France & Flanders in December, 1916.
1/7th Battalion DWR; killed in action 21 11 1917, aged 30 (3rd Battle of Ypres, Passchendaele).

Buried – Dochy Farm New British Cemetery, 3, B, 23.
Commemorated – Marsden War Memorial; CVA; M Stansfield, page 483, and the **7 DWR Drill Hall WM panel 7, column 2.**
Brother of John Wimpenny, Private 305189.

WIMPENNY, John – 305189 Private.
Born at Golcar, Huddersfield, the son of Mrs B Wimpenny, of Chain, Marsden, Huddersfield. Enlisted at Marsden in August, 1914. Pre war Colne Valley battalion Territorial. Embarked for France & Flanders in April, 1915.
1/7th Battalion DWR; reported missing (killed in action) 23 11 1916, aged 20 (Battle of the Somme).
Buried – Shrine Cemetery, Bucquoy, France, 1, B, 25.
Commemorated – Marsden WM; CVA; M Stansfield, page 483, and the **7 DWR Drill Hall WM panel 7, column 2.**
Brother of Joe Wimpenny, Private 307856.

WINCKLE, Henry – 5540 Private.
Son of Mary W Winckle, of Sheffield. Enlisted at Sheffield.
1/7th Battalion DWR, B Company; died of wounds 11 7 1916, aged 26 (Battle of the Somme).
Buried – Forceville Communal Cemetery and Extension, France, 2, D, 15.
Commemorated – the **7 DWR Drill Hall WM panel 5, column 3.**
WM shows name as WINKLE.

WINPENNY, Arthur – 306777 Private.
Enlisted at Bradford.
2/7th Battalion DWR; killed in action 03 5 1917 (Battle of Bullecourt).
Commemorated – Arras Memorial, France, and the **7 DWR Drill Hall WM panel 2, column 3.**
WM shows name as WIMPENNY.

WINTERBOTTOM, Josiah – 3291 Private.
Resided in Oldham. Enlisted at Greenfield.
1/7th Battalion DWR; killed in action 03 9 1916 (Battle of the Somme, Thiepval).
Commemorated – Thiepval Memorial, France, and **7 DWR Drill Hall WM panel 5, column 3.**

WISHART, Donald Mackenzie – 3723 Private.
Born in Manchester. Enlisted at Bradford.
1/7th Battalion DWR; killed in action 03 9 1916 (Battle of the Somme, Thiepval).
Commemorated – Thiepval Memorial, France; the 5 DWR Drill Hall WM, panel 12, column 3, and the **7 DWR Drill Hall WM panel 6, column 1.**

WOOD, Ernest – 1616 Private, Military Medal.
Born in Marsden, the son of Mr and Mrs John Henry Wood, of 12 Royds Terrace, Binn Road, Marsden. Enlisted at Meltham in May/June, 1914. Pre war local Territorial, mobilised on 05 8 1914.
1/7th Battalion DWR; died of wounds (shellfire) at No 16 General Hospital, Le Treport, France on 23 9 1916.
Buried – Mont Huon Military Cemetery, Le Treport, France 2, E, 8.
Commemorated – Marsden WM; J Fisher, page 114; CVA; M Stansfield, page 490, and the **7 DWR Drill Hall WM panel 5, column 2.**
Mentioned in the London Gazette (MM award) 10 11 1916, page 11144; the Huddersfield Examiner (died of wounds) 25 10 1916.

WOOD, Frank – 2466 Private.
Born in 1897 in Uppermill, the son of Robert and Frances Wood, of 5 Webster Street, Mossley.
Enlisted on 05 11 1914 at Mossley.
1/7th Battalion DWR; died of wounds 03 12 1916, aged 19.
Buried – St Sever Cemetery, Rouen, France, A, 34, 2.
Commemorated – Saddleworth WM; Mossley Town Hall WM; St George's Church WM; St John the Baptist Church WM; Calico Printers Association WM; Micklehurst Liberal Club RoH; R Vaughan, pages 24, 53 & 169, and the **7 DWR Drill Hall WM panel 4, column 3.**
"PEACE, PERFECT PEACE"

WOOD, Frank – 11861 Private.
Born, resided and enlisted at Bradford, the son of Jane and James Wood, of 733, Little Horton Lane, Bradford.
2/7th Battalion DWR; killed in action 03 12 1917, aged 25.
Commemorated – Cambrai Memorial, Louverval, France, and the **7 DWR Drill Hall WM panel 2, column 1.**

WOOD, Gilbert – 305472 Corporal.
Born on 25 3 1892 in George Street, Lindley. Resided in Lindley, the son of Albert and Hetty Wood, of 41 Quarmby Fold, Lindley, Huddersfield. Enlisted at Milnsbridge in 1914.
1/7th Battalion DWR; killed in action 11 4 1918, aged 26 (German Spring Offensive).
Commemorated – Tyne Cot Memorial, Belgium; Lindley WM; St. Stephen's Church, Lindley; M Stansfield, page 491, and the **7 DWR Drill Hall WM panel 7, column 1.**

WOOD, Hubert – 4455 Private.
Resided in Grassington, the son of Hubert and Jane Wood, of 'Laburnum House', Grassington. Enlisted at Skipton.
1/7th Battalion DWR; killed in action 14 11 1916, aged 22 (Battle of the Somme).
Buried – Foncquevillers Military Cemetery, France, 1, H, 4.
Commemorated – the **7 DWR Drill Hall WM panel 5, column 2.**
"TO LIVE IN HEARTS WE LEAVE BEHIND IS NOT TO DIE"

WOOD, Lewis – 306678 Private.
Resided in Brighouse, the son of Enoch and Alice Wood, of 23 St Jude's Place, Manningham, Bradford. Enlisted at Bradford.
2/7th Battalion DWR; died of wounds 17 5 1917, aged 22 (Hindenburg Line).
Buried – Achiet-Le-Grand Communal Cemetery, France 1, H, 5.
Commemorated – the **7 DWR Drill Hall WM panel 7, column 3.**
"LOVED AND EVER REMEMBERED"

WOOD, Thomas – 5534 Private.
Born and enlisted at Leeds.
1/7th Battalion DWR; died of wounds 03 7 1916 (Battle of the Somme).
Buried – Authuile Military Cemetery, France, E, 29.
Commemorated - the **7 DWR Drill Hall WM panel 5, column 1.**

WOODALL, Alfred – 5429 (later 7224 & 308068) Private.
Born at Rowley Regis, Staffs. Resided in Springfield, Staffs, the son of William and Annie Woodall. Enlisted at Old Hills.
1/7th Battalion DWR; killed in action 03 8 1917, aged 27 (Nieuport Sector).
Buried – Coxyde Military Cemetery, Belgium, 2, D, 2.
Commemorated - the **7 DWR Drill Hall WM panel 6, column 1.**

"HOME AT LAST THY LABOUR DONE, SAFE AND BLESSED, THE VICTORY WON"
SDGW shows number as 30868.

WOODCOCK, George Henry – 26649 Private.
Born in Wakefield, the son of John and Elizabeth Woodcock, of 13 Tavora Street, Wakefield. Enlisted at Wakefield.
1/7th Battalion DWR; died of wounds 28 4 1918, aged 19 (German Spring Offensive).
Buried – Boulogne Eastern Cemetery, France, 9, A, 52.
Commemorated – the **7 DWR Drill Hall WM panel 2, column 2.**
"HIS SLEEP SHALL BE SWEET LIKE UNTO HIS LIFE, MOTHER"
WM shows initials as G E.

WOODHOUSE, Joseph James – 2091 (later 268586) Private.
Born in 1881 in Mossley. Resided in Mossley, the son of Edward and Mary Ann Woodhouse, of 66 Micklehurst Road, Mossley. Husband of Martha Ann Woodhouse, of 95 Huddersfield Road, Stalybridge. Enlisted at Milnsbridge. Embarked for France & Flanders on 15 4 1915.
1/7th Battalion DWR; killed in action 29 4 1918, aged 36 (German Spring Offensive).
Commemorated – Tyne Cot Memorial, Belgium; Vaughan R, pages 24, 125 & 169, and the **7 DWR Drill Hall WM panel 6, column 2.**

WOODROW, Francis William – 26358 Private.
Born in Wells-next-the-Sea, Norfolk. Resided and enlisted at Norwich.
2/7th Battalion DWR; killed in action 27 11 1917, (Battle of Cambrai).
Commemorated – Cambrai Memorial, Louverval, France, and the **7 DWR Drill Hall WM panel 2, column 2.**
Formerly T4/041651 Private, Army Service Corps.

WOODWARD, F G – 3499 Private.
2/7th Battalion DWR; died 01 1 1916.
Buried – Newcastle-upon-Tyne (All Saint's) Cemetery, D, U, 595.
Commemorated - the **7 DWR Drill Hall WM panel 4, column 3.**
No trace in SDGW.

WOOLMAN, Joe – 1378 Private.
Born in Blackpool, the son of A and E Woolman, of Blackpool. Resided in Oldham. Enlisted at Lees.
1/7th Battalion DWR; died of wounds 04 7 1916, aged 22 (Battle of the Somme).
Buried – Forceville Communal Cemetery and Extension, France, 2, C, 3.
Commemorated – the **7 DWR Drill Hall WM panel 4, column 3.**

WORSNOP, Alfred – 306567 Private.
Son of Albert and Edna Worsnop, of 36 Haycliffe Hill, Great Horton, Bradford. Husband of Annie Worsnop, of 5 Speeton Avenue, Horton Bank Top, Bradford. Enlisted at Bradford.
1/7th Battalion DWR; killed in action 26 4 1918, aged 29 (German Spring Offensive).
Commemorated – Tyne Cot Memorial, Belgium, and **7 DWR Drill Hall WM panel 6, column 3.**

WRIGHT, Anthony – 307419 Private.
Born in Keighley, the son of James and Paulina Wright, of Keighley. Enlisted at Keighley.
1/7th Battalion DWR; killed in action 29 4 1918, aged 24 (German Spring Offensive).
Buried – La Clytte Military Cemetery, Belgium, 5, C, 11.
Commemorated – the **7 DWR Drill Hall WM panel 6, column 3.**
"OUT OF THE STRESS OF THE DOING, INTO THE PEACE OF THE DONE"

WRIGHT, Fred – 938 Private.
Born and resided in Waterhead, the son of Mrs Sarah Jane Wright. Enlisted at Uppermill.
1/7th Battalion DWR; killed in action 14 7 1916, aged 22 (Battle of the Somme).
Commemorated – Thiepval Memorial, France, and **7 DWR Drill Hall WM panel 4, column 3.**
WM shows number as 930.

WRIGHT, Leonard – 306619 Lance Corporal.
Resided in Gomersal, the son of Arthur and S J Wright, of 150 Popeley Terrace, Oxford Road, Gomersal, Leeds. Enlisted at Heckmondwike.
2/7th Battalion DWR; killed in action 13 6 1918, aged 28.
Buried – Bienvillers Military Cemetery, France, 20, D, 4.
Commemorated – Cleckheaton WM and the **7 DWR Drill Hall WM Panel 3, column 2.**
"REST IN PEACE"

WRIGHT, Walter – 2436 Private.
Born in 1894 in Mossley. Resided in Mossley. Enlisted on 31 10 1914 at Uppermill.
1/7th Battalion DWR, posted to 1/5th Battalion, King's Own Yorkshire Light Infantry from Infantry Base Depot on arrival in France; died of wounds (GSW to thigh on 28 7 1916) 01 8 1916, aged 21 (Battle of the Somme).
Buried – Etaples Military Cemetery, France, 9, B, 16A.
Commemorated – St George's Church WM; St John the Baptist Church WM; United Methodist Church WM; R Vaughan, pages 24, 55, 160, 161 & 169, and the **7 DWR Drill Hall WM panel 5, column 3.**

WRIGLEY, Henry – 305867 Private.
Resided in Oldham, the son of John Robert and Priscilla Wrigley, of 121 Redgrave Street, Oldham. Enlisted at Uppermill.
1/7th Battalion DWR; killed in action 28 2 1918, aged 22.
Buried – Oxford Road Cemetery, Belgium, 3, D, 6.
Commemorated – the **7 DWR Drill Hall WM panel 7, column 3.**

WRIGLEY, Howard – 306051 Private.
Resided in Oldham. Enlisted at Thoresby Camp, Nottinghamshire.
2/7th Battalion DWR; killed in action 21 3 1918 (German Spring Offensive).
Buried – Bois-Carré British Cemetery, Thelus, France, 2, C, 15.
Commemorated – the **7 DWR Drill Hall WM panel 3, column 1.**

WRIGLEY, Lewis – 306274 Private.
Born on 20 7 1896 at Filbert Street, Birkby, the son of Albert and Selina Wrigley, of 62 Corby Street, Fartown. Enlisted at Milnsbridge on 15 10 1915.
2/7th Battalion DWR; killed in action 28 11 1917, aged 21 (Battle of Cambrai).
Commemorated – Cambrai Memorial Louverval, France; Fartown and Birkby WM; M Stansfield, page 500, and the **7 DWR Drill Hall WM panel 2, column 1.**

WRIGLEY, R - see RIGBY Richard.
Commemorated – the **7 DWR Drill Hall WM panel 6, column 1.**
CWGC & SDGW show surname as RIGBY.

YOULE, Edward – 5545 (later 307347) Private.
Born in Sheffield, the son of Mrs Henriette Smith, of 45 North Church Street, Sheffield. Enlisted at Sheffield.
1/7th Battalion DWR; killed in action 18 9 1916, aged 19 (Battle of the Somme).
Buried – Lonsdale Cemetery, Authuile, France, 5, N, 9.
Commemorated – the **7 DWR Drill Hall WM panel 6, column 1.**
Formerly 27265 Private, King's Own Yorkshire Light Infantry.

2/5th DWR, Henham Park. July 1916.

2Lt CC BAIN with periscope

C Coy. YPRES 1915
The "Sniperscope" in action

ADDENDA

In addition to the names above, the following twenty one names appear to have been left off the 7th Battalion War Memorial during the original compilation of the Roll of Honour and the engraving process. We have compiled this list of our comrades from the Colne Valley district, who died having served in the 1/7th or 2/7th Battalions, to commemorate them alongside their comrades listed above and to perpetuate the memory of their sacrifice.

After discovering a number of men who were missed from the 5th DWR War Memorial, the Trustees agreed to create an additional panel to commemorate their sacrifice. A similar project is being considered for the men listed below. Lest We Forget:

BOOTH, James Frederick – 240799 Private.
Born on 08 11 1895, at Salendine Nook, the son of Mr and Mrs Albert Booth, of Bank End Farm, Dalton, Huddersfield. Enlisted at Huddersfield in October, 1914.
1/7th Battalion DWR; reported missing (killed in action) 12 4 1918, aged 22 (German Spring Offensive).
Buried – Cabaret Rouge British Cemetery, Souchez, France, 20, D, 26.
Commemorated – Almondbury WM and M Stansfield, page 49.
Mentioned in the Huddersfield Examiner (official casualty list) on 07 8 1916, (information request by the family) on 30 5 1918.

BOWER, Edward – 20239 Private.
Born at Meltham, the son of Isabella Bower, of Green End, Meltham, Huddersfield. Enlisted at Huddersfield.
1/7th Battalion DWR; killed in action 02 1 1918, aged 30.
Buried – Lijssenthoek Military Cemetery, Belgium, 26, D, 13.
Commemorated – St Bartholomew's Church, Meltham, and M Stansfield, page 54.
"WORTHY OF EVERLASTING LOVE"

BRELSFORD, John – 1528 Sergeant.
Born in 1896 in Carrbrook, the son of Joseph and Harriet Brelsford, of 8 Mayall Street, Mossley. Enlisted at Mossley, a pre war Territorial. Wounded in action 09 8 1916 at Thiepval during the Battle of the Somme. Discharged on 03 3 1917 and awarded the Silver Wound Badge (number 181251).
1/7th Battalion DWR, originally F Company; died, home, 15 7 1920, aged 23.
Buried – Mossley Cemetery, C of E 781.
Commemorated – R Vaughan, pages 20, 24, 152 & 153.
"THY WILL BE DONE"

DRANSFIELD, Fred – 2668 (later 305876) Private.
Born in 1897 in Mossley. Resided in Mossley. Enlisted at Milnsbridge. Embarked for France & Flanders on 15 4 1915.
1/7th Battalion DWR; killed in action 29 4 1918 (German Spring Offensive).
Commemorated – Tyne Cot Memorial, Belgium; St Augustine's Church RoH; St George's Church RoH; St John the Baptist Church WM and R Vaughan, pages 24 & 124.

ESCOTT, Richard – 2449 (later 305751) Private.
Born in 1896 in Uppermill. Resided in Mossley. Enlisted at Uppermill. Embarked for France & Flanders on 15 4 1915.
1/7th Battalion DWR; killed in action 14 4 1918 (German Spring Offensive).
Commemorated – Tyne Cot Memorial, Belgium, Mossley Town WM; Uppermill (Pots and Pans) WM; Uppermill (St Chad's Church) WM; St George's Church WM and R Vaughan, pages 16, 24 & 119.

Related to ESCOTT, C, see main list, and ESCOTT, W H, 2/6th Battalion DWR.

EVENNETT, Keble (Keeble?) Thomas – 204359 Private.
Resided in Huddersfield. Husband of Rosetta Evennett, of Lower Denby, Huddersfield. Enlisted at Huddersfield.
2/7th Battalion DWR; died of pneumonia on 25 2 1918 at 42 CCS, aged 33.
Buried – Aubigny Communal Cemetery Extension, 3, C, 25.
Commemorated – M Stansfield, page 142.
CWGC & SDGW (page 55) shows unit at 2/7th Battalion, SDGW (page 27) & M Stansfield (page 142) state 2/4th Battalion. SDGW has spellings of surname as EVENETT & EVENNETT.
"WE ASKED LIFE OF THEE AND THOU GAVEST IT, EVEN LIFE EVERLASTING"

FARR, Fred – 305395 Private.
Born in 1897 in All Saints, Mossley, Cheshire, the son of Matthew Burrow Farr, of 110 Breeze Hill, Micklehurst Road, Mossley. Enlisted at Mossley.
1/7th Battalion DWR; killed in action 13 4 1918, aged 21 (German Spring Offensive).
Commemorated – Tyne Cot Memorial, Belgium; All Saints Church WM; St George's Church WM; Abney Congregational Church RoH and window, and R Vaughan, pages 118, 154, 155 & 159.

HINCHCLIFFE, Sam – 305638 Private.
Resided in Holmbridge. Enlisted at Milnsbridge.
1/7th Battalion DWR; killed in action 18 9 1916 (Battle of the Somme).
Commemorated – Tyne Cot Memorial, Belgium; Hospital Memorial (Holme and Holmbridge plaque) WM; Memorial in Hade Edge Burial Ground, Huddersfield, and M Stansfield, page 211.

HOLLIDAY, Friend – 2214 Private.
Son of Tom and Mary Hannah Holliday, of 34 Thomas Street, Northgate, Huddersfield. Enlisted at Huddersfield on 07 9 1914. Embarked for France & Flanders on 15 4 1915.
1/7th Battalion DWR; discharged, unfit for further service 11 11 1915, died, home, 18 11 1916, aged 20.
Buried – Edgerton Cemetery, Huddersfield, 18B, C, 133.
Silver War Badge (No 89090) awarded 11 11 1915.
Commemorated – M Stansfield, page 224.
Not recorded in SDGW.
"EVER IN OUR THOUGHTS"

KING, John Henry – 1584 (later 305368) Private.
Resided in Diggle. Enlisted at Uppermill.
1/7th Battalion DWR; killed in action 12 4 1918 (German Spring Offensive).
Commemorated – Tyne Cot Memorial, Belgium.
Mentioned in G Howcroft, page 40.

LLOYD, Thomas (Jack) – 17393 Corporal.
Born in Derby. Resided 21 Nabbs Lane, Slaithwaite. Enlisted at Huddersfield.
1/7th Battalion DWR; killed in action 11 10 1918, age 37 (Advance to Victory, Battle of Iwuy).
Buried – Wellington Cemetery, Rieux-En-Cambresis, France, 2, C, 12.
Commemorated – Slaithwaite WM; St James's Church, Slaithwaite, and M Stansfield, page 281.
Mentioned in the Huddersfield Examiner (official casualty lists) on 06 9 1918 & 09 11 1918. Also served in the 10th Battalion, see - **tunstillsmen.blogspot.com** (last accessed August, 2020).

MARLAND, Joseph Lawton – 20528 Private.
Husband of Ellen Marland, of 25 Cheshire Street, Mossley.
12 (Labour) Battalion DWR; died 12 3 1919, aged 31.

Commemorated All Saints Church WM, St George's Church WM, Micklehurst Conservative Club WM; and R Vaughan, page 148.
Also 371617 Labour Corps.

MILNES, Harry – 306997 Private.
Born on 15 7 1888 at Lindley, Huddersfield. Resided at Lea Green, Holywell Green, Halifax. Enlisted 28 3 1916.
2/7th Battalion DWR; died of wounds, at home, on 12 9 1920, aged 42.
Buried – Edgerton Cemetery, Huddersfield, AC Screen Wall.
Commemorated – St Stephen's Church, Lindley, and M Stansfield, page 303.
Silver War Badge (No B155982) awarded 13 3 1919.

NUGENT, Stanley – 24131 (also 2542) Lance Corporal.
Resided in Greenfield. Enlisted at Uppermill.
2/7th Battalion DWR; killed in action 27 11 1917 (Battle of Cambrai).
Commemorated – Cambrai Memorial, Louverval, France; Saddleworth WM.

RAMSDEN, Joe – 11912 Private.
Born on 27 4 1895 in Charles Street, Crosland Moor, Huddersfield, the son of Mr and Mrs Jimmy Ramsden, of 83 College Street, Crosland Moor. Enlisted at Huddersfield on 14 8 1914.
1/7th Battalion DWR; killed in action 11 10 1918, aged 23 (Advance to Victory, Battle of Iwuy).
Buried – Wellington Cemetery, Rieux-en-Cambresis, France, 1, E, 2.
Commemorated – St Barnabas Church, Crosland Moor; Crosland Moor Wesleyan Church; CVA and M Stansfield, page 348.

SHAW, Jepson – 562 (re-engaged as 308194) Corporal.
Born in 1892 in Micklehurst in 1892. Resided in Mossley.
1/7th Battalion DWR; died 08 1 1920.
Buried – Mossley Cemetery, NC 2442.
Commemorated – Micklehurst Liberal Club WM and R Vaughan pages 14, 16, 24, 151 & 156.

SHAW, William – 305224 Corporal.
Resided in Oldham. Enlisted at Lees.
1/7th Battalion DWR; killed in action 13 4 1918 (German Spring Offensive).
Commemorated – Tyne Cot Memorial, Belgium.

THORPE, Turner – 1036 (later 24793) Private.
Born in Holmfirth, the husband of Edith Thorpe, of Yew Tree, Holmfirth. Resided in Holmbridge. Enlisted into the 5th Battalion in 1908. Mobilised with F Company, 7 DWR, at Holmfirth, on 05 8 1914.
1/7th Battalion DWR; died as Prisoner of War on 19 7 1918, aged 29.
Buried – Conde-sur-L'Escaut Communal Cemetery, France, A, 72.
Commemorated – Memorial Hospital (Holme and Holmbridge plaque) WM; 5 DWR Drill Hall WM panel 11, column 3, and M Stansfield, page 441.
Mentioned in the Huddersfield Examiner (reported missing on 13 4 1918 and subsequently POW, not returned from captivity) on 20 1 1919.

WADDILOVE, Robert – 2358 (later 305704) Private.
Resided in Mossley.
1/7th Battalion DWR; killed in action 13 4 1918 (German Spring Offensive).
Commemorated – Tyne Cot Memorial, Belgium.

WHITWAM, Wilfred – 6743 (later 307860) Private.
Born at Golcar, Huddersfield. Enlisted at Huddersfield.
1/7th Battalion DWR; killed in action 29 4 1918 (German Spring Offensive).
Commemorated – St John's Church, Golcar, and M Stansfield, page 475.

WILKINSON, Arthur – 267618 Private.
Born in 1893 in Slaithwaite, the son of Mr and Mrs Clarence W Wilkinson, of Rose Cottage, Outlane. Enlisted at Huddersfield in June, 1917.
1/7th Battalion DWR; killed in action 11 4 1918 (German Spring Offensive).
Commemorated – Tyne Cot Memorial, Belgium; Outlane Trinity Methodist Church; Salendine Nook Church; Memorial in Salendine Nook Churchyard, 423E, and plaque in the Chapel, adjacent to the organ, and M Stansfield, page 478.

7 DWR Band.   Nov 1918.

THE BATTLES

Wherever possible we have listed the battle in which the men fell. Extraordinarily, the majority of the men commemorated did appear to fall in battle, rather than the smaller number who fell in the daily grind and attrition of trench warfare, and still fewer men who succumbed to disease and sickness. Disease had been the major killer in previous wars, far more soldiers died of enteric fever during the South African War than were killed by Boer bullets or shells. By April, 1914, inoculations had been introduced into the British Army and the incidence of deaths from disease dropped dramatically. Only up to ten of the men who are named on this War Memorial died of disease, two died as Prisoners of War and it is not known if these succumbed to wounds or disease.

Three of the men listed on the memorial fought with the 10th Battalion and were killed at Veldhoek, a very successful action in 1917.

A total of 104 Battle Honours were awarded for the whole of the Western Front during the war, 72 of which were awarded to the various battalions of the Regiment, ten of these are emblazoned on the Regulation Colours. There were eight major battles in which the first and second line battalions of the 7th DWR were involved:

The Battles for Ypres.

There were three officially accepted Battles for Ypres, although some historians consider the second German Spring Offensive, Operation *Georgette*, in Flanders, as being the Fourth Battle of Ypres:

1st Ypres: 19th October – 22nd November, 1914;
2nd Ypres: 22nd April – 25th May, 1915;
3rd Ypres: 31st July – 10th November, 1917 (commonly known as the Battle of Passchendaele).

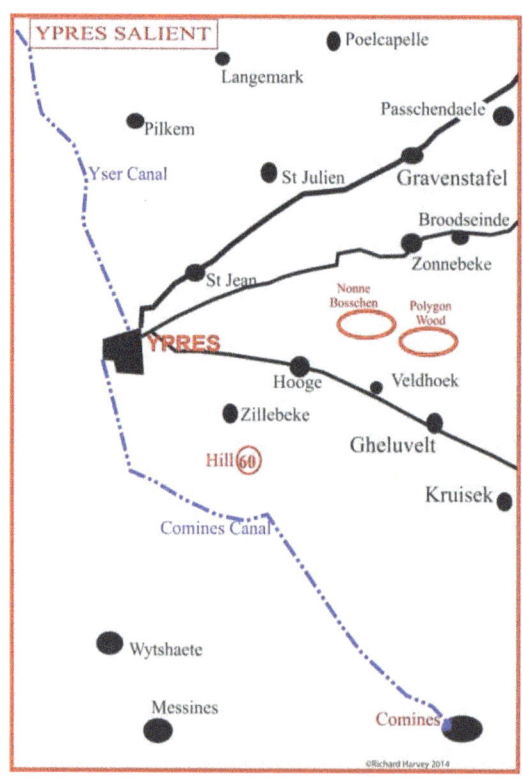

The First Battle of Ypres was fought in 1914 and none of the DWR Territorial Force battalions were in France and Flanders at that time. The Second Battle of Ypres, between April and May, 1915, was at a time when the 1/5th Battalion was under instruction for trench warfare in the Fleurbaix Sector, and a number of men were killed or died of wounds during this period, before moving to the Ypres Sector in early July, 1915. There were many casualties in this sector during the time that the 49th Division was holding the line until December, 1915.

See also Battle of Passchendaele, below:

The Battle of the Somme.
1st July – 18th November, 1916.

The Battle of the Somme was actually a series of forty two separate battles or actions, for which thirteen Battle Honours were awarded to Regiments after the war for their involvement in these major attacks.

The 1/5th DWR was involved mainly in the Battle for Thiepval in 2nd Corps (2nd – 28th September, 1916) and went 'over the top' on 3rd September as part of a much larger operation, the Battle of Pozieres, with 14th Corps attacking Guillemont and 15th Corps attacking Delville Wood, further to the south, on the same day.

The Battalion was further involved in the Somme battle, particularly around 17th September, until moving to the Nieuport Sector, see below, in July 1917.

The Hindenburg Line and the Battle of Bullecourt.

3rd May, 1917.

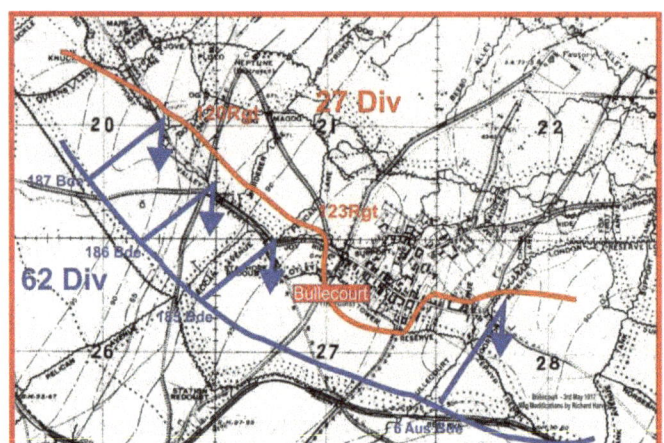

Battle of Bullecourt.

R Harvey

By February, 1917, the second line Territorial Force Battalions in 62nd Division had completed their trench warfare instruction and were ready to take their place in the line, moving into the trenches at Beaumont Hamel on 13th February, 1917. On 27th February, the 2/5th DWR successfully attacked and captured a German trench, Orchard Alley, which raised their morale.

Shortly afterwards the Germans carried out a deliberate withdrawal to the Hindenburg Line, destroying everything behind them and leaving many booby traps and poisoned wells These measures were considered so brutal that even some German generals considered resigning.

The British followed up cautiously until they were brought to a halt by the formidable defences of the Hindenburg Line (actually known by the Germans as the Siegfried Line). Plans were soon made to break through this line.

On 11th April, 1917, the Canadians attempted to breach the German Hindenburg line at Bullecourt but had been repulsed and a major German counter-attack had taken ground from the Allies. In May, reinforced with the 62nd (TF) Division, they were to have another go. The second Battle for Bullecourt was one of the worst days in the war for the 2/5th Battalion, 145 men listed on the War Memorial were reported as missing, killed or died of wounds as a result of a few hour's fighting (with another man who is not on the Memorial but is commemorated in this book).

The Nieuport Sector.
13th July – 24th September, 1917.

This Sector, on the Belgian coast (also known at the time as the Lombartzyde Sector) was scheduled to be the start line for a major attack eastwards in support of an amphibious landing further along the coast by the British 1st Division. This was due to be a major part of what was to become the 3rd Battle of Ypres, commonly called the Battle of Passchendaele. Unfortunately, the Germans launched a spoiling attack in this area and pushed the Allied forces back from the proposed start line on the right bank of the canal, overwhelming two battalions occupying the bridgehead.

The Nieuport (Lombartzyde) Sector

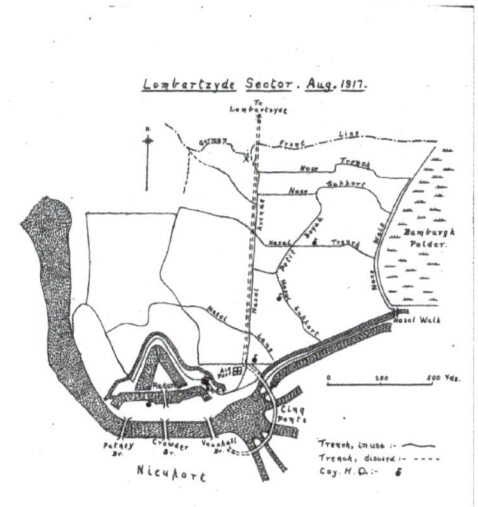

Capt P G Bales   *Captured German photograph*

The 49th Division arrived in Dunkirk by rail on 13th July, 1917, as this attack took place. Following some training on the beaches and in the dunes for an attack, 147 Brigade took their place in the front lines on 3rd August, 1917, and heavy casualties were suffered by the Division from heavy German artillery fire and gas during the next fifty two days. The Brigade started to move out of the area on 23rd September and 49th Division left 15 Corps, Fourth Army. Twelve men are recorded on the War Memorial who were killed here, however, the Archives Volunteers Team has recorded a total of 5 Officers and 107 ORs who died in this sector between 25th July and 6th October, 1917, from all four DWR Battalions in 147 Brigade.

The Battle of Passchendaele (3rd Battle of Ypres).
31st July – 10th November, 1917.

This Battle was one of the largest battles fought on the Western Front, certainly in terms of casualties. As with the Battle of the Somme, it, too, consisted of many battles and actions, with a total of eight Battle Honours being awarded for this period.

The 49th Division reached this battle area again in mid November, 1917, being in action until relieved on 3rd April, 1918. Their rest period was to be short lived, by 10th April the Division was helping to stem the German Spring Offensive, Operation *Georgette*, in the Erquinghem Lys/Nieppe area, although the 1/5th Battalion had, by then, moved to 62nd Division.

The Battle of Cambrai.
20th November – 3rd December, 1917.
The Germans were not expecting an assault of this size, supported by tanks in force and they fled in disarray initially. However, mechanical failure and the German realisation that tanks were not proof against artillery brought the attack to a halt, along with the winter weather. The German counter attack regained most of the ground lost but the scope and daring of the attack had shattered their 'impregnable' defences and was another crack in their belief of invincibility, leading to eventual victory.

The German Spring Offensive.
March to July, 1918.

Actually a number of German offensives at different times and in different areas, which were designed to break through to the Chanel Ports and force Britain out of the war, by cutting off the supply lines, (Operations *Michael*, 21st March – 4th April and Operation *Georgette*, 9th – 25th April) and then to seize Paris (Operation *Blucher-York*, 27th May – 4th June; Operation *Gneisnau*, 9th – 11th June, and Operation *Friedensturm*, 15th – 17th July, 1918). A final assault, to take Ypres and the Channel Ports (Operation *Hagen*), was cancelled when the German High Command realised that the Allied counter-attack in the Soissons region (18th July) was much greater than they believed to be possible at that stage of the war and that they were facing defeat. Their forces for Operation Hagen were redirected to the Rheims area in July, 1918.

87 men from the 7th Battalion are recorded as having died in this period, who are also commemorated on the War Memorial, which is an indication of how desperate a time it was.

Battle of Tardenois.
20th – 30th July, 1918

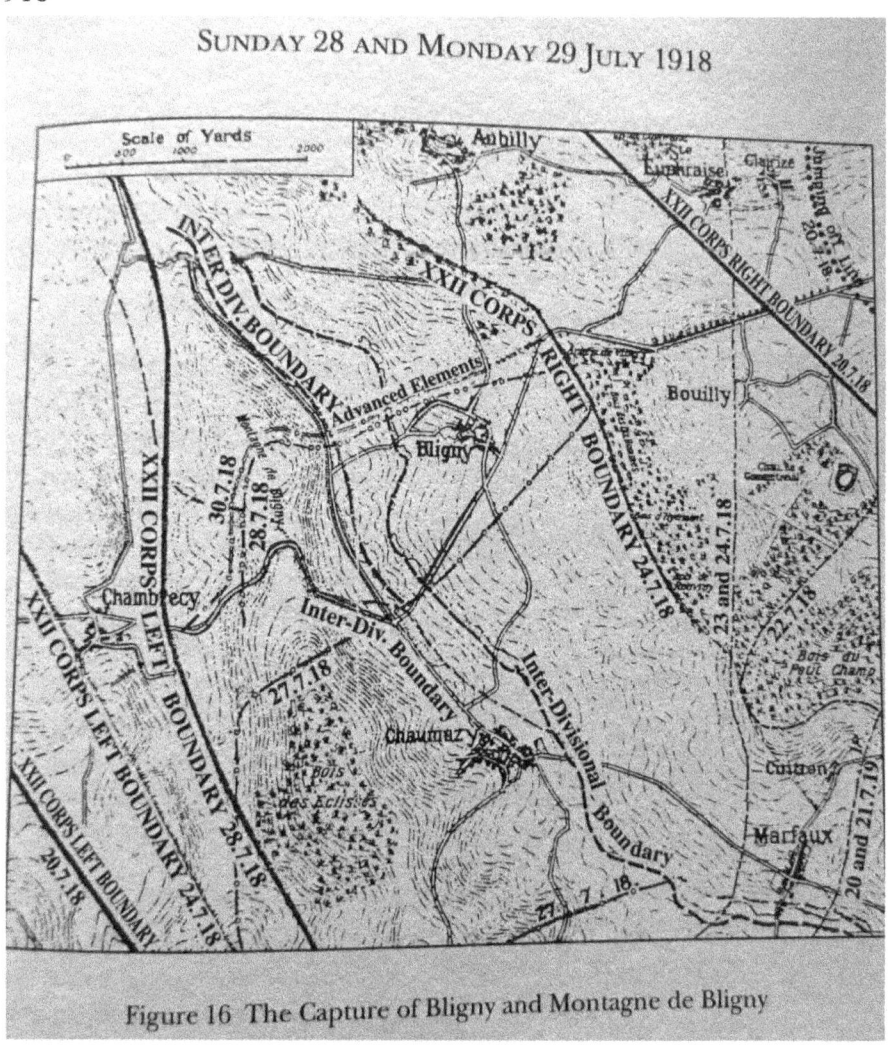

Figure 16 The Capture of Bligny and Montagne de Bligny

Extract from the Official History of the War

The French were aware of a large German build up of troops released from the Russian Front after the collapse of the Russian Army and the Treaty of Brest Litovsk. The German objective of Operation *Blucher-York* was Paris. The French requested assistance from the British and the 9th British Corps was soon in action in the Ardre Valley in May, 1918, helping to stem the German assault. Another request for British support, as a result of intelligence of another major German offensive, resulted in the 22nd Corps, with 62nd Division, being entrained to join General Berthelot's French 10th Army. The Germans launched Operation *Friedensturm* in the Rheims Sector on 15th July and the 62nd, alongside the 51st

Highland Division, arrived to take over from the exhausted Italians fighting with the French in time to stem the German advance and then counter-attack, retaking the village of Bligny before being relieved and returning to the British area. By this time the 1/5th and 2/5th Battalions had been amalgamated and were fighting as the 5th Battalion in 62nd Division. Forty seven men are recorded as having been killed during this battle who are commemorated on the War Memorial. Research shows that the two DWR Battalions engaged, the 2/4th and 5th DWR, suffered between 100 and 140 (CWGC and SDGW, respectively) deaths overall in this ten day battle. The Battle Honours 'Marne 1918' and 'Tardenois' were awarded for this action.

The Advance to Victory.
8th August – 11 November, 1918.

Once more, this was a series of battles and actions, for which twenty Battle Honours were awarded, post war. The Germans dubbed the 8th August as the Black Day for the German Army and saw the beginning of the collapse of their fighting force and its morale, which had been sapped from the end of the Battle of the Somme in November, 1916, and through a series of Allied victories in 1917, culminating in the Battle of Cambrai in November of that year. Their early collapse was only prevented by the arrival of approximately a million battle hardened reinforcements from the Eastern Front, who brought new ideas and tactics and higher morale with them. However, after the blunting of each of their major Operations, due to the tenacity of the troops fighting against them and the arrival of fresh American troops who proved to be just as tough, if not as experienced, in the final actions during the German Spring Offensive, German morale began to crumble. This was hastened by the unrest, food riots and strikes in the Fatherland, since 1916 and which were growing in tempo and becoming more widespread in 1917, laying the seeds of their complete collapse and the Armistice of 1918. The Germans had been outfought, outgunned and blockaded to a standstill both on the Western Front and at home. The Germans were pushed back to a line close to where the British and German armies had clashed on August 23rd, 1914. The 2nd Battalion DWR ended up about 11 kilometers from Mons, where they had started, a mere sixty six of the original 992 men remained with that Battalion on the 11th November, 279 of these 'original' soldiers had been killed and 247 had been taken prisoner. It is worth remembering that, by this stage of the war, the majority of soldiers were conscripts rather than the eager volunteers of the first sixteen months of the war.

156 men commemorated on the 7th Battalion War Memorial tablets died during this period. The Germans may have been withdrawing and even surrendering in large numbers, but they were still resisting strongly in defence of the Fatherland, leaving much destruction and many booby traps behind them, in the same way as they had done in early 1917 during their withdrawal to the Hindenburg Line, after the Battle of the Somme.

An important battle for the Regiment during this period was the Battle of Iwuy, 10th-11th October, 1918. Here the Germans fielded five of the twenty A7V tanks that they managed to put into operation around this time in four different sectors along the front. At Iwuy these five monster battle wagons were supported by three captured British tanks, taken at Cambrai the year before.

The two German tank groups put in their counter attack against the Canadian attack of the day before, just as 49th Division took the lead and launched their attack to seize Villers en Couchies from their start line along the road to the east of the cross roads on the Rieux-Iwuy road. The 1/7th Battalion's right flank rested on the cross roads and the two assaulting Companies started their advance from where the boundary wall of the Wellington Cemetery was started after the battle (see rear cover).

The British infantry attack went well at first, crossing the ridge half way between the start line and Villers en Couchies. The German tanks appeared on the left flank of the Divisional attack and caused a great number of casualties, forcing a withdrawal to the ridge. However, a gallant defence, assisted greatly by the Canadian artillery, one of their officers was awarded the VC for knocking out one of the tanks, left the British troops in possession of the ridge from where, the next morning, the advance was resumed. The Germans lost one of the A7V tanks which was not able to be recovered and was destroyed and the rest were withdrawn that night and moved off by rail to prepare for a further action east. The three British tanks were destroyed or broke down.

We have identified 38 men from the 1/7th Battalion who were killed that day. There were doubtless more who would have died of wounds in the Casualty Clearing Station of Hospitals which would be difficult to identify. One of those who was badly wounded during this battle died of his wounds back in Sheffield, Yorkshire, in 1924. Sargeant Arthur Loosemoor had been awarded the Victoria Cross for gallantry at the Battle of Passchendaele in 1917.

Battle of Iwuy, 10-12 October, 1918

More battles were fought in the next month but the Allies were defeating the German field army and the numbers of prisoners were increasing as their forward units and formations disintegrated and the German High Command were forced to accept an armistice.

The only disturbing element was the fact that after the Armistice the German Army was allowed to march back into Germany, carrying their weapons and with banners flying. Very little damage had been done inside Germany, compared to the devastated area astride the trench lines in Belgium and France, as well as naval shelling and the aerial bombing of Britain between 1915 and 1918. This left the prospect for German nationalists to claim that the Army had not been defeated in the Great War but had been betrayed by politicians and communist factions which were involved in six general strikes, mutinies in ten German Naval bases, along with workers' takeovers in seven major cities and the declaration of the Bolshevik Free State of Bavaria, in 1918.

WEAPONS

The causes of death of many of the men commemorated on the War Memorial have been recorded where possible. The weapons and terminology of the First World War differed from later conflicts and the major differences are set out, below:

WW1	WW2
Aerial torpedo.	Bomb.
Bomb.	Hand Grenade.
Gas: Chlorine. Lachrymatory - White, Black or Green. Sneezing - Blue Cross. Phosgene - White C, White D. Mustard - Yellow Cross. (German colour codes, as used on shell casings).	Not used, officially. CS Tear gas.
Mine - subterranean, using Tunnelling Companies to dig under the enemy front line. Extensively used.	Land mine - normally surface laid or shallowly concealed. Very extensively used, in mine fields.
Shellfire - high explosive, gas.	Shellfire, high explosive, illuminating, smoke.
Shrapnel - air burst munitions scattering numerous 'ball bearings'. Extensively used.	Shrapnel - VT fuse for proximity explosions.
Trench Mortar.	Mortar.
Stokes Mortar.	3" Mortar.
Livens Projector.	Nebelwerfer (copied by the Germans for WW2 after they eventually captured some Livens Projectors in 1918).
Large Gallery Flame Projector - dug in underground near Mametz for the first day of the Battle of the Somme.	Tank flame throwers.
Tanks - Introduced during the Battle of the Somme, 15th September, 1916 by the British. The French built a fleet of 800 light tanks which were used en masse during the counter attack in July, 1918, and came as a shock to the Germans, which disrupted their Spring Offensive at a critical point. The Germans only built and used 20 A7V tanks, alongside a number of captured British tanks, in late 1918.	German blitzkrieg tactics were devised in the 1930s, largely as the result of the commander of A7V 560, Lt Volkheim, which had been disabled and destroyed on the 11th October, becoming a senior instructor at the German Tank School. German tank division in the Second World War were powerful combat formations.

Illustration 9: Ernst Volckheim in front of his A7V with his crew (Public domain)

Courtesy of Monsieur M L'Espagnol, Iwuy, 2021.

THE SHELL HOLE BOY

(A TALE OF THE 'DUKES')

By Edwin Peel

Price 2d each
all proceeds to be given to the Wounded Soldiers.

Express Office, Idle

Pte J W Taylor, of 4, Wellington Street, Eccleshill, and of the Duke of Wellington's Regiment, has been severely wounded in both arms and legs and is now in the Northern General Hospital, Leicester, where he arrived on Sunday, May 20th. He was 20 years of age in February last, and had been in the army fourteen months, seven months of which has been in France. While training in England he won a beautiful silver cigarette case, presented by Colonel Tennyson, for the highest aggregate score for shooting. Previous to joining the army he was employed in the stock rooms of Messrs Graham, Blundell and Co, Ltd, Chapel Street, Bradford. The senior Chaplain, in a letter to Pte Taylor's father, says young Taylor had a terrible experience, laying out in a shell hole for eight days without food. Everybody was amazed at his great pluck and endurance. When two Germans came to him on the 8th day, he had the wonderful presence of mind to threaten them with his rifle, so that they surrendered to him, and he made them carry him towards our line.

The Shell Hole Boy

I looked on his face 'neath that counterpane white,
Which was lit with a sweet, boyish smile –
It seemed to speak happiness, for his face was so bright,
That I longed to stay and chat for a while.

"What a curious title your pals call you by,
'Shell Hole Boy'! Why what does it mean?"
But he curiously smiled and, heaving a sigh,
Said, "My pals have made such a scene."

A sturdy chap in the next bed, he heard
My question, so came to my aid.
"He's a hero. I'll tell you every word
Of how the title was made.

"His duty took him to our very first line,
And the Huns, they were making it hot.
The shells all around us bursting, our chaps were fine,
How they stood it and ne'er left the spot.

"The Order came, "Over!" We went with a bound,
The enemy marked us to a man;
And just as we mounted the highest ground, the straffing and hell-fire began

"Twas then he was wounded, but would not give way,
Until he'd used up his bombs one by one.
Again he was wounded, still he would stay,
And stick his duty like a true British son.

"Yet again he was hit and he tottered and fell,
Nigh dead with pain, he dropped into the mud
Of a large crater, made by a shell.
There he lay moaning, and covered with blood.

"The enemy was strong, and we had to give way,
And leave our wounded and dead;
The scene it was terrible, how I remember that day".
Then he shivered and covered his head.

"But our hero," he started to tell me again,
Was left in that shell-hole to lie,
Half buried, and in such terrible pain –
Left, as we thought, there to die.

"For eight days and nights in that shell hole he lay,
By day the hot sun, by night the cold frost;
Overhead the shells still whizzed on their way, when he gave himself up for lost.

"On the eighth day two figures came creeping up near,
So he gripped his rifle by his side
And levelled it at them; how they trembled with fear.
'Have mercy, oh Kamerad, we're weary and worn.
One held out a picture, 'See my wife and boy.
Three years we've been parted, how my heart is torn.
Both in London – to see them would give me great joy'.

"Then surrender your arms, our hero replied,
And carry me back to our men."
They bore him so gently, but with pain he cried,
And that's how I saw him again."

So, that is his story and, I think you'll agree,
That he's made a name which none can destroy;
Though a boy in years a hero is he.
So proudly shake hands with the brave 'Shell Hole Boy!"

E O P

Copy held in the DWR Regimental Archives.

HERITAGE AND LEGACY

The Volunteer Movement soon recovered from the trauma of the war years and the Territorials were reconstituted, as the Territorial Army, in 1921. The 7th Battalion, with its Headquarters again in Milnsbridge, had Companies at Milnsbridge and Mossley.

The first camp of the 7th Battalion was held in the summer of 1920 at Scarborough. The great number of the decorated soldiers who had once again volunteered, after what they had gone through, including some whose camp had been so rudely interrupted by German dreams of empire and conquest six years previously, enjoyed another period of soldiering and, undoubtedly, tale telling which the newer recruits would listen to in awe.

The Territorials were also invited to furnish recruits for the Defence Corps for the National Emergency of April, 1921, before heading for camp in Whitby that July.

Numbers and recruiting fluctuated during the inter war period but, by 1939, the 'Terriers' were once again prepared to defend King and Country, and in the numbers to furnish both the first and second lines of Territorial Divisions – but that is another story.

Territorial Camp, Redcar, 1934 - 272 years Territorial Service

The Milnsbridge Drill Hall was sold off by the Ministry of Defence and part of it has been turned into a private museum, the Bullecourt Museum, in honour of the men of the 2/7th Battalion who fought and fell at the battle of Bullecourt, on 3rd May, 1917, their first major engagement in the war.

ACKNOWLEDGEMENTS

The compilers would like to thank all those who have helped and supported this book; the Trustees of the Huddersfield Drill Hall, for their encouragement and support; Richard Harvey, for his invaluable help with the images and maps; Ron Hartley, who has supported this venture with his vast knowledge of the men of the 7th Battalion; Rita Vaughan who has supplied a wealth of information concerning the upper reaches of the Colne Valley and made some valuable comments on the text; Paul Sims, of the Archives Volunteers Team; Alan Stansfield, for allowing us to use the information painstakingly gathered by his late wife, Margaret, for her book 'Huddersfield's Roll of Honour 1914 - 1922'; Graham Sargeant, for his painstaking research; Dr Bill Smith, for allowing us to use information from his internet blog – **tunstillsmen.blogspot.com**; Monsier Michel L'Espagnol, for details of the Battle of Iwuy and image; Jean Hancock, for her help with the layout and compilation of the facts, and, not least, Derek Alexander for his time, patience and expertise in publishing this book.

Finally, I would like to thank the relatives of those who are commemorated on the Drill Hall War Memorial Tablets for making arrangements to visit the Drill Hall to pay their respects and, thereby, giving us the original idea that these names should be remembered with pride. This led to the project for the refurbishment of the 5 DWR War Memorial, in 2018, and the inspiration for the two books - to make available more information concerning the men whose names are recorded on the two First World War Memorials shown below.

Mr Derek Alexander, Valence House Museum Volunteer, visiting the Drill Hall in 2017

SELECT BIBLIOGRAPHY

Anon – *Commemorating the Great War, Ripponden Remembers* booklet, privately published.

Bales P G – *History of The 1/4th Battn Duke of Wellington's (WR) Regiment*, (Halifax, 1928).

Barber S – *Guiseley Terriers a small part in the Great War* (Pen and Sword, 2018) ISBN 978-1-52670-352-1

Binns C – *A soldier of the Great War: Joseph Sykes O'Hara,* H&D FHS Journal Vol 32, No 1, page 30.

Clayton J T – *Craven's Part in the Great War* (Craven Pioneer and Chronicle, 1919).

Commonwealth War Graves Commission – on line database (accessed March 2020).

CVA – *Colne Valley Almanac,* a series of publications printed annually throughout the war. Copies held in Huddersfield Central Library.

Edited – *Huddersfield Drill Hall Albums,* a series of Albums/scrapbooks compiled by members of the 5th and 7th Battalions between 1907 and 1965 (unpublished as yet).

Fisher, J J – *History of the Duke of Wellington's West Riding Regiment, from Aug 1914 to Dec 1917* (G T Whitehead, 1917).

Flaving M S & Green M – *5 DWR WW1 War Memorial,* (Valence House, 2020).

Ford C – *Honley in the Great War 1914 - 1918,* (Honley Civic Society, 2014). IDBN 13-978-0-9572638-5-7.

Goodall T – Goodall Collection (unpublished, 1914-1919), copy held in the Royal Armouries, Leeds).

Green, Michael – *Nominal Roll of Territorial Force War Medal awards* (unpublished papers)
- *Nominal Roll of Brighouse Tribute Medal awards* (unpublished papers)
- *Nominal Roll of Honour, Bailiffe Bridge & Brighouse War Memorials* (unpublished papers)
- *Nominal Roll of Honour, Coley & Norwood Green War Memorials* (unpublished papers)
- *Nominal Roll of Honour, Queensbury Holy Trinity Church & Queensbury War Memorial* (unpublished papers)
- *Nominal Roll of Honour, Rastrick War Memorial* (unpublished papers)

Green, Michael & Susan, Flaving S, Harvey R – *Battle of Iwuy*, DWR Archives (2020) dwr.org.uk.

Hornshaw, C R & Fowler, M W – *Calderdale War Dead a biographical Index of the War Memorials of Calderdale,* Privately published (1995).

Howcroft, G B – *The First World War 1914 - 1918,* Hirst, Kidd & Rennie, Oldham (1986).

Edited – *Huddersfield Drill Hall Album 7 DWR Volume 1,* (unpublished albums held in the Mess).

Lyall S, Slaven D – *From Mills to Marching and Back Again Gargrave 1900-1925*, Gargrave Heritage Group (2019) ISBN - 978-1-9161058-0-5.

NA – *National Archives Nominal Roll,* accessed from the Internet (2018).

Sharp M – *Clifton War Memorial,* self published book, ISBN 978-0-9573416-1-6.

Smith Bill – *Internet Blog 10th Battalion* - tunstillsmen.blogspot.com (last accessed Aug 2019).

Stansfield M J – *Huddersfield's Roll of Honour 1914-1922,* University of Huddersfield Press (2014) ISBN 978-1-86218-126-7.

Thompson P I – *Barnoldswick, a small town's history 1800-2014,* privately published booklet (2014).

Turpin C – *Cleckheaton's Finest - Spenborough War Memorial,* unpublished pamphlet (undated).

The Naval & Military Press Ltd – *Soldiers Died in the Great War 1914-19* CD Rom V2.0 format (undated). Prepared from the books published by The War Office (1921) & J B Hayward & Son (1989).

Vaughan R – *Remember all the Boys, The Men of Mossley, Carrbrook and Luzley In The Great War (including 63 men born in Saddleworth).* Unpublished booklet – mossley@btinternet.com, (2011), a copy was kindly donated to the DWR Regimental Archives. A .pdf document titled *Mossley: The Duke of Wellington's Regiment and the Great War*, by Rita Vaughan and Kathryn Young, has recently been donated to the DWR website by the author - accessed from **dwr.org.uk,** family history page. In addition, a website - **findagrave.com** - has been published on the internet with details of Mossley Soldiers who fell in the war.

7 DWR lapel badge for the post war Old Comrades Association

THE STATISTICS

The following chart and statistics illustrates the casualties suffered by the two front line battalions from the Colne Valley and district during the war. The war weariness that set in during 1916 was accentuated by the even larger casualty list of 1917. However, the authorities had stopped the publication of large casualty lists in the Press and were producing weekly HMSO booklets available, at a cost, to the public, as announced in the Huddersfield Examiner:

Mon 30 Jul 1917

CASUALTY LIST TO BE OBTAINED BY PUBLIC THROUGH BOOKSELLERS.

The Secretary of the War Office states that, as it has become impossible owing to the limitation of space imposed by the shortage of paper for newspapers to publish the full casualty list which is supplied to them, daily arrangements have been made for the issue of these lists by the Stationery Office in a weekly edition. Copies will be obtainable through any bookseller or from branches of the Stationery Office. The first issue will appear on Tuesday August 7th and this will be sold at the price of 3d per copy to cover cost of production or post free at 4d. Subscriptions will be received by the Stationery Office at the rate of 4 shillings per quarter including postage.

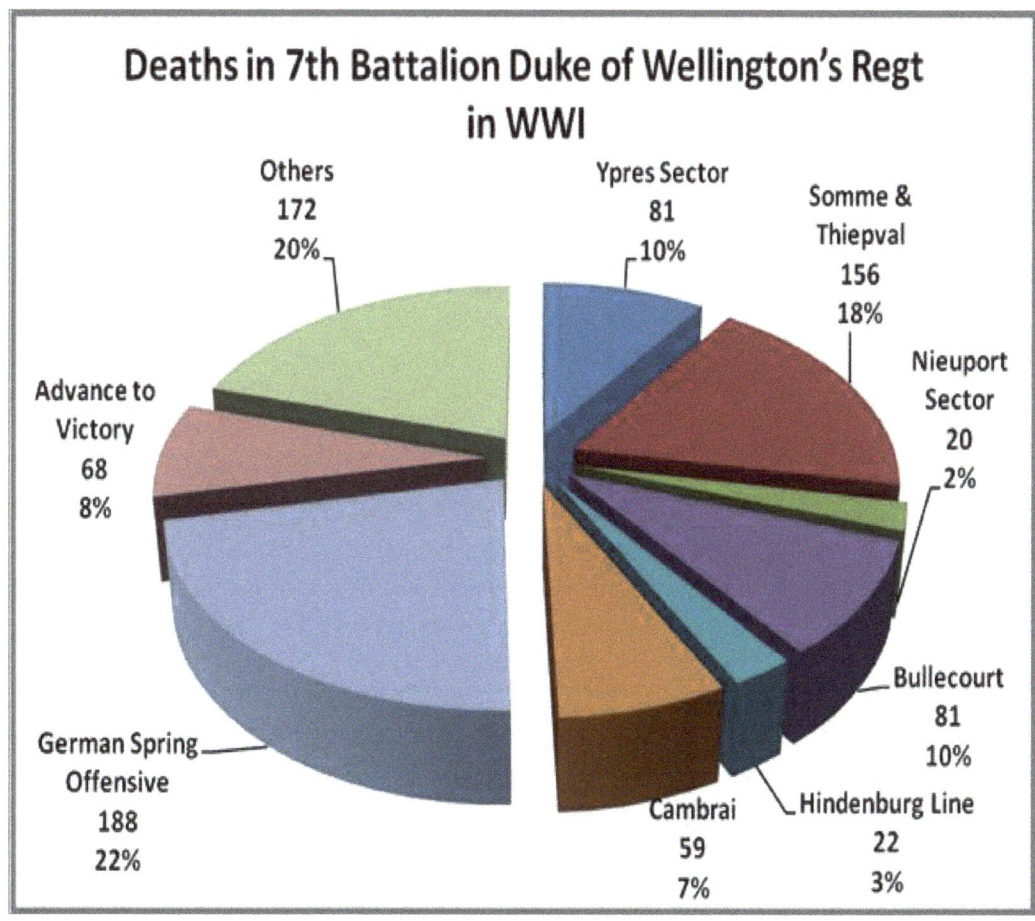

The Battle of the Somme was by far the greatest battle fought by the British Army, in scale if nothing else. It received great publicity, with picture houses screening films of the combat, which were very popular, found its way into the national psyche and is still remembered by school children today, by name if not for any detail. However, the German Spring Offensives caused even more casualties for the

7th Battalion in 1918, including the thirty eight who were killed in action at the Battle of Iwuy, the largest and most unique of the desperate battles for the survival of the Army and its defeat.

Year	Deaths
1915	81
1916	156
1917	182
1918	256

Major Battles	Deaths
Somme	156
Nieuport Sector	20
Bullecourt	81
Hindenburg Line	22
Cambrai	59
German Spring Offensive	188
Advance to Victory	68
Other deaths 1915 to 1918	172

Statistics for the chart compiled by Graham Sargeant.

Soldiers were still dying of their wounds in 1920 and beyond (see Sgt Brelsford, who was wounded by shellfire in August 1916, had his right leg amputated later that year and died on 15th July, 1920, due to a piece of shrapnel which had lodged close to his left lung) and there were approximately 578,000 soldiers in hospital at the signing of the Armistice, according to the Director General of Army Medical Services, as reported in the Huddersfield Examiner on Friday, 3rd October, 1919.

The Regiment has 5,965 recorded awards of the Silver War Badge from its inception, on 12th September 1916, until the end of the war.

www.ingramcontent.com/pod-product-compliance
Lightning Source LLC
Chambersburg PA
CBHW042016090526
44588CB00023B/2878